Exchange-Traded Derivatives

Wiley Finance Series

Exchange-Traded Derivatives

Erik Banks

WILEY

Other Wiley Editorial Offices

John Wiley & Sons Inc., 111 River Street, Hoboken, NJ 07030, USA

Jossey-Bass, 989 Market Street, San Francisco, CA 94103-1741, USA

Wiley-VCH Verlag GmbH, Boschstr. 12, D-69469 Weinheim, Germany

John Wiley & Sons Australia Ltd, 33 Park Road, Milton, Queensland 4064, Australia

John Wiley & Sons (Asia) Pte Ltd, 2 Clementi Loop #02-01, Jin Xing Distripark, Singapore 129809

John Wiley & Sons Canada Ltd, 22 Worcester Road, Etobicoke, Ontario, Canada M9W 1L1

Wiley also publishes its books in a variety of electronic formats. Some content that appears
in print may not be available in electronic books.

British Library Cataloguing in Publication Data

A catalogue record for this book is available from the British Library

ISBN 0-470-84841-3

Typeset in 10/12pt Times by TechBooks, New Delhi, India
Printed and bound in Great Britain by Biddles Ltd, Guildford and King's Lynn
This book is printed on acid-free paper responsibly manufactured from sustainable forestry
in which at least two trees are planted for each one used for paper production.

Contents

Acknowledgements

I greatly appreciate the assistance supplied by various individuals and organizations, including members of the global futures trading teams at Merrill Lynch and Citicorp, who provided constructive comments on different aspects of the book, and officials at Chicago Mercantile Exchange, Eurex, Euronext Paris, Hong Kong Exchanges and Clearing, London International Financial Futures Exchange, Mercado Mexicano de Derivados, Osaka Securities Exchange, and Sydney Futures Exchange, who took the time to provide information and answer detailed queries. Similar thanks are due to several regulatory authorities/self-regulatory agencies, including the US Commodity Futures Trading Commission, the National Futures Association, and the Commodity Futures Association of Japan.

I am very grateful, as always, to have the wonderful help and support of the John Wiley & Sons team. Specifically, I am indebted to Samantha Whittaker, Publisher, for supporting the project with her usual enthusiasm and providing ongoing direction and assistance as the book progressed. Thanks are also due to Carole Millett, Editorial Assistant, for helping out on all the things that matter and Samantha Hartley, Production Editor, for her tremendous contributions during the editing process.

And I am, of course, extremely grateful to my wife Milena for her patience and support on yet another project!

E. Banks
ebbrisk@netscape.net

This book is dedicated to the memory of my father
Robert B. Banks

"So sad, so strange, the days that are no more."
Tennyson

Biography

Erik Banks has held senior risk management positions at several global financial institutions, including XL Capital, where he was Partner and Chief Risk Officer of the Bermuda reinsurer's derivative subsidiary, and Merrill Lynch, where he spent 13 years as Managing Director of Corporate Risk Management, leading credit and market risk teams in Tokyo, Hong Kong, London, and New York. Mr Banks, an Adjunct Professor of Finance at the University of Connecticut, has written various books on risk management, emerging markets, derivatives, merchant banking, and electronic finance. He lives in Southern Connecticut where he is working on several other book projects.

Introduction

I.1 OVERVIEW

Exchange-Traded Derivatives provides an overview of the global listed futures and options markets, and how individual exchanges and products are adapting to a new operating environment – an environment characterized by rapid, almost continuous, change. The book also serves as a general reference for products and instruments offered by various global exchanges.[1]

- In *Part I – The Changing Marketplace* – we focus our attention on the overall marketplace, discussing the forces that are altering the operating environment and how exchanges must cope in order to prosper.
- In *Part II – The Established Exchanges* – we describe, in summary form, the major global exchanges, their origins and structure, the range of products and services they offer, and the manner in which they employ technology to benefit members and clients.
- In *Part III – The New Marketplaces* – we review emerging exchanges – traditional forums based in emerging markets as well as those that are purely "electronic" in nature – that are likely to increase in importance over the coming years.

Depending on one's specific definition of a "futures exchange," there were between 70 and 100 such forums operating around the world at the start of the twenty-first century – each one trying to play a role in the development of local, regional, and global markets. While they are all important in some way, we limit our focus in this book to 22 of the world's largest established exchanges, along with 5 emerging, and 5 electronic, exchanges.

Before embarking on our discussion, we present a brief primer on exchange-traded contracts for those who may be less familiar with the instruments, or who need a "refresher." The primer focuses on:

- Market fundamentals
  - Exchanges
  - Exchange-traded instruments
  - Clearing
  - Margin
  - Hedging versus speculating

---

[1] Since contract specifications change periodically we have chosen to provide exchange website links rather than details which might soon be out of date; the reader is encouraged to consult website links included in each chapter (along with supplementary links listed in the Reference section) for the most current contract details.

  – Cost of carry, basis, and expectations
  – Exchange-traded derivatives versus over-the-counter derivatives
• Sample futures and options strategies
  – Futures strategies
  – Options strategies

We supplement the review discussion with a basic glossary, which appears at the end of the book; all italicized items in the book refer to glossary entries. Those already conversant with the material can skip this section without any loss of continuity.

I.2   MARKET FUNDAMENTALS

I.2.1   Exchanges

Exchanges are central marketplaces, approved by relevant regulatory authorities, which exist in either physical or electronic form. These marketplaces provide the facilities needed to bring together buyers and sellers of financial or physical commodities for future delivery. Exchanges do not set prices, nor do they participate in trading for their own accounts, they simply supply the infrastructure needed to facilitate *price discovery* in relevant instruments. Physical exchanges feature trading floors (or pits) with brokers who buy and sell contracts on an *open-outcry* basis – through hand signals or verbal communication. Those that exist in electronic form function in the same way, except that buying and selling are done through screen-based technologies. Some exchanges feature both physical and electronic trading in order to extend trading hours or support specific contracts that cannot generate enough volume in the trading pit. Physical or electronic exchange trading flows through exchange members, who have acquired the right to transact on behalf of their own accounts and for client accounts. Broadly speaking, exchange members may be *clearing members* or *nonclearing members*; clearing members can clear proprietary and client trades directly with the clearinghouse, while nonclearing members can only clear their own trades; we discuss the clearing process below. Client (end-user) trades may be routed to exchange members through a *futures commission merchant* (FCM), a specialist intermediary that deals with exchange members, or directly to members through electronic interfaces. Exchanges may be structured as *mutual organizations* (owned by the membership) or private/public corporations (owned by investors).

I.2.2   Exchange-traded instruments

An *exchange-traded derivative* is a standardized financial contract, traded on an established exchange, that derives its value from an underlying financial or physical/commodity reference. Financial references can include interest rates/bond prices, equities/indexes, and currencies, while commodity references can include agriculturals (e.g. grains, livestock, dairy), "*softs*" (e.g. coffee, cocoa, sugar, orange juice), hard assets (e.g. lumber, chemicals), energy (e.g. oil, natural gas, electricity) and other references (e.g. weather, catastrophe, transportation prices, and so on).

As the value of the underlying reference moves up or down based on supply and demand forces, the value of the derivative contract moves up or down as well.

Table I.1   Long/short futures relationships

Position	Reference asset ↑	Reference asset ↓
Long futures	Gains value	Loses value
Short futures	Loses value	Gains value

Exchange-traded contracts are offered in the form of:

- futures
- options
- futures options

A *future* is a contract that represents an obligation to buy or sell:

- a specific quantity of an underlying reference asset
- at a price agreed, but not exchanged, today
- for settlement at a future time

A future can thus be considered a contract for deferred payment and delivery. The contract might feature *financial settlement* (i.e. cash exchange) or *physical settlement* (i.e. underlying commodity/asset exchange).[2] A *long position* – one that is purchased or owned – in a futures contract increases in value as the reference price rises and loses value when the price falls; a *short position* – one that is borrowed or sold – increases in value as the price falls, and decreases in value as the price rises. For example, a company might buy one gold futures contract (representing 100 ounces (oz) of gold) for \$350/oz for settlement in 3 months; in 3 months, unless the contract is *closed out* by taking an opposite position (e.g. selling the same position), the company will deliver \$35 000 and receive 100 oz gold. If the price of spot gold in 3 months is greater than \$350/oz, the company will have earned a profit; if not, it will suffer a loss.

Futures profit and loss (P&L) relationships are summarized in Table I.1 and depicted in Figures I.1 and I.2.

An *option* is a contract that gives the purchaser:

- the right, but not the obligation, to buy (*call option*) or sell (*put option*) the underlying reference asset
- at a specified price level known as a *strike price*
- at any time until an agreed expiry date (*American option*) or only on the expiry date (*European option*)

In exchange for this right the buyer pays the seller a *premium payment*. By accepting the premium the option seller has an obligation to buy or sell the underlying asset at the specified strike if the option is exercised.

---

[2] The individual/institution that is short the futures contract and intends to deliver a physical commodity can select from among various delivery options (e.g. the kind of commodity or asset deliverable into the contract) and then delivers notice to the clearinghouse of its intent to deliver (typically through the FCM or broker); if the FCM does not receive delivery notification from the short seller, it can close out the position unilaterally. The last notice day is usually the last trading day of the contract. Cash-settled, rather than physically settled, contracts are typically closed out through wire transfers.

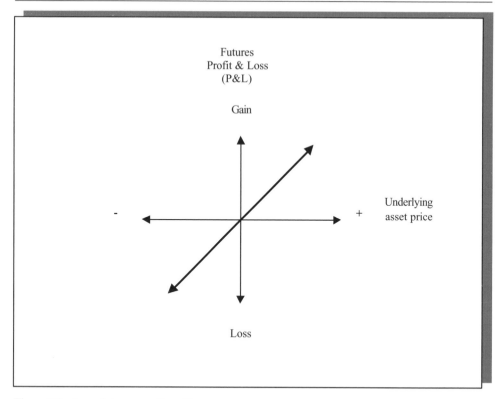

Figure I.1   Long futures payoff profile

For instance, instead of buying the gold future in the example above, a company might buy a 3-month European call option on gold struck at $350/oz. If, 3 months hence, the price of gold is above $350/oz, the company can exercise the option at a profit (i.e. it can exercise the call, buy the gold at $350/oz, deliver the $35 000 in cash proceeds and then sell the gold at a higher price in the *spot*, or cash, *market*). If the price of gold is below $350/oz, the company will let the contract expire unexercised (e.g. there is no economic value in the option, as gold can be purchased cheaper in the spot market than through the option). The difference between the long future and the long call relates to the downside exposure: while the long future generates a loss once gold falls below $350/oz, the long call has no such downside. If gold falls below $350/oz, the owner of the call will simply choose not to exercise the option. The maximum downside of any long option position is thus the premium paid to secure the option. As with futures, options may be settled in financial or physical terms.

Options P&L relationships are summarized in Table I.2 and depicted in Figures I.3–I.6.

A *futures option* is simply an option granting the purchaser the right to enter into an underlying futures transaction in exchange for a premium. A *futures put* gives the purchaser the right to sell a futures contract at a set strike price, while a *futures call* gives the purchaser the right to buy a futures contract at a set strike price. Long and short futures options are summarized in Table I.3.

Table I.2   Long/short options relationships

Position	Reference asset value ↑	Reference asset value ↓
Long call	Gains value	Loses value (but limited to premium paid)
Short call	Loses value	Gains value (but limited to premium earned)
Long put	Loses value (but limited to premium paid)	Gains value
Short put	Gains value (but limited to premium earned)	Loses value

Table I.3   Long/short futures options

Position	Right/Obligation
Long futures call	Right to buy a futures contract at the strike price
Short futures call	Obligation to sell a futures contract at the strike price, if exercised
Long futures put	Right to sell a futures contract at the strike price
Short futures put	Obligation to buy a futures contract at the strike price, if exercised

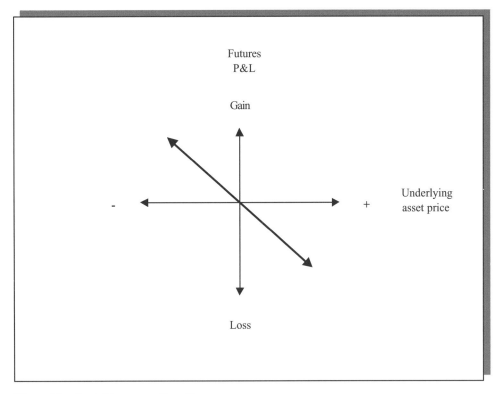

Figure I.2   Short futures payoff profile

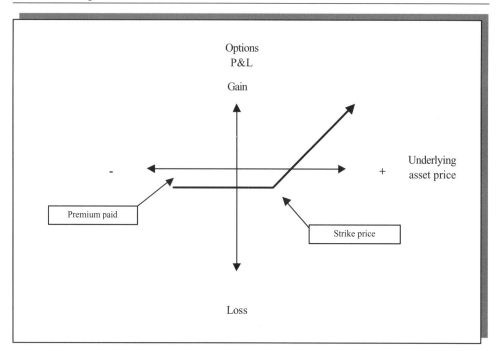

Figure I.3   Long call payoff profile

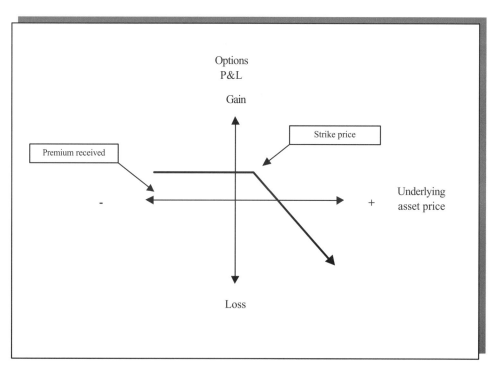

Figure I.4   Short call payoff profile

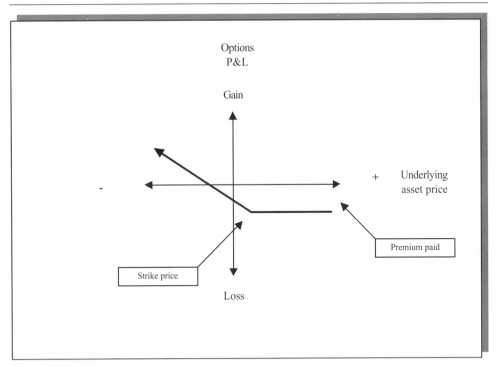

Figure I.5 Long put payoff profile

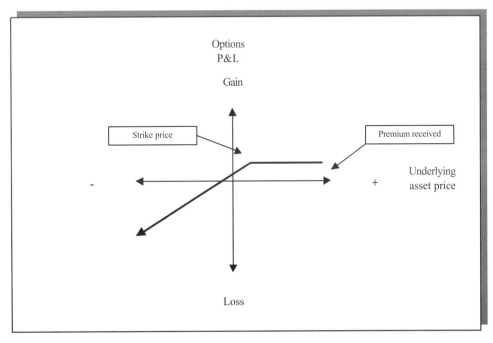

Figure I.6 Short put payoff profile

Table I.4   NYMEX light sweet crude oil futures contract specifications

Term	Description
Trading unit	1000 US barrels (42 000 gallons), minimum price fluctuation $0.01/barrel
Delivery date	Last calendar day of the delivery month
Deliverable grades	Domestic crude streams with 0.42% sulfur by weight or less, no less than 37° American Petroleum Institute (APIn) gravity nor more than 42° gravity, including: West Texas Intermediate, Low Sweet Mix, New Mexican Sweet, North Texas Sweet, Oklahoma Sweet, South Texas Sweet. Foreign crude streams no less than 34° APIn gravity nor more than 42° APIn gravity, including: UK Brent and Forties, Norwegian Oseberg Blend, Nigerian Bonny Light, Nigerian Qua Iboe and Colombian Cusiana (at relevant discounts or premiums)
Delivery point	Cushing, Oklahoma at any pipeline or storage facility with access to TEPPCO, Cushing storage or Equilon Pipeline
Contract months	30 consecutive months plus long-dated contracts with original maturities of 36, 48, 60, 72, and 84 months
Last trading day	Third business day prior to the 25th calendar day of the month preceding the delivery month
Price limit	$3.00/barrel in all but the first two months; $6.00/barrel if previous settlement price is at $3.00 limit. In event of $7.50/barrel rise in the first two months, all limits set at $7.50/barrel

All exchange-traded contracts – whether futures, options, or futures options – are characterized by standard terms, including:

- *Trading units*: the size of the contract (also known as *notional value*) and the minimum price fluctuation per contract (also known as *tick value*)
- *Delivery date*: the date when the contract settles/matures
- *Deliverable grades*: the classes and types of assets that are acceptable for delivery against a contract[3]
- *Delivery points*: the approved location where physical commodities can be delivered
- *Contract months*: the month(s) on which contracts are offered for trading[4]
- *Last trading day*: the final date on which trading in a given contract can occur
- Other terms and conditions as applicable, including:
  - *Price limits*, or the maximum amount a contract is permitted to fluctuate during a given trading session
  - Strike price/exercise style (for options/futures options)

Note that each standard contract specifies the *initial margin* (or collateral security) that must be posted. We discuss margining at greater length below.

For instance, the New York Mercantile Exchange (NYMEX's) light sweet crude oil futures contract features the standard terms outlined in Table I.4.

---

[3] Since contracts' terms often allow different assets to be delivered, participants generally seek the "*cheapest-to-deliver*" (lowest cost) asset and use that as the basis for pricing a given contract.

[4] Multiple month/quarter contracts may be quoted at the same time, particularly for actively traded references. The *nearby* and *next-nearby* contracts – meaning the two contracts with the shortest time until expiry – are often the most active. *Open interest*, which measures the number of open contracts on an exchange, is a popular measure of activity, or liquidity.

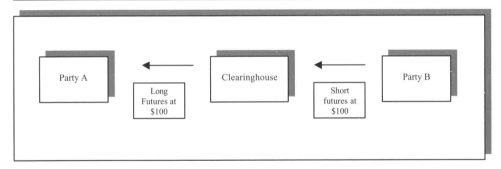

Figure I.7 Clearinghouse intermediation

I.2.3 Clearing

One of the main characteristics, and advantages, of the listed derivatives market is a centralized clearing process that reassigns all trades to the exchange's clearinghouse, a creditworthy central counterparty. *Clearing* is the process of recording a trade passing through the exchange and assigning it to the clearinghouse so that it becomes the counterparty to that transaction (note that if the recording yields discrepancies between what buyers and sellers believe they have executed, an "*out-trade*" is noted and must be reconciled by the relevant brokers or FCMs). The clearinghouse is responsible for computing and collecting margins on new and existing trades (as described below) and organizes processes related to physical or cash delivery of futures and options contracts that are not closed out prior to maturity. A clearinghouse is typically structured as a wholly owned, but legally independent, subsidiary of the exchange in order to protect the exchange operation from possible losses; however, in some cases it may be constituted as an integrated division of an exchange or an independently operated entity that is minority owned by a number of exchanges and/or exchange members.

By routing all trades through a central clearinghouse participants eliminate *credit risk* (or the risk of loss due to counterparty default); this is a key consideration for those who prefer not to be exposed to the credit performance of other parties. From a practical perspective a clearinghouse *intermediates*, or stands between, every buyer and seller so that they do not face each other directly. For instance, if Party A wants to buy a futures contract worth $100 it enters an order into the exchange.[5] The exchange matches the $100 buy order with a $100 sell order from Party B, which might wish to sell a contract at that price, and passes the trades to the clearinghouse. The clearinghouse then becomes a party to both trades: it provides the buyer with a long futures contract and a seller with the equivalent short contract, in exchange for initial margin payments. Note that the $100 value is not exchanged at trade date, simply the margins associated with the positions. This is consistent with the fact that a futures contract represents deferred delivery and, thus, deferred payment. At the end of each trading day the clearinghouse revalues the positions and might request additional margin from the buyer or the seller, depending on which way the market has moved. If required margins are not posted, the clearinghouse closes out the position. Figure I.7 illustrates the basic intermediation function of a clearinghouse.

---

[5] In practice it may enter the order through an FCM, which passes it through a clearing member; for simplicity, however, we assume Party A faces the exchange directly.

Since a clearinghouse acts as counterparty to all futures and options trades, it must be of sufficient credit standing (e.g. strong liquidity and capital) to attract customers. A strong credit rating can usually be gained through various levels of security, including:

- Initial and variation margins from clearing members
- Clearing funds/liquidity facilities
- Member guarantee deposits
- Insurance policies
- Capital on hand
- Exchange parent guarantees

Two basic models are generally used to provide the clearinghouse with security, including the "*defaulter pays*" *model* (which first seizes exchange-based assets of the defaulting party but may ultimately require enough capital within the clearinghouse to cover the loss) and the "*survivor pays*" *model* (which pools risk and losses across clearinghouse members). In the US, clearinghouses are authorized by the Commodity Futures Trading Commission (CFTC)[6]; in the UK the Financial Services Authority (FSA) approves clearing roles, and in other countries national financial regulators generally set minimum operating standards for their own clearers.

I.2.4 Margin

As noted above, the credit exposure on listed contracts is mitigated through margins posted with the exchange clearinghouse. Margins are determined by each exchange and vary by contract: the more volatile the asset underlying the contract, the higher the margin, since the probability of large market movements and, hence, unsecured credit exposure, is greater. Three elements govern the margining process:

- Initial margin
- Variation margin
- Maintenance margin

Initial margin must be posted on every new position based on a set percentage of its value at time of execution in order to secure the core risk of the transaction. In general, clearing members post *clearing margins* on behalf of their customers when a trade is executed and simultaneously collect *customer margins* from FCMs or clients.[7] At the end of each day the position is revalued and *variation margin* may be called or returned. Variation margin is required when the value of the position has fallen below the *maintenance margin* – or minimum trigger – level, but can be returned when it exceeds the maintenance level. If a party fails to post variation margin within a predefined period the clearinghouse liquidates the underlying contract.[8] Initial and variation margins thus secure the potential exposure of an exchange contract, thereby limiting maximum market moves to one day. Margin must generally be posted in the form of secure, high-grade assets, such as cash, US Treasury securities (or other high quality government bonds), acceptable bank letters of credit, and so forth.

---

[6] For instance, the CFTC has approved the Board of Trade Clearing Corp (BOTCC) as clearer for CBOT, CME Clearinghouse for the CME, Intermarket Clearing Corp for the Philadelphia Board of Trade, NY Clearing Corp for the NY Board of Trade, the Options Clearing Corp (OCC) for five separate options exchanges, and so forth.

[7] Customer margins might be set higher than clearing margins in order to protect the clearing member from client credit risk.

[8] In fact, some participants simply use the variation margin call as a mechanism to close out a losing position; failure to post the required increment simply results in liquidation of the position.

A simple example best illustrates the margining process. Consider a speculator who purchases 10 contracts of gold at $400/oz (with each contract equal to 100 oz, for a notional value of $400 000). The position requires initial margin of $2500 per contract ($25 000 total) and a maintenance margin of $1500 per contract ($15 000 total).

- End of day 1:
  - Gold price falls to $393/oz, so the position has lost $7000
  - The maintenance margin balance is now $18 000 (e.g. $25 000 − $7000), but since it remains above the $15 000 requirement, no variation margin call is made
- End of day 2:
  - Gold price falls to $388/oz, so the position has lost another $5000
  - The maintenance margin balance is now $13 000 (e.g. $18 000 − $5000), below the $15 000 level; variation margin is thus required
  - A variation margin call is made for $12 000, to bring the margin back up to $25 000
- End of day 3 (close out):
  - Gold price rises to $402/oz, so the position has made $14 000
  - Close out value of the contact yields a net profit of $2000 (e.g. −$7000 − $5000 + $14 000)

The different components of exchange structure and trading/clearing/margining are summarized in Figure I.8.

I.2.5 Hedging versus speculating

Participants in futures and options can act either as hedgers or speculators. A *hedger* enters into a derivative trade in order to reduce or eliminate a risk exposure. If a hedge is effective (i.e. perfectly matched) it produces a "breakeven" result: when the derivative gains in value, the underlying reference asset being protected loses value, and vice versa. A hedger may

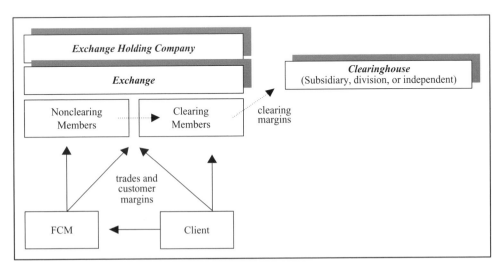

Figure I.8   Exchange structure

establish a *long hedge* by purchasing a derivative contract to cover a natural short position or a *short hedge* by selling a derivative contract to cover a natural long position. A *speculator*, in contrast, enters into a derivative trade to earn a profit based on the direction of the market, asset spreads, or volatility. By taking a position in one or more contracts, the speculator hopes only to profit – no underlying reference asset exists to offset potential losses. Since hedgers and speculators are motivated by different goals, both are essential to the smooth functioning of the marketplace. An overabundance of hedgers or speculators can create supply/demand imbalances, price anomalies, and illiquidity.

I.2.6   Cost of carry, expectations and basis

Several important relationships exist between *spot prices* (i.e. current, or cash market, prices) and futures prices and help explain why hedgers and speculators might choose to participate in the marketplace.[9] Key concepts include cost of carry, expectations, and the basis.

The first concept relates to futures pricing under a cost of carry framework. The *cost of carry* is simply the cost of maintaining a position. For a physical commodity this involves:

- The cost of financing, storing, and insuring the commodity
- The benefit of lending the commodity

For a financial asset it involves:

- The cost of financing the financial asset
- The benefit of lending the financial asset

The total cost of carry is simply the future value of the costs less the benefits. Thus, a *theoretical futures price* must equal the spot price plus the future value of costs, less any benefits associated with the position. Intuitively, this makes sense: if a company owns an asset and is asked to sell it for future delivery, it will want to be compensated not only for its known value today (i.e. the spot price) but also the costs it must bear to hold the asset until the future date, less any benefit it can derive from the asset over that period.

In order to prevent continuous *arbitrage* (or riskless trading), the theoretical price of the futures contract must at all times be less than the spot (or current) price plus the total cost of carry:

$$F < S + C$$

where F is the futures price, S is the spot price, and C is the total cost of carry (i.e. future value of costs less benefits). If the actual futures price quoted in the marketplace is greater than the theoretical futures price an arbitrage profit can be made by:

- Selling the futures contract
- Borrowing and purchasing the underlying asset
- Lending the asset

Consider the following example: spot oil is quoted at $24/barrel, the borrowing rate for a company is 7%, and oil can be lent at 2%. Based on the cost of carry model, the theoretical

---

[9] Many excellent works, which address the mathematical aspects of futures and options in great detail, are available. Readers may wish to consult the works of Daigler, Dubovsky, Duffie, Hull, and Stoll and Whaley, among others, for additional quantitative information; these works are cited in the reference section.

one-year futures price is $25.20 (e.g. $24 + $1.68 − $0.48). If one-year oil futures are quoted in the market at $27 rather than $25.20, a company can earn a riskless profit by:

1. Selling the one-year futures contract at $27
2. Borrowing $24 from its bank at 7% (for one year)
3. Purchasing oil in the spot market at $24
4. Lending the oil to another party at 2% (for one year)

In one year, the company:

1. Repays the $24 loan (total $25.68, or $24 * 1.07)
2. Receives proceeds from the oil it lent out (total $0.48, or $24 * 0.02)
3. Delivers the oil it purchased in the spot market into the contract at $27

This yields a net arbitrage profit of $1.80 (e.g. +$27 − $25.68 + 0.48). When the reverse scenario holds true (i.e. the actual futures price is less than the theoretical price) a similar arbitrage structure can be created. Arbitragers constantly search for opportunities to capitalize on a breakdown in this rule – when an opportunity arises, it is exploited very quickly, bringing the relationship back in line.

A second important concept relates to *expectations*[10] and centers on the relationship of futures prices to the expected spot price at contract maturity – rather than the prevailing spot price. Under the expectations model the current futures price is precisely equal to the expected spot price at maturity; if accurate, a speculator's expected profits are equal to zero. In order to induce speculators to buy futures from short hedgers, expected returns need to exceed the risk-free return – meaning the futures price needs to be below the expected spot price, rising as maturity approaches; this is known as *normal backwardation*. In the case of long hedgers, speculators must be induced to sell futures; this means the futures price must be above the expected spot price and fall as maturity approaches – this is known as *contango*.

Regardless of the theoretical pricing approach, futures players must always cope with a concept known as the *basis*, or difference between futures and spot prices. As a contract nears maturity, *convergence* occurs: the futures price and the spot price draw closer together until they are precisely equal. Basis convergence – as related to maturity – occurs because the cost of carry declines as contract maturity draws nearer: the shorter the holding period, the lower the storage/insurance/financing costs, as illustrated in Figure I.9. A hedger that covers a position with a futures contract replaces *directional risk* (e.g. risk of upward or downward movements in price) with *basis risk* – the risk of fluctuations between futures and spot prices. Basis risk arises when a hedger covering a position liquidates the futures position prior to contract maturity; if the contract can be held to maturity, basis risk between perfectly matched cash/futures references will ultimately "zero out." Differences in the basis come from various sources, including:

- Changes in futures and spot price convergence
- Change in the cost of carry (e.g. insurance, storage, transportation or daily "time decay" in net financing)
- Hedge mismatches (e.g. different references between hedge instrument and underlying exposure)
- Random changes in the cost of carry relationship

---

[10] Economist John Maynard Keynes originally put forth the framework.

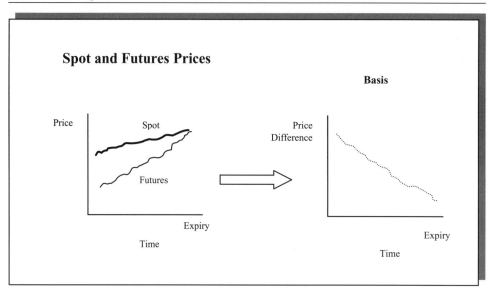

Figure I.9   Spot, futures and the basis as contract expiry approaches

I.2.7   Exchange-traded derivatives versus over-the-counter derivatives

Over-the-counter (OTC) derivatives are customized derivative contracts, originally developed in the early 1980s, which are traded directly between two parties rather than through an exchange.[11] While exchange and OTC derivatives are similar – both, for example, give hedgers and speculators the means to express a view or manage an exposure – they are different in several key areas. OTC derivatives can be written as:

- *Forwards* (similar to futures contracts without daily settlement, simply one settlement at maturity[12])
- *Swaps* (two-way exchange agreements with intervening settlement periods[13]) and
- Options (as discussed above)

---

[11] The market for OTC derivatives started with currency swaps/options and, over the next two decades, expanded into interest rates, commodities, equities and credits.

[12] A forward contract is a principal-to-principal transaction with an agreement to exchange an asset at a set price on a set date in the future. The transaction is highly customized and features no intervening revaluation (or mark-to-market). Futures, as we have noted, are revalued daily, with gains and losses realized immediately. Futures and forwards can be made identical, however, by *"tailing the hedge"* through a present value discount factor. Thus, for a multiperiod contract, futures gains can be reinvested and losses can be funded, causing a future to look like a forward. Forwards and futures can be used to hedge risk exposures and can receive similar accounting treatment under certain scenarios. For instance, a "fair value" hedge, which relates to risk exposure associated with the price of an asset or liability, requires that the derivative and underlying risk exposure both be marked-to-market into current income. This can be done with a forward as well as a future (as long as the additional "tailing" step is tied to the transaction). "Cash flow" hedge accounting is often more appropriate when the cash flow of the exposure is uncertain. Under this scenario the results of a forward or futures derivative hedge need to be evaluated to determine how much of the hedge is effective or ineffective. The ineffective component is reflected in current income, the effective portion in "other current income" and then reclassified as income when forecast cash flows affect earnings.

[13] Settlement periods are often set quarterly, semiannually, or annually. In essence, a swap is similar to a "bundle" of forward contracts.

Table I.5   Primary differences between exchange-traded and OTC derivatives

	Exchange-traded	OTC
Terms	Standardized	Customized
Trading forum	Central exchange (physical or electronic)	OTC (telephonic or electronic)
Price transparency	Good	Poor
Liquidity	Reasonable–strong	Limited
Credit exposure	Negligible	Significant unless collateralized
Margins	Required	Negotiated
Settlement	Generally closed-out	Generally held until maturity
Regulation	Full	Partial to full

Key features of OTC contracts include:

- Customization: While exchange-traded derivatives feature standardized terms, OTC contracts can be "tailor-made" to the precise reference, size, maturity, and price requirements of the two parties. Accordingly, they are much more flexible (and often more complex), and can be targeted at a much broader range of underlying references.
- Liquidity and transparency: Since OTC derivatives are customized, secondary liquidity tends to be much lower than in comparable exchange contracts (though certain exceptions exist – short-term forward rate agreements and "vanilla" interest rate swaps, for instance, are very liquid). The homogeneity that characterizes exchange contracts acts as a "two edge" sword, alternately increasing liquidity but reducing exposure flexibility. Since OTC contracts are not traded in a central forum (with some "electronic" exceptions, as we shall note in Chapters 1, 2, and 30–34) price transparency is not as strong as in the listed market, where trading prices are readily apparent.
- Settlement: While most exchange contracts are actually closed out prior to expiry (e.g. reversed), OTC contracts are often held to maturity.
- Counterparty credit risk: Since OTC contracts are traded "off exchange" the parties to the trades typically face each other's credit (rather than the credit of a central clearinghouse); this means that, unless separately negotiated margin/collateral is taken, performance risks are much higher.

It is worth noting that OTC derivatives are not always subjected to the same level of regulatory scrutiny as listed contracts; this is particularly true when transactions are booked through offshore subsidiaries. If OTC dealers choose to operate in an onshore, regulated environment they must, of course, adhere to applicable rules. Table I.5 summarizes key differences between exchange and OTC derivatives.

I.3   SAMPLE FUTURES AND OPTIONS STRATEGIES

We have noted above that exchange-traded contracts can be used to hedge or speculate. In order to demonstrate the practical application of these instruments, we present several hedging and speculating strategies that might be employed in either the financial or commodity markets. The examples we include are by no means exhaustive – many others can be developed – but are representative of typical transactions.

I.3.1 Futures strategies

I.3.1.1 Long hedge on soybeans

A hedger can use a long futures position (e.g. long hedge) to protect an input exposure (which, by definition, is a short position). Consider, for example, a small commercial manufacturer of salad oils that uses soybean oil as the primary feedstock in the production of soybean-based salad oil. The company might find that consumers are very sensitive to the price of salad oil, so that any price increase passed on will result in much lower demand (e.g. consumers will use some other substitute rather than paying a higher price). Accordingly, the only way to control profit margins is to manage expenses, including raw material input costs, e.g. soybean oil. If soybean oil prices rise, the company's cost of production increases and its profit margins suffer; conversely, if soybean oil prices fall, profit margins expand. In fact, when soybeans are priced at 16.10 cents/pound (lb), the firm meets its profit targets – any price above that erodes margins, any price below that improves margins. In order to produce its next run of salad oil, in 3 months, the company needs 6 000 000 lb of soybean oil. The company has three choices. It can:

- Leave the exposure unhedged and hope that the price of soybean oil does not rise above 16.10 cents/lb
- Enter the spot market and purchase 6 000 000 lb of oil at 16.00 cents/lb (but pay an additional 0.10 cents/lb for storage and insurance, since it does not need the oil for 3 months)
- Establish a long futures hedge by purchasing soybean oil for delivery in 3 months

If it elects the third option, we further assume that the company can buy 100 contracts of October Chicago Board of Trade (CBOT) soybean oil futures at a price of 16.07 cents/lb (or $9642/contract based on 60 000 lb contract size ($600/tick)) (for simplicity we ignore the effects of initial and variation margin in this, and other, examples).

We can now consider the following two market scenarios, which occur when the company closes out the long futures position just prior to contract expiry in 3 months.

Scenario 1
- Soybean oil settles at 16.75 cents/lb
- Futures gain: +$40 800
  - (100 contracts * $600 tick * (16.75 − 16.07))
- The company purchases oil in the spot market at 16.75 cents/lb actual ($1 005 000), but only 16.07 cents/lb effective ($964 200) after taking account of the profit on the long futures hedge.

Scenario 2
- Soybean oil settles at 15.75 cents/lb
- Futures loss: −$19,200
  - (100 contracts * $600 tick * (15.75 − 16.07))
- The company purchases oil in the spot market at 15.75 cents/lb actual ($945 000), but 16.07 cents/lb effective ($964 200) after taking account of the loss on the long futures hedge.

By establishing the long futures hedge the company is indifferent to what happens in the spot market 3 months hence: it has locked in its costs and, thus, its profit margin.

I.3.1.2   Short hedge on interest rates

As noted earlier, a hedger can protect a natural long position by establishing a short futures position. Assume that on January 1 a company knows it will need to borrow $100 000 000 under its bank facilities at Libor (London Interbank Offer Rate, an offshore interbank interest rate) plus a spread of 25 *basis points* (1/4 of 1%, which we denote as L + 25). It does not need the funds until the end of March and is thus exposed to the direction of interest rates over the 90-day period: if rates rise, its borrowing costs will be higher, and if they fall costs will be lower. The company can remove this interest rate uncertainty by "locking in" today's rates with an appropriate futures hedge. This means it needs a contract that provides compensation if interest rates rise (i.e. the compensation will offset its higher borrowing costs) or requires a payment if interest rates fall (i.e. the payment will be offset by lower borrowing costs). A Eurodollar future, which is tied to Libor, gains in value as Libor falls and loses value as Libor rises; it thus serves as the proper hedge for the company.

On January 1 the company sells March Eurodollar futures to cover the anticipated $100 000 000 borrowing obligation. Since the Chicago Mercantile Exchange's (CME's) 3-month Eurodollar future trades in $1 000 000 notional size the company needs to sell 100 March contracts. Assuming Libor is trading at 5% on January 1, the value of the contract at trade date is 95.00 (100 − 5%) (in reality the Eurodollar price may, or may not, match the current Libor rate – we simply assume they match for ease).

We now consider two market scenarios, which occur at expiry in 3 months.

Scenario 1
- Libor is 6%, meaning Eurodollar futures price settle at 94.00 (100 − 6%)
- The company's net borrowing cost amounts to −$1 3125 000 for the quarter
  ○ Funding cost: −$6 250 000 annualized, or −$1 562 500 for the quarter ($100 000 000 @ 6.25% (e.g. L + 25))
  ○ Futures gain: $250 000 for the quarter (100 contracts ∗ $2500 tick ∗ (95.00 − 94.00))

This is equal to 5.25% annualized, identical to the "Libor plus spread" at inception of the trade on January 1.

Scenario 2
- Libor is 4%, meaning Eurodollar futures price settle at 96.00 (100 − 4%)
- The company's net borrowing cost amounts to −$1 312 500 for the quarter
  ○ Funding cost: −$4 250 000 annualized, or −$1 062 500 for the quarter ($100 000 000 @ 4.25% (e.g. L + 25))
  ○ Futures loss: −$250 000 for the quarter (100 contracts ∗ $2500 tick ∗ (95.00 − 96.00))

This also equals 5.25% annualized, and is identical to both Scenario 1 and the borrowing rate at inception. Through this short Eurodollar hedge the company crystallizes its borrowing costs in advance of its funding needs and is thus indifferent to what happens in the short-term interest rate market.

This simplified example does not illustrate the potential impact of basis risk that might occur as a result of "imperfect hedging" in terms of:

- Size: perhaps the company needs to borrow $100 700 000, meaning the residual $700 000 piece would be unhedged or overhedged

- Maturity: perhaps the company needs to borrow in 4 months instead of 3 months, meaning that it will be exposed to potential rate movements during the remaining 1-month period
- Reference: perhaps the company is borrowing on the basis of *commercial paper rates* (CP, short-term unsecured rates for high-quality companies) or some other non-Libor index, indicating an imperfect mismatch between the borrowing reference and hedge

Though basis risks may exist through any, or all, of these differences, they will be much smaller than the directional risks (e.g. the direction of interest rates) already covered through the short hedge.

I.3.1.3   Extensions of the short hedge on interest rates

Extending this example, we can imagine a scenario where the company has to borrow $100 000 000 every quarter for the next four quarters – March, June, September, and December. In order to protect this exposure it can enter into a *strip hedge* – a hedge comprised of sequential futures contracts corresponding to the incremental quarterly borrowing schedule. The balance of the analysis follows the one presented above (with the same caveats related to potential basis risk if amounts, maturities, or references are not perfectly matched).

When a company needs to borrow in the more distant future, but cannot hedge through long-dated futures contracts as a result of *illiquidity* – or lack of contract volume/activity – it might choose to use a *rolling hedge* (or "*stack and roll*" *hedge*) by continuously selling/repurchasing the nearest contract month (which generally features the greatest *liquidity*, or activity). For instance, if the company needs to borrow in 2 years but trading volume in the 2-year futures sector is nonexistent, it can continuously "roll" its hedge from one contract date to the next; in our original example it might sell March futures, repurchase them just prior to expiry and sell June contracts, repurchase those just before expiry and sell September contracts, and so forth, until the long-dated exposure it is attempting to hedge appears in the liquid part of the curve. In practice Eurodollar, Euribor (Euro Interbank Offer Rate), light sweet crude and a handful of other futures are liquid out to many years; however, other financial and commodity contracts are not as liquid, meaning that a rolling hedge is often a requirement. While a rolling hedge can remove directional risk it can create an exposure to *curve risk*, or risk of changes in the price of the reference asset at different maturity intervals.

A *cross-asset hedge* might be employed when a company, wanting to hedge its risk but having no direct mechanism for doing so, identifies a futures contract that can act as a proxy. This allows potentially large directional risk to be substituted with more manageable basis risk. For instance, if a company borrows based on CP rates rather than Libor, it cannot directly hedge its CP rate exposure as the exchange marketplace features no CP futures contract. Accordingly, it needs to select the best proxy hedge – that is, the one with the highest *correlation* to CP rates. Since different interest rate indexes tend to move in tandem – albeit at different magnitudes – the company can find the one that best suits its needs by:

- Identifying interest rate indexes that feature futures contracts
- Analyzing, through historical data, the correlation between the interest rate indexes and CP rates
- Selecting the one with the highest correlation as a cross-asset hedge (knowing that the higher the correlation, the better the match, and the more effective the resulting hedge)

For instance, a company might note that Treasury bill futures (based on Treasury bill rates) and Eurodollar futures (based on Libor rates) are actively traded, and would examine historical price data to find the one with highest correlation against CP. If Libor features the higher correlation, Eurodollar futures would form an acceptable cross-asset hedge. However, since the price relationship between Libor and CP is not identical, the company must find the correct number of contacts for its hedge. It can do this by:

- First running a statistical process (e.g. linear regression) to determine the precise relationship between the movement of the underlying exposure and the price of the proxy future; the resulting *hedge ratio* indicates how many Eurodollar futures will be required to cover a given CP exposure
- Then estimating the financial impact of unit changes in the underlying CP exposure and proxy Eurodollar futures (e.g. sensitivity level), which allows the proper number of contracts to be executed, and
- Then "tailing the hedge" – or reducing it to take account of the fact that the position is revalued daily rather than at maturity (meaning that the *present value* (discounted future value) of the hedge is equal to the exposure); this is obtained by discounting the number of contracts required by a factor that reflects the risk-free rate and time to maturity

Consider an example where a company needs to hedge a $100 000 000 1-month CP exposure with 3-month Eurodollar futures. Following the process summarized above:

- The company computes a CP/Eurodollar hedge ratio of 0.8 (based on historical prices), meaning it will need 80 Eurodollar contracts ($80 000 000 notional) to cover a $100 000 000 CP exposure
- However, the company notes that a basis point move (1/100th of 1%) in 1-month CP equates to $8.33/month/$1 000 000 versus $25 for 3-month Eurodollars; it therefore needs to adjust the 80 contracts by a sensitivity level of 0.33 ($8.33/$25). Accordingly, it only needs 26.4 contracts for a proper hedge
- Finally, it "tails the hedge" over a 3-month period, reducing the requirement to 26 contracts

By selling 26 Eurodollar contracts as a cross-asset hedge the company removes the directional risk associated with a general movement in interest rates, but preserves a residual CP–Libor basis risk. Though we have illustrated the concept of a cross-asset hedge using interest rates, it is applicable in many other markets, including currencies, equities, commodities, and so forth.

I.3.1.4   Speculative long position in gold

A speculator can express a market view by going long or short in a particular financial or physical asset. Indeed, the simplest speculative strategy is to establish a *naked position* (i.e. an outright, or unhedged, position) in an underlying futures contract in expectation that the price will move favorably: up for a long position, or down for a short position.

For instance, a Japanese investor might be "bullish" on gold, expecting the price to rise over the next few months. To express this view, the investor might purchase gold futures through the Tokyo Commodity Exchange (TOCOM). Assume that TOCOM's June gold contract is trading at ¥1200/g (¥1 200 000/contract or ¥1000/tick) and the investor purchases five contracts. Just

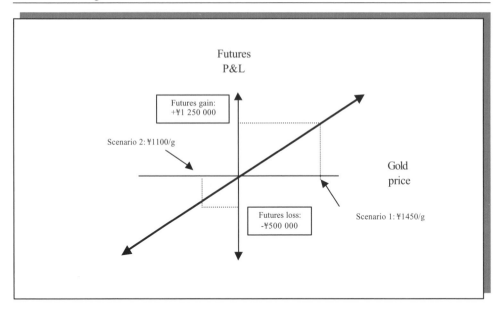

Figure I.10   Speculative long futures position in gold

prior to contract maturity the investor closes out the contract (so as not to take physical delivery of the gold) under two different scenarios.

Scenario 1
- Spot gold rises to ¥1450/g
- Futures gain: ¥1 250 000
  - (5 contracts * ¥1000 tick * (¥1450 − ¥1200))

Scenario 2
- Spot gold falls to ¥1100/g
- Futures loss: −¥500 000
  - (5 contracts * ¥1000 tick * (¥1100 − ¥1200))

It is easy to imagine the opposite scenario – a speculative short position – where the investor sells the June TOCOM contracts, profiting as spot gold falls to ¥1100/g at settlement and losing as it rises to ¥1450/g. Figure I.10 illustrates the futures gains/loss from the speculative long futures position under the two scenarios.

I.3.1.5   Speculative intermarket spread position in crude oil

Speculative positions can also be taken in other forms, including *intermarket spreads*. A spread position seeks to profit from any price convergence or divergence in the spread, or basis, between contracts in related markets. Spread differentials can be caused by a number of factors. For instance, lack of supply in one market might drive prices up, lack of demand in another market might force prices down, storage or transportation costs related to the two references might diverge as a result of labor actions or transport fuel prices, and so on.

Assume that a speculator thinks that the spread between West Texas Intermediate (WTI) oil (one of the US light sweet crude streams deliverable under the NYMEX contract) and Brent oil (the crude benchmark underlying the International Petroleum Exchange's (IPE) futures contract and one of the foreign crude streams deliverable under NYMEX) will narrow over the next 3 months. To take advantage of this view, the speculator sells 1000 September NYMEX crude contracts at \$24.95/barrel and buys 1000 September IPE Brent contracts at \$24.66/barrel, for a net spread of 29 cents per barrel.

We can consider the following scenarios prior to contract close-out in September.

Scenario 1
- WTI falls to \$24.45/barrel, Brent falls to \$24.24/barrel, creating a spread differential of 21 cents
- Futures gain (on NYMEX short position): +\$500 000
  - (1000 contracts ∗ \$1000 tick ∗ (24.95 − 24.45))
- Futures loss (on IPE long position): −\$420 000
  - (1000 contracts ∗ \$1000 tick ∗ (24.24 − 24.66))
- Net gain on intermarket spread: +\$80 000

Even though the speculator lost on the IPE position, it accomplished its goal of gaining on the entire intermarket spread; had the speculator maintained a position in only NYMEX or IPE, the gain or loss would have been much larger.

Scenario 2
- WTI rises to \$25.05/barrel, Brent rises to \$24.70, creating a spread differential of 35 cents
- Futures loss (on NYMEX short position): −\$100 000
  - (1000 contracts ∗ \$1000 tick ∗ (24.95 − 25.05))
- Futures gain (on IPE long position): +\$40 000
  - (1000 contracts ∗ 1000 tick ∗ (24.70 − 24.66))
- Net loss on intermarket spread: − \$60 000

Under this scenario the spread widened from the original 29 cents to 35 cents, contrary to the speculator's view, creating a loss.

I.3.1.6   *Speculative calendar spread position in corn*

A speculator may wish to take advantage of perceived discrepancies in different parts of the maturity curve for a given commodity and can do so by establishing a *calendar spread* (sometimes known as a *time spread*). If futures in one part of the curve appear overly "cheap" relative to other contracts, a speculator can purchase the "cheap" contracts and sell the "expensive" contracts; if the strategy is correct, the speculator will gain as prices between the two calendar contracts converge. As with the intermarket spread discussed above, a calendar spread eliminates exposure to directional movements (e.g. different contract months on the same underlying asset should move in the same general direction) and allows the speculator to focus solely on differences in the curve.

Consider an example where a speculator feels that December corn traded on the Chicago Board of Trade (CBOT) appears cheap relative to June corn, and establishes a calendar spread by purchasing 1000 contracts of December corn at \$2.05/bushel and selling

1000 contracts of June corn at $2.00/bushel (e.g. a spread of 5 cents/bushel). The following scenarios ensue.

Scenario 1
- June corn settles at $2.01/bushel, December corn trades at $2.11/bushel, creating a net spread of 10 cents/bushel
- Futures loss (on June contracts): −$50 000
  - (1000 contracts ∗ 5000 bushels/contract ∗ (2.00 − 2.01))
- Futures gain (on December contracts): +$300 000
  - (1000 contracts ∗ 5000 bushels/contract ∗ (2.11 − 2.05))
- Net gain on calendar spread: +$250 000

Scenario 2
- June corn settles at $1.99, December corn trades at $2.06, creating a net spread of 7 cents/bushel
- Futures gain (on June contracts): +$50 000
  - (1000 contracts ∗ 5000 bushels/contract ∗ (2.00 − 1.99))
- Futures gain (on December contracts): +$50 000
  - (1000 contracts ∗ 5000 bushels/contract ∗ (2.06 − 2.05))
- Net gain on calendar spread: +$100 000

I.3.2 Options strategies

The hedge and speculation strategies discussed above can be replicated using options or futures options; in addition, various unique strategies can be designed to take advantage of the structural features of options. Though we will not consider an exhaustive list of option-based strategies, we define some of the most common in this section.

I.3.2.1 Simple positions

Hedge or speculative positions can be created by simply buying or selling put or call options. A hedger with a natural long position can purchase a put option that generates a protective gain as the market price of the asset falls; in this sense the long put option acts as a "one-sided"[14] short futures position. For example, an agricultural producer with unsold corn inventory can protect against a possible price decline by purchasing a CBOT put option on corn. If the put is struck at $2/bushel, the producer gains as the price of corn falls below $2; although the stock of unsold corn will suffer from the same decline, the option functions as a hedge by providing a compensatory payment. If the price of corn rises to $3, the put becomes worthless but the corn inventory can be sold at the higher price. The only cost to the hedger under this strategy is the premium paid to secure the option. In the same light, a hedger with a natural short position can protect its position by purchasing a call option.

---

[14] Recalling the payoff profiles illustrated earlier in the section, the payoff is only "one-sided" since the buyer of the option will always leave the worthless option unexercised. However, the cost of creating this "one-sided" payoff profile is the premium payment. Note that combining long and short option positions yields "synthetic" futures positions. For instance, a *synthetic long position* is established through a long call and a short put struck at the same price, while a *synthetic short position* is established through a long put and a short call struck at the same price.

A speculator who believes the price of an asset will change can purchase a call option (benefiting as the price increases) or a put option (benefiting as the price decreases). Alternatively, a speculator who thinks the price of the underlying asset will remain relatively stable can sell an option; as long as the option does not move *in-the-money* (i.e. as long as the price of the asset does not move above the strike price for a call, or below the strike price for a put), the speculator gains from the premium income received from selling the option. If, however, the option moves in-the-money, the option buyer will exercise against the speculative seller. In the case of a call option, the speculator will have to deliver the underlying asset; if it does not own the asset it will have to purchase the required quantity in the higher-priced spot market, so suffering a loss. In the case of a put option, the speculator will have to accept the underlying asset; if it does not require the asset for its operations it may be forced to dispose of it in a lower-priced environment, again suffering a loss.

I.3.2.2   Multiple positions

Complex option positions can be created to protect against price changes or express different speculative views. Some of the most common multiple option strategies include long and short call and put spreads, straddles, strangles, butterflies and collars. In general, short option strategies result in a net inflow of premium, and are thus widely used by speculators hoping to generate income.

Call spread

A *call spread* is a combination of a long call option and a short call option, each with different strike prices but identical expiry dates. A long call spread combines a long at- (or near-) the-money call and a short out-of-the-money call, and provides the purchaser with a limited economic gain on the upside. By purchasing the "more expensive" closer-to-the-money option and selling the "cheaper" out-of-the-money option, the spread buyer is a net payer of premium; by selling the second option, however, the overall cost of the position is defrayed. Protection or gain is, of course, limited to the differential between the long and short strikes. For instance, if a hedger with a natural short wishes to protect against rising Brent crude oil prices over a relatively small range (not believing, perhaps, that the market will move a great deal), it might purchase an IPE Brent call struck at $22/barrel and sell a second call struck at $28/barrel; the underlying position will be hedged within the $6 range, but will become unhedged again if oil exceeds $28/barrel. A speculator who is bullish, but not expecting a large market breakout, can also establish a long call spread position, achieving financial gains in the range defined by the two strikes (but not having to pay the same amount of premium as if it simply purchased a long call). A short call spread, created by selling the more expensive call and buying the cheaper one, is taken to express a neutral to bearish view. Figure I.11 summarizes the payoff profile of a long call spread on oil.

Put spread

A *put spread* is a combination of a long put option and a short put option, each with different strike prices but identical expiry dates. A long put spread strategy combines a long at- (or near-) the money put with a short out-of-the-money put to provide the purchaser with an economic gain on the downside, within a range bounded by the two strikes. A short put spread is created by selling the more expensive, closer-to-the-money put and

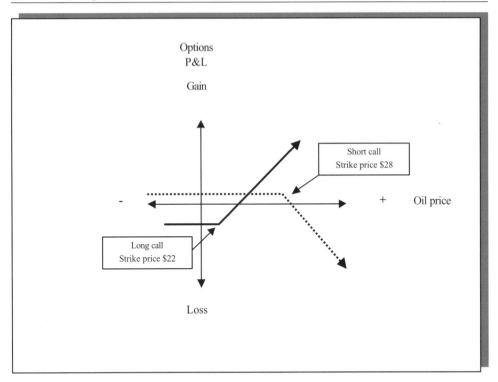

Figure I.11   Long oil call spread payoff profile

buying the cheaper, farther out-of-the-money put, and is taken to express a neutral to bullish view.

Straddle
A *straddle* is a combination of a put option and a call option struck at the same price and expiring on the same date. A long straddle is created by purchasing the call and put, and gives the buyer protection/gain whether the market goes up or down. Indeed, straddles are often bought by those who feel the market will move by a considerable amount, but are unsure in which direction; as a result, they are commonly referred to as a "volatility strategy," seeking to protect against market volatility rather than direction. A hedger can use a long straddle to protect a position, while a speculator can use it to express a view on volatility. For example, a speculator who is unsure whether the broad stock market (as measured by the Standard and Poor's 500 index), will rise or fall over the coming quarter – but expecting that it will be volatile – can purchase a CBOE S&P 500 index call and put struck at the same level (e.g. 850). As long as the market moves up or down by an amount that is large enough to compensate for the premium paid, the position will result in a profit. A short straddle, created by selling the equal strike put and call options, might be taken by a speculator believing the market will remain calm. Figure I.12 illustrates the payoff profile of a long index straddle.

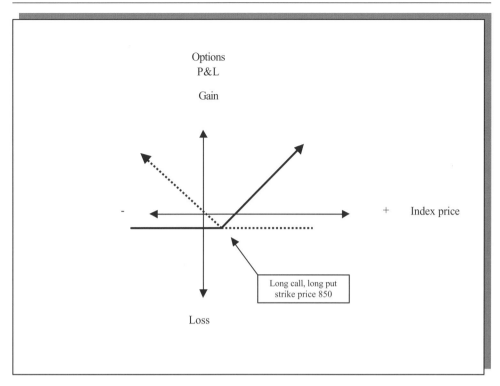

Figure I.12   Long index straddle payoff profile

Strangle

A *strangle* is similar to a straddle, except that the individual put and call options have different, rather than identical, strike prices. A long strangle is thus formed by purchasing a put and a call with different strikes and, depending on the level of the market in relation to the put and call strikes, may require more volatility before generating a payoff; a strangle may thus be cheaper than an equivalent straddle. A short strangle is created by selling a put and a call with different strikes.

Butterfly

A *butterfly* is a combination of long and short options with varying strikes but the same expiry date. A long butterfly, which can be formed by purchasing low- and high-strike options and selling two middle-strike options, creates a payoff profile that resembles a short straddle without the extreme downside. For instance, a firm may buy a CBOT call on wheat at $4/bushel, sell two calls at $4.15/bushel and purchase a fourth at $4.30/bushel; the sale of the two middle-strike calls reduces the cost of the purchased low- and high-strike calls. The greatest gain to the purchaser of a butterfly occurs when the market trades in a relatively narrow range around the short strikes; the downside of the combination is limited to the premium paid. A short butterfly can be constructed by selling a low- and a high-strike option and purchasing two middle-strike options, and thus resembles a long straddle without the extreme upside. Variations on the theme can, of course, be created. For instance, when the two middle-strike options are spread apart the resulting payout, known as a *condor*, approximates a strangle with limited upside/downside (thus, a long condor is equivalent to a short strangle with limited downside and a short condor is akin to a long strangle with limited upside).

Collar

A *collar* can be structured as a long call option/short put option with the same expiry date, or a short call option/long put option with the same expiry date, and is designed to protect a hedger's core downside exposure while giving up some of its upside profit; this reduces the overall cost of the strategy. In the extreme, a firm can create a "*zero cost collar*," where the premium expense of the long option is completely offset by the premium income of the short option. For instance, if a gold producer is trying to protect against a decline in the price of gold, it might purchase a NYMEX gold put struck at $350; to offset the cost of the put (which we assume is $10), it might be willing to give up some of its upside by selling a NYMEX gold call struck at $410 (for a premium receipt of $4). The gold producer may be comfortable giving away gold price "upside" through the short call in exchange for a lower-cost hedge on the downside (e.g. $6 versus $10), since it will be able to sell its own gold in the higher-priced spot market if needed.

This introductory section is intended only to introduce basic concepts related to exchange-traded derivatives. We urge the reader to consult additional works that address specific topics in far greater depth; many of the references listed at the end of the book contain detailed treatments of futures and options pricing, hedging and trading strategies, deliverable asset techniques, risk management approaches, and so forth.

Part I
The Changing Marketplace

1

Forces of Change

1.1 INTRODUCTION

The exchange-traded derivative market has developed into an integral component of the global financial system. The liquid and price-competitive nature of listed futures and options gives institutions the ability to hedge exposures or take speculative positions in volatile markets very efficiently, and has resulted in a steady increase in the dollar value and volume of business flowing through exchanges.

Despite success in creating an effective marketplace, however, exchanges are facing a series of significant challenges – challenges that threaten to alter the "status quo" of the derivatives marketplace and the role of established exchanges. In particular, exchange markets – and the surrounding community of clearinghouses, brokers, and market-makers – are being forced to cope with:

- Deregulation
- Globalization
- Product/market competition
- New technologies
- Disintermediation
- Commercialization

These forces are creating an operating environment that is quite different from the one that characterized the sector from its origins in the eighteenth and nineteenth centuries until the late 1990s. In this chapter we consider each of these "forces of change" by analyzing how they impact exchange operations. In Chapter 2 we extend the discussion by reviewing how exchanges are dealing with these forces – in essence, how they are realigning their operations to remain relevant in the financial world of the twenty-first century. In the balance of the text we describe, in summary form, the operation of the world's leading exchanges, as well as some of its new and emerging marketplaces, to see how they are meeting the competitive threats of the new environment. Figure 1.1 summarizes the major forces at work in the marketplace.

The exchange-traded sector features a large number of authorized, regulated trading forums; as noted in the Introduction, this amounts to at least 70, and as many as 100, exchanges operating throughout the Americas, Asia, Europe, and Africa. While most are important in their respective local marketplaces, many are quite small and fail to attract international participation; they may be subject to sovereign regulations that prohibit offshore activity or lack products that appeal to international institutions. The world's most influential exchanges, in contrast, generally have appealing, liquid products that attract a large number of domestic and international clients. Our focus in this book, in the interest of both content and space, is therefore on the major exchanges of the world (including some very important operations located in emerging markets, as noted in Chapters 25–29).

While our primary focus is on traditional exchanges, we would be remiss if we did not include some discussion of the "new breed" of *electronic communication networks* (ECNs, part of a

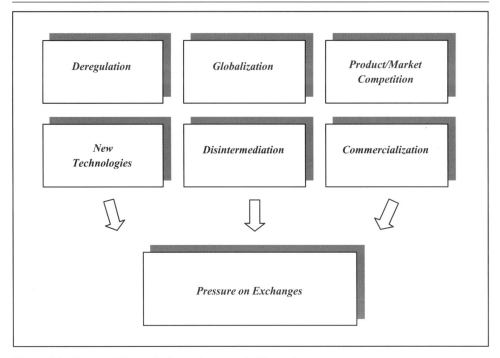

Figure 1.1   Forces of change in the exchange-traded derivative sector

broader group of *business-to-business (B2B) exchanges*) that have developed in recent years through advances in distributed technologies and communication networks; Chapters 30–34 are devoted to a brief review of several of these platforms; some of these new electronic exchanges have evolved into viable conduits and may ultimately emerge as important challengers of traditional exchanges. As we shall note in the next few chapters, the traditional exchange-traded market is changing form rapidly, and will one day contain elements of the ECN world that make it a true "hybrid" marketplace.

Table 1.1 contains a summary of the exchanges discussed in this text; the acronyms appearing in the table are used throughout the book to refer to specific exchanges.

1.2   DEREGULATION

Deregulation means a flexible and global derivatives market that is characterized by lower barriers to entry, greater competition, profit pressures and volatility, and stricter regulatory reporting, compliance, and financial requirements. It can lead to greater liquidity if competitors build mechanisms to promote business, or less liquidity if new efforts simply serve to fragment the marketplace.

As deregulation takes greater hold, institutions (including exchanges and their participants) face a markedly different operating environment:

• Exchange competition increases as barriers to entry are lowered
  – New products, trading/dealing forums, and mechanisms are granted licenses or authorization by local regulators

Table 1.1   Major global exchanges

Exchange	Location
Bolsa de Mercadorias e Futuros (BM&F)	São Paulo
Borsa Italiana (BI)	Milan
BrokerTec Futures Exchange (BTEX)	New York
Chicago Board of Trade (CBOT)	Chicago
Chicago Board Options Exchange (CBOE)	Chicago
Chicago Mercantile Exchange (CME)	Chicago
Eurex	Frankfurt, Zurich
Euronext	Amsterdam, Paris, Brussels, Lisbon, London
European Electricity Exchange (EEX)	Frankfurt, Leipzig
Hong Kong Exchanges and Clearing (HKEx)	Hong Kong
International Petroleum Exchange (IPE)	London
Intercontinental Exchange (ICE)	Atlanta, London
International Securities Exchange (ISE)	New York
Korea Futures Exchange (KOFEX)	Seoul
London International Financial Futures Exchange (LIFFE)	London
London Metal Exchange (LME)	London
Malaysian Derivatives Exchange (MDEX)	Kuala Lumpur
Mercado Español de Futuros Financieros (MEFF)	Madrid
Mercado Mexicano de Derivados (MEXDER)	Mexico City
Montreal Exchange (MX)	Montreal
New York Board of Trade (NYBOT)	New York
New York Mercantile Exchange (NYMEX)	New York
OM Stockholmsborsen (OM)	Stockholm
OneChicago (OC)	Chicago
Osaka Securities Exchange (OSE)	Osaka
Singapore Exchange (SGX)	Singapore
South African Futures Exchange (SAFEX)	Johannesburg
Sydney Futures Exchange (SFE)	Sydney, Wellington
Tokyo Commodity Exchange (TOCOM)	Tokyo
Tokyo Grain Exchange (TGE)	Tokyo
Tokyo International Financial Futures Exchange (TIFFE)	Tokyo
Tokyo Stock Exchange (TSE)	Tokyo

- Volatility in the financial markets increases as capital moves in search of profitable opportunities
- Regulatory reporting requirements increase as regulators seek information regarding the safety and security of those providing financial services
- New capital and liquidity rules are imposed to ensure appropriate financial security

Though the specific characteristics of regulatory change are broad and dynamic, they directly and indirectly force exchanges to alter their approaches to business.[1]

Deregulation of markets often lowers barriers to entry. While regulation is typically intended to protect participants (e.g. exchanges, intermediaries, and end-users) by ensuring a robust framework of controls, it can also have the added "side effect" of keeping new competitors at bay. For instance, strict requirements related to exchange licensing, membership, capital and

---

[1] This is true even when a national authority grants local exchanges "self-regulatory" status. Self-regulation is relatively prevalent in the exchange-traded world, where individual forums seek to protect their operations by applying certain safety standards and controls to their business; many of the controls look strikingly similar to those recommended by regulators.

liquidity levels, clearing or market-making responsibilities, mandatory technology investment, and so forth, may all be part of the regulatory protection scheme; new competitors may be unwilling, or unable, to meet these hurdles. Deregulation measures that result in a lowering of some (or all) of these requirements can spawn new exchange competitors. New competitors, in turn, can create profit pressures for established exchanges as they enter the market and squeeze margins; cutting prices is not an uncommon strategy for competitors hoping to gain market share at the expense of established leaders. In certain cases this can also lead to lower liquidity – particularly when new exchanges or ECNs introduce competing products that cause fragmentation; a fragmented market often lacks a central pool of liquidity, and can lead to price inefficiencies in the medium term. If new exchanges choose to offer complementary, rather than competitive, products/services, market breadth can expand and liquidity deepen.

As deregulation leads to the elimination of investment restrictions, capital moves more freely across borders and new participants join the marketplace. While liquidity may or may not improve – depending on whether or not competition induces price cuts or market fragmentation – volatility is almost certain to increase. As investors, hedgers, and speculators gain access to new markets, they can put their capital to work in the pursuit of new profits; some of this activity may be very short term in nature, driven by perceived speculative opportunities. In addition, market economies operating without capital restrictions must take greater command of monetary and fiscal policies through their marketplaces, meaning financial indicators can rise and fall with greater speed, and by greater amounts. Greater volatility typically benefits risk management instruments – including listed derivatives – as institutions hedge away, or position for, market movements. Exchanges must thus be prepared to meet the business opportunities generated by increased capital flows and associated market volatility.

In general, most countries and their national regulators appear to be adopting a "less is more" approach to regulation, dismantling rules which are no longer useful or can better serve the industry when applied less onerously. Deregulation can occur by discarding existing rules or updating ("redrafting") aspects of regulatory code. For instance, in the US the 1981 Shad–Johnson Agreement (which formalized the division of regulatory powers between the Securities and Exchange Commission (SEC)[2] and the Commodity Futures Trading Commission (CFTC)[3]), effectively banned trading of single stock futures;[4] the Agreement was discarded in 2000 and US exchanges can now offer single stock futures.[5] An example of a more extensive regulatory "overhaul" – designed to make rules more equitable and applicable in the local marketplace – is found in the passage of the Commodity Futures Modernization Act (CFMA) of 2000, which replaced the Commodity Exchange Act (CEA), and its forerunner, after nearly 80 years.[6] The CFMA has been a catalyst for change in the exchange world, permitting: the creation of new technology-based exchanges to offer standardized and custom products; the development of legally independent clearinghouses to clear exchange and OTC derivatives;

---

[2] The SEC is an independent government agency charged with overseeing the US securities markets. It has jurisdiction over markets and securities, including OTC derivatives and certain listed derivatives (e.g. options on securities and stock indexes).

[3] The CFTC is an independent government agency that was established in 1974 to administer federal commodity laws. CFTC has authority over futures, options, and leveraged contracts involving commodities and indexes of securities. It is responsible for reviewing terms/conditions of national markets/contracts, ensuring that contracts meet normal market flows and conducting daily surveillance. The CFTC works closely with, and audits, the National Futures Association (NFA), an industry body supporting self-regulation.

[4] Under the Shad–Johnson Agreement (named for the chairmen of the SEC and CFTC presiding over the divisions in the early 1980s), the SEC, which already had explicit regulatory authority over the country's securities and OTC derivative markets, was given regulatory authority over options on securities and stock indexes; the CFTC was granted explicit authority for options on futures.

[5] While this is an important advance for the US and its competitive position, trading of stock futures is hardly new: since the late 1980s, nearly a dozen local exchanges around the world have introduced their own single stock futures contracts.

[6] The CEA was an enduring piece of futures legislation, having been created in 1922 as the Grain Futures Act and renamed the CEA in 1936.

the use of cross-margin agreements across products to improve management of member margins; and so forth. This type of regulatory "updating" is a form of deregulation that effectively allows forums and participants to do more, rather than less, under the overall national regulatory framework. Similar deregulation measures are afoot in Japan, other parts of Asia and Europe. For instance, Japanese laws have been amended to allow exchanges to become "for profit" corporate institutions, enter into exchange partnerships and alliances, and introduce new products for the retail sector; European laws have been altered to allow clearinghouses to operate across national borders without significant restriction; and so forth.

Though deregulation is under way, there remains a certain lack of clarity and uniformity. For instance, regulations are still largely focused on familiar national/regional boundaries rather than cross-border realities. Though an exchange's business may emanate from various remote international locations, it is simpler for a single national regulator to assume responsibility for these activities than for a regulatory panel or "cross-border" regulator to form and police the business. Cooperative regulatory arrangements, which reflect twenty-first-century trading realities, must be formed to cope with business that is becoming ever more global. In addition, some countries still feature more regulation than others. While this may exist for good reason, there is a danger that some "overregulated" exchanges will be placed at a competitive disadvantage in the global marketplace. For instance, US regulation is more stringent than that of many other countries. While this is unlikely to be an issue when dealing with very liquid contracts on US financial references (after all, participants, have little choice if they want to trade liquid US contracts such as the S&P 500, light sweet crude oil, or Eurodollars), it is likely to be a more serious consideration when dealing with instruments that are freely traded elsewhere (e.g. gold, coffee, sugar); in such cases overregulation might drive business to exchanges with more liberal regulations. Consider NYMEX and the LME. Both exchanges trade gold contracts, but the NYMEX contract is much more heavily regulated; indeed, the LME contract has no price transparency, no formal audit trail, and no member-posted margins (margins are granted through credit limits) – participants wanting this relative "flexibility" may well direct their business to the LME. Similar examples can be found in other marketplaces.

Interestingly enough, deregulation can actually increase regulatory reporting requirements for exchanges and participants. In order to ensure appropriate financial security for participants, regulators and self-regulatory organizations are apt to require more information on the status of positions, risks, market movements, and so forth; this additional "reporting burden" might be seen as one of the costs of operating in a freer environment. In some cases regulators might also require participants to possess greater financial strength (i.e. more liquidity, more capital). This allows markets and institutions to bear the costs of possible problems created by a more liberal operating environment (e.g. member default on the exchange).

All forums need to adapt to changing regulation. Though institutions most often fear excess regulation (which can constrain business and stifle market and product expansion), a dearth of regulation can be equally disruptive. Exchanges have to be able to react to these regulatory changes by: meeting new competitive threats created by lower barriers to entry; coping with greater market volatility; adhering to new reporting requirements; and, ultimately, adapting business focus. Though complex, broad efforts at deregulation might ultimately lead to regulatory harmonization and rationalization. In some countries, for instance, exchange and securities markets are governed by different regulatory authorities and receive different treatment for instruments that essentially perform the same function (e.g. equity, equity options, equity futures, equity futures options, equity forwards, equity swaps). As the pressure to deregulate continues, national regulators will have to synchronize their views by determining how to oversee their products and markets. If logic prevails, the end result should be uniform rules across markets and products that perform the same basic risk management or investment function; we consider this topic in greater detail in Chapter 2.

1.3 GLOBALIZATION

Globalization means interconnected financial markets that promote cross-border capital movement – this requires exchanges to deliver products that support international capital flows and trading platforms that permit "around the clock" access. Globalization also means a renewed focus on development of national exchange platforms that can link into the industrialized mainstream.

The globalization of institutions, markets, and products means exchanges are again faced with a new set of challenges:

- Pressure to remain at the "leading edge" of product and market development is acute
- Redesign of operations and business strategies to support a global, 24-hour business becomes a priority
- Redefinition of business focus when the underlying operating environment changes becomes vital
- Development of national futures/options efforts assumes added importance and urgency

Global financial markets, linked by pools of free-moving capital, characterize the twenty-first-century financial environment and large institutional players are a central element of this global capital "linkage." In an increasingly borderless world driven by deregulation, technology, and shareholder demands, these institutions use their capital to obtain the best possible returns or hedges; for instance, they might use derivatives to create a risk position, hedge an exposure, or leverage the returns on an investment. Any marketplace (and its underlying instruments) that allows an institution to obtain a proper hedge/speculative position efficiently stands to benefit.

In order to capture this business, exchanges need to be at the "leading edge" of product and market development; any delay or error can prove costly, as business can easily be lost to the larger and more flexible OTC market, or to newer ECNs. While most established exchanges are constantly trying to improve existing products or introduce new ones, they must be even more diligent in an era of rapid global change. This might require the creation of more sophisticated instruments or entirely new business lines, or a merger or alliance with another exchange in order to fill a time-zone or product void. The global nature of markets means institutions cannot wait for an exchange to be "open" in order to execute trades. Eight-hour trading days are a relic of the past – market activity does not stop with the sounding of a bell on an exchange floor. To properly address the requirements of global institutions it is now necessary for an exchange to provide trading day coverage spanning 18–24 hours. If an exchange cannot do so through its own structure and platform, it might be forced to develop a cross-border alliance that fills the time-zone gap. Institutions are also unlikely to want to "shop around" for the best pricing or product selection; in a rapidly changing market environment they want immediate access to the tightest pricing and broadest product selection. This, again, means that an exchange has to offer a suite of well-priced products, or develop seamless interfaces to other exchanges or alliance partners that can.

Globalization necessarily leads to redefinition. When the environment changes as a result of significant political or economic forces, the markets and conduits supporting them must adapt in order to remain relevant. European monetary harmonization serves as a good case study. Monetary integration, signaled through the introduction of the euro and the coordination of monetary policies among participating countries, forced many financial institutions (including exchanges) to redefine their roles. Once integration was agreed, many of the regional financial markets and exchanges that had played an important role in domestic financial policy were forced to look for new ways of doing business – or risk becoming irrelevant. For instance, regional exchanges that featured local bond contracts that became part of the euro were suddenly left without a critical mass of liquidity – hedgers and speculators no longer needed to position, or hedge with, Spanish or Italian government bond futures through the local exchanges, for instance, but could turn directly to the very liquid German Bund contracts traded on Eurex or Euronext. Much the same happened with those that once relied heavily on trading of individual European currency rates; 12 currencies have condensed into one (and more will follow over the coming years as the European Union grows larger), meaning those relying on currency derivatives have had to redefine their roles in order to remain relevant.

Globalization and industrialization are almost synonymous – the industrial nations of the world are the primary drivers of global development and investment. As countries join the "developed mainstream" they need financial markets and instruments that support their economies; this often leads to the creation of national exchange markets. Though the US was the dominant force in the exchange-traded markets during the 1970s and early 1980s, its share of the world market has declined steadily since the mid-1980s as new exchanges have formed. For instance, the US accounted for 79% of world exchange-traded volume in 1986, but only 43% by 1998.[7] The decline is not due to the fact that US markets are still somewhat overregulated or that product innovation has been stifled or squeezed out by OTC alternatives. Rather, it is because countries such as Spain, Sweden, Malaysia, China/Hong Kong, South Africa, Brazil, Mexico, and others – realizing the importance of conduits and contracts in furthering national economic and business goals – have actively created their own exchanges. Local exchange capabilities allow countries to address national needs very specifically: they provide local government and commercial participants with the tools to manage monetary policy, commercial exposures, and financial positions. Success at a local level can lead to a greater state of financial and economic readiness – a state that characterizes an industrialized country. Growth through this "national interest" is evidenced by the fact that the most active international contracts are those that reference non-US financial indicators, including:

- Exchange rates
- Local short-term deposit rates
- Local medium/long-term government bond rates
- Local equities and equity indexes

Physical commodity references are typically of "secondary" importance in new or emerging local marketplaces (the only real exceptions tend to be global commodity indicators such as crude oil and gold).[8] Most resources and efforts are targeted toward financial indicators that allow active management of micro- and macro-exposures, and participation by local and

---

[7] Commodity Futures Trading Commission (1999), *The Global Competitiveness of US Futures Markets Revisited*, Washington DC.

[8] Even in advanced futures markets, such as those of the US and Europe, the bulk of futures and options activity has moved toward financial indicators. Most growth over the past decade has been in interest rate and equity contracts, which now account for two-thirds to three-quarters of all global exchange activity. In the US, for instance, the most actively traded contracts are on US Treasuries and 3-month Eurodollars (together accounting for nearly 50% of exchange-traded volume), followed by light sweet crude oil and the S&P 500.

offshore institutions. The fact that many countries are successfully introducing their own exchanges and contracts (many of which can be traded nearly 24 hours a day through a multitude of electronic links), suggests that globalization is, indeed, spreading. Any country that wishes to be a contender in the global economy of the twenty-first century needs a complete and robust financial system to attract institutional capital and manage its economy. A sophisticated, exchange marketplace is now virtually a requirement for joining the global marketplace.

1.4 PRODUCT/MARKET COMPETITION

Product/market competition means hedgers, investors, and speculators can substitute exchange contracts with other alternatives. To preserve, and ultimately gain, market share in the risk management and investment sectors, exchanges must create innovative and liquid products and deliver them efficiently, securely, and cost-effectively. Exchanges must also create new business lines in order to diversify revenues and protect against margin erosion and market cycles.

The exchange-traded sector is not a monopoly market, but operates in a world with risk and investment substitutes; this means competitive pressures are large – and growing:

- The OTC derivative market is larger, and more creative, than ever – and can often be the lowest-cost provider of risk management or investment instruments
- Newer electronic marketplaces, which can support a broad range of products and services, are providing participants with very flexible and cost-effective alternatives. These platforms are also attempting to replicate through various means some of the structural advantages of exchanges – such as centralized clearing – in order to become more "perfect" substitutes
- Developing and introducing new exchange products is a time-consuming and expensive – but ultimately necessary – process. Adding new business lines – another expensive proposition – is becoming a requirement in order to balance exchange revenue sources

The OTC market, which traces its origins to the early 1980s when parallel currency loans were repackaged as standardized currency swaps, has grown rapidly in both depth and breadth. As noted in the Introduction, OTC contracts give users the ability to customize transaction parameters, including notional size, currency, maturity, underlying reference, payment frequency, and so forth; this flexibility has allowed it to capture a large share of the institutional risk management and investment business. Though participants generally bear the credit risk of a counterparty (rather than a clearinghouse) and liquidity for some instruments can be thin, OTC derivatives compete aggressively against exchange derivatives[9] – particularly in products that fall just outside of the "mainstream." While trading in Eurodollars, Bunds, US Treasuries, the S&P 500 and a handful of other references can be done very cost-effectively with exchange contracts, trading in certain other assets can often be handled more efficiently through the OTC market. For instance, an institution seeking to cover medium-term Canadian dollar interest rates, or longer-dated Eurosterling, Swiss francs or French equity volatility, might obtain better execution levels in the OTC market. In addition, the OTC market is often a product leader, introducing instruments that are not available in exchange-traded form – thus forcing

---

[9] The relationship between OTC and exchange markets is not always adversarial. Indeed, the two depend on each other for liquidity and management of residual risk exposures – an established futures market benefits from a strong OTC market, and vice versa (and both can benefit from a strong cash market). For instance, when an OTC dealer executes a large OTC transaction it often turns to the exchange market for a cost-effective hedge. But even this relationship has limits. If the OTC dealer can execute the hedge more cheaply and efficiently in the OTC market, it is likely to do so. This means the exchange markets have to remain viable, effective, and efficient.

exchanges to "catch up." The OTC market, for instance, was the first to feature interest rate swaps (in the early 1980s, just after the introduction of currency swaps); after a 20-year delay, some exchanges (e.g. LIFFE, CME, SFE) have started introducing their own swap contracts. The OTC market also features a thriving business in *credit derivatives* (e.g. default/credit spread derivatives referencing the credit performance of individual counterparties) – one that does not yet exist in listed form. With many institutions actively managing their credit risk exposures, the ability to execute credit derivatives is increasingly important – but exchanges have not yet created a competing product of their own. The same is true in more esoteric asset classes, including catastrophe risk and weather risk. Though certain exchanges (e.g. CBOT, CME, LIFFE) have offered contracts on these risks for the past few years, liquidity has been thin to nonexistent; activity in the OTC market is far greater. Financial structures with any degree of complexity (e.g. exotic options, structured notes with embedded derivatives, and so on) are the preserve of the OTC market – and will continue to be in the future. The arrival of ECNs that facilitate dealing in OTC structures (as discussed in greater detail below), will give the OTC market an even bigger boost over the coming years, placing even greater pressures on the exchange-traded sector.

Since the OTC marketplace has grown so rapidly and proven to be such a product innovator, the pressure on exchanges, and exchange leadership and members, is formidable. Exchanges do not want to lose their "bread and butter" business – the liquid benchmark contracts they have developed over the years – to the OTC markets and they do not want to be seen as lacking the capacity to create new products: it is important that they be viewed as product innovators and market leaders, not just "reactive" followers. Development of new products is generally a time-consuming and expensive process that relies on months, or even years, of research and development based on market analysis, end-user consultation, pricing/analytics development, technology programming and support, advertising and marketing, and so forth. Though expensive in terms of time and dollars, exchanges really have no alternative if they want to remain competitive.

Creation of alternate services – such as OTC and third-party clearing, technology, data/analytics, market information, and so forth – is also a growing requirement. Exchanges that confine their business solely to derivative products may be missing opportunities to maximize revenues and create cash flows that can be used for technology investment and further product research and development. They are also more susceptible to revenue downturns when derivative trading slows. Associated value-added business services play to the strengths of exchanges that are willing to develop and market them commercially. If they fail to do so many third-party providers are willing to "fill the void"; indeed, exchanges are already experiencing pressure from alternative competitors such as technology companies, independent clearing firms and market information and data providers – just as they are from the OTC and electronic markets in their core product base of derivative instruments.

1.5 NEW TECHNOLOGIES

New technologies mean more efficient and convenient ways of executing business – a benefit to new electronic platforms designed around such architecture and an obvious threat to traditional physical, open-outcry businesses that fail to adapt. New technologies are a large, but increasingly necessary, cost of doing business, and the redesign of operations to accommodate automated client interface, execution, clearing, and delivery is becoming an integral part of the twenty-first-century business model.

Many exchanges were taken aback by the arrival of distributed technologies and advanced communications that appeared in earnest during the latter part of the 1990s. While some were prepared for the changes that accompanied these advances, many were not – and have been placed in a difficult position. In fact, new technologies represent the single greatest force impacting exchange operations:

- New technology-based business models have reshaped the commercial and financial environment
- Market structures have been altered, causing fragmentation in some sectors, consolidation and massing of liquidity in others
- Disintermediation of different participants in the exchange "chain" has accelerated
- Long-standing physical, open-outcry mechanisms are being called into question
- Capital demands to fund vital technology projects have increased dramatically

The rise of new technologies in the latter part of the twentieth century marked a key turning point for many in the financial industry, including those in the exchange community. The advent of new technology has lowered barriers to entry and created a new "breed" of competitor. In the process it has forced – and continues to force – exchanges to rethink their business strategies, product offerings, and delivery mechanisms, and has demanded a new commitment to technology – generally at a considerable cost. Indeed, failure to respond by altering operating mechanisms, trading access, and product design can diminish any competitive advantage an exchange possesses.

The creation and rapid expansion of *electronic commerce* – or business conducted solely or primarily in an electronic environment – started in the mid-1990s and gained momentum into the millennium. A move toward direct B2B technology platforms, capable of delivering virtually any product and associated service through flexible electronic mechanisms, changed many of the established operating rules of the business world. Rather than conducting business through traditional methods and relationships, new technologies – based on powerful and fast computer hardware, flexible computing languages, new communications protocols, and rapid routing and networking infrastructure – allow companies to deal with each other directly, and for intermediaries to provide clients with more efficient ways of doing business. While the electronic commerce movement started in the retail sector (with consumers using the Internet to purchase a broad range of goods), it quickly spread to the much larger institutional marketplace, with technologies enhanced to handle the rigorous dimensions of institutional dealing.[10] As a result, a new wave of competitors has entered the commercial arena generally, and the financial arena specifically. New B2B financial companies – many lacking the traditional "physical presence" commonly associated with banks, brokers, and exchanges – now offer the same products and services as traditional "physical" institutions. In 1998 the SEC approved the creation of *alternative trading systems* (ATSs, or ECNs) – electronic forums for conducting financial business; regulators in many other countries have done the same (e.g. the UK's Financial Services Authority, Japan's Ministry of Finance, Hong Kong's Monetary Authority, and so on). ECNs can be structured in different forms: execution systems or "destination networks," order routing mechanisms, crossing networks, routers and executers, and so forth. Regardless of specific form, these platforms have encroached on territory that was once the exclusive domain of established securities and derivative exchanges (as well as OTC market-makers,

---

[10] Though most B2B platforms feature the same communications and security features as retail-based Internet platforms, they are far more secure, dedicated, and robust.

such as large financial institutions); specifically, ECNs provide the framework for listing and trading financial instruments/contracts on a variety of underlying references.

Some of the new entrants have successfully achieved critical mass in certain instruments. Since they are so flexible, they have the advantage of being able to offer both common and customized contracts that might not otherwise achieve the requisite level of liquidity in an exchange-traded marketplace. Those that have succeeded – i.e. those that survived the "dot com" bubble of the late 1990s and early 2000 by proving the economic viability of their business models and the technical capability of their technology architecture – have been able to address many of the demands of buyers and sellers, including simple and flexible access and execution, transparent pricing, and front-to-back processing – all at a low cost. This represents a considerable threat to established exchanges.

While the early efforts of some platforms have proven successful, broader issues related to market structure, fragmentation, and liquidity have arisen; the role of formal exchanges versus flexible platforms in a new marketplace has not yet been determined. For instance, short- and long-term financial markets are driven by different dynamics. Short-term activity is heavily influenced by pricing and liquidity created through the interaction of buyers and sellers, brokers, dealers, and other intermediaries; business is often driven by standalone or discrete transactions that reflect tactical response, and may benefit from flexible trading mechanisms. Long-term markets, in contrast, are often based on strategic actions and established corporate relationships; quick reaction is less likely to occur and the need for flexible trading mechanisms may be of less importance. Since short-term markets are so dynamic (and, to a great extent, "self-organizing") it is unclear whether a rigid, center-based exchange structure (Figure 1.2), can continue to work effectively – particularly in an era when a more fluid structure, that takes account of different participants and execution platforms (Figure 1.3), is available. How end-users and intermediaries ultimately use ECNs and other flexible mechanisms will help dictate how organized exchanges and markets evolve, and which players become dominant. The "end-game" might, in fact, be a combination of traditional exchanges and ECNs, direct exchange-to-client contact and intermediated business, and so forth. Market structure may also reveal whether market fragmentation will be a persistent problem. As more providers use technology to overcome barriers to entry and introduce new markets/products, participants may gravitate to different forums to achieve their goals; in the absence of fungibility across platforms, markets, and products, fragmentation may appear – by market, product, or geography. The creation of

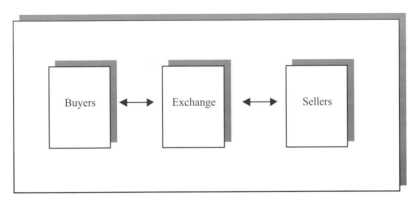

Figure 1.2   Center-based marketplace and technologies

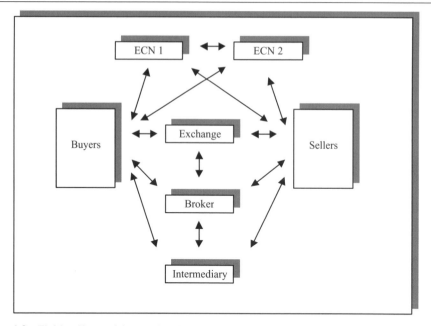

Figure 1.3   Fluid, self-organizing marketplace

multiple liquidity pools in the same product or marketplace, without a critical mass of trades, may lead to less favorable pricing. Less favorable pricing, in turn, might lead to a decline in business in certain marketplaces and, ultimately, broader marketplace consolidation.

Though the ECN world is still developing, we can consider three broad categories of platforms for purposes of our discussion:

- Dealer market ECNs
- Regulated ECNs
- Hybrid ECNs

Some ECNs have a degree of structure and standardization (e.g. uniform contract specifications and central clearing facilities) that makes them look like traditional exchanges. Others lack product standardization or are dependent on the creditworthiness of the sponsoring institution(s), and are thus quite different from traditional exchanges; in fact, these *dealer market ECNs* are actually cash or OTC "execution conduits," backed by individual counterparties/consortia, where the sponsor(s) posts prices on products or brings together multiple buyers and sellers. Different types of dealer market ECNs have been created since the late 1990s to service individual segments of the electronic financial markets (e.g. Atriax, Volbroker, Swapswire, Creditrade, Creditex, UBSW Online (the former Enron Online platform), and so on). Though most lack the structural advantages of exchanges (e.g. clearinghouses to mitigate the effects of credit risk) and a critical mass of liquidity, some have succeeded and proven that there is market demand for the product or service platform.

A distinction between dealer market forums and those offering derivative trading that approximates or replicates that of an established exchange is important: not every online exchange is a direct substitute forum for futures and options trading. *Regulated ECNs*, which enjoy specific regulatory authorization to operate as electronic futures exchanges, can be considered electronic versions of traditional exchanges, offering products (but perhaps not yet the liquidity) that are effectively fungible. This is an important distinction for those who specifically want to deal in a regulated exchange environment because of the advantages offered – namely standardized contracts, centralized clearing, transparent pricing, and regulatory approval and oversight. Electronic platforms such as OneChicago (OC), BrokerTec Futures Exchange (BTEX), and the European Electricity Exchange (EEX), for instance, have been approved by their respective national regulators to operate as designated electronic futures markets, or regulated ECNs.

In some cases electronic exchanges are acting as *hybrid ECNs*, merging the dealer market and regulated ECN models by delivering customized and standardized products through unregulated and regulated units. For instance, the Intercontinental Exchange (ICE, owned by a group of prominent energy companies and financial institutions) has successfully introduced a dealer market platform with OTC energy, metals, and weather trading (some contracts have standardized features); it also owns IPE, the regulated UK energy exchange, and is gradually migrating the IPE's established contracts to an all-electronic platform. As part of its overall business plan ICE is also seeking to operate in the US as a regulated exchange.

Though many ECNs have been created since the late 1990s, few have yet to succeed in a meaningful way; some invariably will, but many others will not. Those that fail are most likely to suffer from one or more of the following flaws:

- Inability to provide a compelling business proposition (e.g. leading-edge products and services delivered in a timely, cost-effective fashion)
- Lack of a critical mass of liquidity (e.g. imbalance between buyers and sellers, coupled with market fractionalization[11])
- Failure to convince customers to abandon "old ways" of doing business
- Inability to provide protection against counterparty credit risk (e.g. lack of centralized clearing or some alternate form of credit protection)[12]

Only when an ECN addresses these concerns can it attract the participation needed to create and sustain a meaningful business. When it does, the competitive challenge it can present established exchanges is likely to be considerable.

With new technology influencing business activities and creating new sources of competition, traditional conduits and intermediaries are under considerable pressure to redesign their business strategies. While delivering financial services through traditional mechanisms was satisfactory several years ago – there really was no other choice – clients increasingly demand a range of options: traditional delivery, electronic delivery, automated execution and confirmation, electronic straight-through processing, cross-platform access, and so forth. Inability to offer at least some of these options leads quickly to a competitive disadvantage. Accordingly, many financial institutions and marketplaces, including exchanges, have spent the past few years examining new technologies, determining which are appropriate for their business lines and executing multiyear, multimillion dollar plans to streamline, enhance, automate, or replace their infrastructure.

---

[11] Though ECNs can be value-added and progressive, they can also fractionalize the market so much that a true, deep pool of liquidity cannot build in a single location – meaning customers will not necessarily get the best execution price. "Centralization versus fragmentation" must therefore be considered. Participants must determine whether a centralized marketplace is essential to best price execution or whether a competitive, though fragmented, market achieves the same benefit (at least in the short run).

[12] Since ECNs typically lack the clearing and settlement facilities of their own, those seeking to replicate the beneficial features of exchange derivatives need to unite with clearing entities that can supply such security (the lack of credit risk is, after all, one of the primary advantages of dealing in exchange contracts). As we shall note later in the book, joint ventures and alliances between ECNs and clearinghouses are becoming more prevalent.

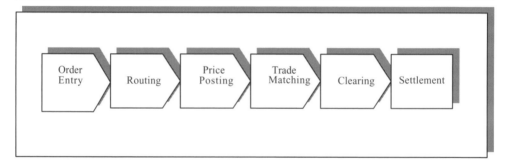

Figure 1.4   Automating the listed futures and options process

As summarized in Figure 1.4, it is already possible for every stage in the listed derivative process to be performed with a high degree of automation (if not perfectly, at least very reliably). Though different stages have been (and continue to be) automated by exchanges at different points in time, Hull Group's 1992 conversion of Deutsche Terminborse's (DTB, now part of Eurex) front- to back order flow marked an early instance of a full electronic platform. The conversion process gathered momentum in the mid-1990s as new technologies became available, and continues to the present time. Exchanges must generally employ technology in every stage of the process in order to remain efficient and cost-competitive. But adapting technology for use in futures trading is an expensive, long-term proposition that strains exchange revenues and resources. Though financial benefits clearly exist – in the form of greater business volumes and cost savings – the upfront costs of partial or complete conversion to an electronic environment are substantial. Smaller exchanges, or those without adequate resources, that are unable to fund the same level of technology investment might have to consider alternate solutions, such as purchasing individual software modules from other exchanges or third-party providers over an extended period of time. In extreme situations such exchanges might even be forced to merge or combine with those that have greater technological capabilities. If established exchanges can successfully implement new technologies they have a considerable advantage over ECNs; they can use their history, experience, contacts, reputations, clients, and market share to help preserve, and even build, on the pool of liquidity that is so essential to efficient pricing. By doing so they may also be able to avoid fractionalization and minimize competition.

The advent of new technology brings to mind one of the central questions facing a number of major exchanges: can physical, open-outcry trading survive? Indeed, should it survive? For many global exchanges physical trading is a mechanism of the past, and conversion to an electronic environment has commenced or has already been completed. For example, influential exchanges such as LIFFE, SFE, Euronext, and HKEx have already determined that the future of the listed derivatives business is electronic and have converted to all-electronic platforms. For others, including many of the world's most powerful, the answer is still unclear. Major forums such as the CME, NYMEX, and CBOE, for instance, have all embraced technology and made considerable strides in implementing new electronic platforms and services – but have not abandoned open-outcry trading.[13] Thus far, these exchanges feel they can provide customers with the best product range, liquidity, and pricing by operating through physical and

---

[13] The CME, for instance, created the PMT Partnership as early as 1987 to operate Globex 1, the exchange's first electronic overnight platform; the exchange revamped and upgraded the platform several times and now features a robust framework that permits electronic trading during day or evening hours.

Table 1.2 Summary of global exchanges
with physical trading floors

Exchange	Physical location
BM&F	São Paulo
CBOE	Chicago
CBOT	Chicago
CME	Chicago
IPE	London
LME	London
NYBOT	New York
NYMEX	New York
SGX	Singapore

electronic platforms, and have refused to abandon open-outcry trading.[14] Whether this will remain true in the future remains to be seen. A summary listing of major global exchanges retaining a partial or total physical presence through 2002 is listed in Table 1.2.

Technology will continue to play a decisive role in the future of all exchanges; the pressure it brings to bear on exchange management, members, and investors is, and will be, considerable – and increasingly difficult to challenge. Platforms that can offer the best liquidity and price, in a safe and efficient environment, should emerge as winners in the provision of financial contracts. Whether this is ultimately accomplished through ECNs or established (but restructured) electronic/hybrid exchanges, or some combination of the two, remains to be seen. In the meantime, all platforms – physical, electronic, hybrid – will be required to commit even more financial resources to funding development and implementation of new technology – an additional financial burden to bear in a very competitive market.

1.6 DISINTERMEDIATION

Distintermediation – a by-product of deregulation, globalization, new technologies, and competition – means the exchange community must search for new ventures in order to remain commercially relevant and financially viable. This may ultimately benefit the client through greater product/service options and lower costs.

Disintermediation is changing the face of exchanges, as well as the surrounding community of brokers and intermediaries. It is a disruptive force with considerable implications:

- New technologies can weaken long-established client relationships, causing exchanges and intermediaries to lose an important competitive advantage; brokers and other agents are thus losing business to direct access platforms
- Commoditized services that can be easily automated are becoming increasingly prevalent; there is less need for exchange agents to "intervene" in different stages of the business process

---

[14] As noted in the Introduction, an exchange – whether physical or screen-based – provides execution and clearing services; execution is based on price discovery, liquidity, and order matching. A long-held belief – that the physical contract is always the most liquid – was shattered when the all-electronic Eurex gained Bund market share from LIFFE at a time when LIFFE was still a physical exchange. The migration to the Eurex contract started when Eurex reduced execution fees and gave members free interfaces and technology advice. Ultimately, however, Eurex's success hinged on giving customers the best liquidity and pricing – these came from the Eurex marketplace, supported by new technology, rather than LIFFE trading pit. Order matching is also central to the argument – there is very little to suggest that orders are matched more efficiently on the floor than via computerized matching systems.

- Customers demand ease of access and intermediaries must respond; participants do not want to maintain multiple memberships, relationships, or access fees and want to be able to tap into any market when needed, with a minimum of inconvenience
- Customers ultimately benefit through lower costs and better services, and the role of the "middleman" is marginalized

The introduction of bond futures in the mid-1970s was an important step in the financial disintermediation process. Powerful US bond dealers, which had historically held a tight grip on the cash Treasury bond market, were no longer able to exert the same control, as virtually anyone could access the new bond futures market (the same was not true of the cash market, which was still dominated by very large institutional players). Growing turnover in the futures market eventually led to greater activity in the cash markets – and led ultimately to greater liquidity and tighter margins that benefited all participants. In a similar way, the new technologies permitting direct client connectivity that are being deployed by new and established exchanges are now disintermediating exchange agents, as well as exchanges themselves, and should lead to greater direct "client-to-exchange" and "client-to-client" business flows.

FCMs, who act as intermediaries between end-users and clearing members (or exchanges), are at particular risk. During the period of strict open-outcry trading FCMs were in continuous contact with clients, providing execution, advice, and reporting services; a strong bond developed between FCM and client, and both benefited. With computers and networks enveloping the financial markets many clients are increasingly following the "do it yourself" model, accessing prices, information, and research that FCMs once supplied, and executing their own trades – more efficiently and cheaply. Relationships have grown weaker, loyalties have faded, and clients are more willing to "shop" for the best services. Customers can act as clearing members and give up their trades directly to general clearing members – obviating the need to go through an FCM (who would normally give up the client order to the general clearing member). This type of structure is already in place on some exchanges (e.g. Eurex), meaning that foreign investment and commercial banks, which once acted as a vital link between clients and general clearing members, are being removed from the process. Similar disintermediation forces are at work with introducing brokers, give-up brokers, and other exchange agents. In fact, these organizations are at even greater risk, as their roles are more specialized. For instance, introducing brokers maintain relationships with customers and work with them on developing futures strategies. However, they are not permitted to hold customer funds, meaning that they must maintain relationships with FCMs, adding another layer to the process – a layer that can easily be removed. Some exchanges also feature specialists that oversee trading and are able to fill portions of orders as they see fit; these specialists are also at risk of being disintermediated.

How FCMs, brokers, specialists, and other exchange intermediaries adapt to the new environment, and how their roles change over time, is still uncertain. Traditional roles are clearly in jeopardy:

- Electronic communications between exchanges and clients are flexible and robust
- Client-friendly trade execution interfaces are increasingly common, allowing clients to directly enter their own trades
- Electronic mechanisms to route orders are prevalent, even among open-outcry exchanges that have not yet converted to full electronic platforms
- Network mechanisms supply sophisticated and timely information and risk pricing

All of these factors threaten traditional intermediaries. Exchange agents that are part of large organizations (e.g. divisions of large commercial or investment banks) may simply see their previous functions disappear; the services they provide are so commoditized and readily available through alternate mechanisms, and the margins they earn are so thin, that it becomes increasingly difficult to justify resource allocation.[15]

Exchange intermediaries might be able to define new roles for themselves by bundling exchange-traded products with cash and OTC products, giving them greater ability to provide customers with "one-stop shopping." This, however, will not be simple, as different regulations govern each market segment. Alternatively, they might be required to offer complete technology solutions to accompany futures market access. Thus, providing a useful client trading interface and back-end electronic position reporting might actually be the "revenue generator" while executing the futures transaction might simply be "the cost of doing business." Independent agents will face significant difficulties. Some may be forced to narrow their focus by dealing with smaller exchanges that do not yet feature the same capabilities, or perhaps by becoming principals (e.g. risk-takers), so supplying exchanges with more liquidity.

Broader distintermediation forces are also at work – affecting not only FCMs and other exchange intermediaries, but also exchanges themselves. As we have noted, competition from the OTC markets and the new wave of ECNs may ultimately squeeze some exchanges out of the process entirely – creating a market structure based on client-to-client access, rather than client-to-exchange or intermediary-to-exchange access. Though exchanges still deliver certain compelling services (e.g. price discovery, liquidity, credit risk mitigation), it is not difficult to imagine new efforts by OTC market-makers and dealer market ECNs neutralizing these advantages and removing exchanges from their risk intermediation role. With disintermediation, customers are gaining real advantages through cheaper execution and improved services; they will continue to be able to "shop" for the best deals among the exchange community, or turn to the OTC or ECN sectors to get the best execution and clearing deals. Exchanges must prepare for this possibility.

1.7   COMMERCIALIZATION

Commercialization means a change in exchange focus and philosophy, from a traditional mutual or "nonprofit" approach to a stockholder/profit-based approach centered on maximizing economic returns. Exchanges must now be very commercial, focused on minimizing costs and maximizing revenues.

Commercialization is a very visible force impacting the way exchanges are approaching their business strategies:

- The goals of exchange members are becoming secondary to the commercial requirements of exchanges. Determining how to deliver profits has become the primary issue for most organizations
- Previous measures of success – including market share and trading volume – need to be replaced by those that reflect true commercial success, including profitability and cost efficiency

---

[15] FCMs must generally support business flowing through electronic, as well as open-outcry, exchanges. They must therefore maintain personnel and infrastructure for both environments, adding to their costs.

- Technology surfaces, once again, as a potential solution – automating as much of the futures/options chain as possible in order to drive costs down and margins up. But, as noted earlier, technology is expensive, consuming valuable exchange resources
- Converting ownership structure from mutual/member-owned to investor-owned opens up the possibility of raising new capital for investment in technology – a process that can ultimately help lower costs

In a world driven by economic forces, the pressure to act commercially by maximizing revenues and profits has never been greater. In the traditional exchange-traded world, profit motivations have generally been considered secondary to the development of products, formation of liquidity, and settlement of trades – these features are the essential characteristics of any successful exchange and have thus been given priority. The member-owned mutual organization structure used by many exchanges generally puts the interests of members and the exchange ahead of any profit considerations (by focusing, for instance, on market share and trading volume rather than profit margins and net operating income). Though generating revenues and profits is necessary for any organization requiring capital expansion, it does not have to be the primary operating goal. This has been a convenient and appropriate ownership (and management) structure, particularly in a world where competitive forces have been relatively mild. Indeed, some regulatory authorities have embraced the mutual structure by requiring that national exchanges be member-owned.

Economic realities are now placing more focus on the commercial aspects of the business and the pressure to deliver profits has mounted. This means exchange operations need to focus on:

- Revenue growth
- Cost control/operating efficiencies
- Capital access

Revenues can come from higher fees or higher volumes. If the products or services offered are very commoditized (or the competitive environment is very intense), generating significantly higher fees is unlikely and only greater volumes will produce the desired results; if a true "premium" product or service is being offered, margins can be expanded. In reality, higher volumes may be a more realistic approach for most; to attract volumes, however, exchanges must be extremely efficient, low-cost producers that are almost error-free in their operations.

Cost controls and operating efficiencies are important in order to lower transaction "round turn" costs and attract more volume. Costs must be held in check by reducing overhead, abandoning nonessential product development, prioritizing contract rollouts, and so on. Exchanges face large fixed costs but "cost per transaction" that declines as volume increases; attracting more volume is therefore a good way of lowering expense. As a result, structural transformations that build volume – including mergers and alliances – are a possible solution for some. Consolidating clearing services and outsourcing technology requirements can also reduce costs.

Accessing capital is a third area of focus, as it permits an exchange to raise funds for technology investment that can be used to automate processes, attract business, and lower costs. Though technology can be funded through retained earnings, it is often more efficient to do so through external sources, such as public equity capital. This means converting mutual exchange structures into public companies, effectively separating member and investor interests. Though some institutions are reluctant to abandon the mutual structure that has served them well over the past few decades, many are finding they have little choice.

As we have illustrated in this chapter, the forces of change facing exchanges and the broader exchange community – brokers, FCMs, banks and other intermediaries, technology companies – are considerable, and span key areas such as deregulation, globalization, product/market competition, new technologies, and commercialization. The operating environment for exchanges and their products is very different than it was 10, or even 5, years ago. The changes have been, and will continue to be, disruptive. But disruption can bring opportunity, and in the next chapter we shall consider how some exchanges have attempted to take advantage of these opportunities.

2

Responding to Challenges

In order to respond to the challenges we have outlined in Chapter 1, and to demonstrate continued relevance in a changing financial environment, exchanges and the associated community have been forced to rethink business structures and competitive strategies. As part of the process they have had to consider a series of very complicated questions:

- Can exchanges still be relevant in a marketplace where OTC derivatives are so dominant?[1] If more OTC products gain a critical mass of liquidity and are cleared centrally will this be an insurmountable challenge to the listed market?
- Will new ECN entrants be so nimble and cost efficient that they will start taking market share? How quickly will they overcome their structural barriers (e.g. regulatory licensing, centralized clearing) and become pure competitors?
- Is the mutual ownership structure a hindrance in the twenty-first century? Can it, or should it, survive? Can a mutual exchange be commercially efficient?
- Should open-outcry trading be abandoned? Can the cost of operating physical and electronic platforms be justified?
- How can profits be maximized and costs minimized? How can revenues be diversified in order to create profit stability?
- How can product scope and market access be broadened, and can 24-hour trading be created and delivered efficiently?
- Is a merger or alliance with another exchange desirable? Is it inevitable?
- How can vital technology investments be funded? Is it better to develop a platform in-house, or outsource it to third parties? What minimum technology capabilities must the operation have in order to succeed?

These are just some of the issues exchanges are grappling with. Most have been hard at work planning and implementing strategic and structural enhancements in response; yet, while some have already adapted their business models and corporate structures, many others have not and thus face even greater pressures. Regardless of the pace of change, most exchanges have come to recognize that to remain static – to operate as a marketplace of the mid- to late twentieth century – is inadequate. Those responding to competitive forces have done what a few years ago might have been regarded as "unthinkable," including:

- Adapting corporate structure
- Abandoning open-outcry trading
- Implementing new technologies
- Enhancing market access and product choice
- Expanding clearing and settlement services

---

[1] OTC derivatives account for approximately two-thirds of all global derivatives activity.

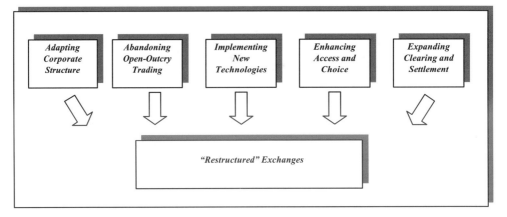

Figure 2.1   Responding to challenges

As exchanges restructure their operations by focusing on the enhancements summarized in Figure 2.1, regulators and institutional participants are trying to adapt as well. It is critical for national regulators and financial intermediaries to "change with the times" – failure to do so leads to regulatory difficulties or lost business opportunities. The entire upheaval is creating winners and losers – both inside and outside the exchange world; how participants fare depends very much on how they react to the realities of the new environment.

2.1   ADAPTING CORPORATE STRUCTURE

Altering corporate structure means discarding organizational models of the past in favor of those that permit efficient and flexible operation. This can involve a considerable change in business philosophy and focus, and may require concessions from members and investors, and cooperation with other organizations.

Adapting corporate structure is one of the most effective (and visible) ways of meeting the challenges of the new business environment. Numerous exchanges have been willing to alter their structures – sometimes radically – in order to remain competitive, by:

- Demutualizing exchange operations
- Floating stock publicly
- Merging with, or acquiring, other exchanges
- Entering into partnership agreements with other exchanges, including alliances, joint ventures and other cooperative agreements

Figure 2.2 summarizes these structural changes.

For decades many exchanges have operated as mutual organizations, with members, rather than outside investors, holding majority ownership interests. Under this organizational structure decisions are often taken to advance the interests of exchange members. Sometimes "optimal" economic and business goals coincide with membership goals, other times they do not. When goals do not match, the debate on how to proceed can be heated and the decisions difficult – but the organization is not answerable to "outsiders." This may, or may not, result in the best allocation of resources, the right decisions on pricing policies and business strategies,

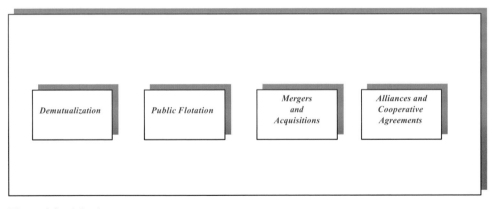

Figure 2.2   Adapting corporate structure

and so on. For instance, mutual owners might decide to raise contract fees in order to boost revenues and deliver more profits back to the membership; however, raising fees might actually drive business away. Likewise, members might decide not to spend money on technological expansion so as not to strain resources; this may be beneficial in the short term, but may have negative implications over the medium term. The mutual organization has a further drawback: lack of access to external capital. Since members contribute capital, the only meaningful way of increasing capital further is by adding new members or levying special contributions on existing members. In an era where capital is needed to fund technology development and global product expansion, the mutual structure can be a considerable hindrance. As a result, it is not surprising to see that some exchanges have converted (or are contemplating conversion) from mutual organizations to "for profit" corporations; some regard this as an essential – even inevitable – step that leads to a change in business philosophy and focus.

The demutualization process is not always easy. Exchange members have powerful "voices" and debate on future corporate structure can be intense and divisive. But some organizations have determined that demutualization is in their best long-term interests and opted to convert. For instance, mutual organizations such as the CME, NYMEX, LIFFE, SFE, HKEx, and SGX have become corporations over the past few years (Table 2.1 summarizes major demutual-izations of the past few years). Other mutuals have rejected change, preferring the status quo of member ownership. For example, exchanges such as CBOE, TOCOM, and TGE have all considered but rejected demutualization, believing they can achieve their revenue goals and funding requirements by continuing as member-owned forums. Whether they will "revisit" the issue at some future time is uncertain.

Exchanges that convert to corporate ownership run the company in the best interests of the shareholders, which can include:

- Seeking new, and possibly diversified, sources of revenue through new products and services
- Negotiating new alliances and other profit-making ventures
- Managing expenses more diligently by finding efficiencies and eliminating excesses
- Sacrificing turnover/market share rankings when they are no longer profitable to maintain

In short, pursuing initiatives that lead to the "age-old" corporate goal of maximizing profits. A corporatized entity, as noted below, also reserves the right to float its shares publicly and

Table 2.1   Major exchange demutualizations

Americas	Europe	Asia
CME	BI	HKEx
ISE	IPE	SGX
MX	LIFFE	SFE
NYMEX	LME	TSE
		OSE
		MDEX

Table 2.2   Major exchange flotations

Exchange	Year of public flotation
HKEx	2000
Euronext	2001
OM	1987
SFE	2002*
SGX	2000

*Representing a full listing on the Australian Stock Exchange.

so raise extra capital. The new structure can also permit broader strategic tie-ups, including mergers and alliances that might not be possible under mutual structures (we discuss this at greater length below). (It is worth stressing that not all global exchanges are, or have been, structured as mutuals; some are already organized as private or public corporations and have been able to avoid one step of the conversion process.)

2.1.1   Public flotation

Following demutualization, some exchanges take a second step and float newly corporatized entities on a national stock exchange – or pave the way to do so in the future by filing appropriate registration statements. Those floating their shares raise equity capital that can be used to fund product development, technological enhancement, or acquisitions/alliances. Members who buy shares in the exchange become investors, but they are not usually required to do so; exchange ownership and membership thus become separate roles. Exchanges that convert from mutual to corporate status, but choose not to float immediately, reserve that option for the future; there is no time limit on converting from a private to public company. Before going public, however, they need to demonstrate a sound business strategy and a strong track record of profitability. Investors are more likely to buy into an exchange if the fundamentals and strategies are strong and selling shares at a higher stock price ultimately yields more proceeds for the exchange. A summary of key exchange flotations is highlighted in Table 2.2.

2.1.2   Mergers and acquisitions

To meet the competitive challenges of the times, some exchanges have chosen to merge with other forums inside, or outside, the industry. Mergers and acquisitions generally bring considerable advantages to the parties involved, including:

- Greater cross-product and client coverage
- Potential expansion in the liquidity pool for a given contract
- More expansive geographic "footprint"
- Greater operating efficiencies
- Increased access to new technologies and other professional expertise
- Elimination of a potential competitor from the marketplace

While a series of exchange mergers occurred between the mid-1980s and mid-1990s (e.g. LIFFE's purchase of FOX and LCE, NYCE's merger with CSCE to form NYBOT, NYMEX's acquisition of COMEX, SFE's purchase of NZFOE, TGE's purchase of TSEx and HGE, and so on) the pace appears to have quickened. In recent years, for instance:

- DTB and SOFFEX merged into Eurex
- HKFE and SEHK merged into HKEx
- SIMEX and SES merged into SGX
- KLOFFE and COMMEX merged into MDEX
- MATIF, Monep, SBF, and Société du Nouveau Marché merged into Paris Bourse, Belgian Futures and Options Exchange and Brussels Stock Exchange merged into the Brussels Exchanges, and Amsterdam Stock Exchange and Amsterdam Options Exchange merged into the Amsterdam Exchanges; the three national groups then combined to form Euronext
- OM purchased Stockholmsborsen
- Euronext purchased LIFFE and Bolsa de Valores de Lisboa e Porto
- ICE purchased IPE
- BM&F acquired the Brazil Futures Exchange of Rio de Janeiro

Each of these combinations has served to redefine the nature and characteristics of the traded derivatives industry. In most cases the end result has been increased product scope, liquidity, and time zone/marketplace access.

Mergers and acquisitions tend to occur in one of three forms:

- Combinations of derivative exchanges within a country
- Combinations of derivative and stock exchanges within a country
- Combinations of derivative exchanges between countries

(Note that in certain exceptional instances mergers/acquisitions can also occur between derivative exchanges and ECNs.)

Mergers between a country's derivative exchanges are reasonably common and are typically driven by the belief that operating efficiencies can be improved and derivative product scope and liquidity expanded. Savings can be considerable as consolidation means eliminating duplicative processes and personnel costs, sharing clearing and settlement services, leveraging technology developments, and consolidating management structure. The KLOFFE/COMMEX, CSCE/NYCE, and TGE/TSEx/HGE combinations are just a few examples of this type of merger. Mergers between a country's national derivative and stock exchanges may also be motivated by the desire to achieve greater economic efficiencies. In addition, when a stock exchange is responsible for listing and trading equity options or futures as well as cash products, integration brings the two markets together, helps build liquidity, and eliminates duplication. Pairing cash instruments with derivative products can also help smooth earnings cycles: when cash markets are quiet an exchange can rely more heavily on its derivative operations, and vice versa. The OM, HKEx, SGX, and JSE/SAFEX mergers (which, in all cases, also included consolidation of clearing functions) serve as examples of this model; more are almost certain to follow. Mergers of derivative exchanges across borders are also becoming more common as regulatory rules are relaxed and the logic of greater global product and market access strengthens. The Euronext/LIFFE, Eurex, SFE/NZFOE, and ICE/IPE mergers are prominent examples of the cross-border solution and should serve as a model for others.

To date, mergers in the clearing sector have been based primarily on cooperative arrangements and cross-margining alliances rather than full-scale mergers. There are, of course, some exceptions to this: the combination of the three Euronext clearinghouses into the consolidated Clearnet platform; the creation of the London Clearinghouse (LCH) as a joint clearinghouse for London's primary derivative/stock exchanges; and, the establishment of SFE Clearing as a clearing umbrella for all SFE and NZFOE trading. Though still relatively rare, these cross-border clearing mergers prove that the "regional clearinghouse" concept can actually work; we discuss this idea at greater length below.[2]

The relative lack of clearing mergers appears to be primarily the result of organizational, geographic, technological, and regulatory complexities. It is occasionally also the result of internal politics – particularly at mutual organizations, where membership voice is all-important (e.g. the OCC and BOTCC nearly merged, but members were unable to agree on terms). It is far simpler to create a mechanism that permits management of margins across exchanges than to merge or consolidate entire corporate bodies. This is particularly true when different regions and countries are involved – each country has its local/national regulatory, accounting, and tax issues. Thus, in the very short term, *cross-margin agreements* between clearinghouses are likely to be a popular form of cooperation. Over the medium term, broader clearinghouse integration should emerge – particularly as parent exchanges merge. Pure clearinghouse mergers that are unrelated to exchange mergers could occur given the right economics; as with exchange mergers, the consolidation of clearinghouses can benefit all parties through reduced risks, lower costs, increased stability/reliability, improved liquidity, and so forth. The defining characteristics of any clearing platform are stability and integrity – these are the qualities that give exchange-traded derivatives an important advantage over OTC products; anything that might disrupt stability and integrity has to be avoided, so consolidations must be handled with care.

Regional clearing alliances (e.g. the Clearnet model) might ultimately pave the way for "superregional" clearinghouse structures – amalgamations of broader regional organizations – perhaps to the point where three or four superregional clearinghouses dominate the entire industry (e.g. US/Americas, Europe, Japan/Asia). The European Securities Forum (ESF), an industry group, has already supported the concept of a single, integrated clearing process, owned/governed by its users, that is capable of servicing a variety of constituents across national borders (quite possibly as a mutual organization, though the advantages of commercialization might dictate otherwise). The ESF supports efforts directed at the creation of a single entity operating under one legal jurisdiction and regulatory regime; this is a complex undertaking given the disparate laws and regulations of countries that might be involved. Nevertheless, over the long term such superregional alliances may appear. The current and potential "stages" of clearinghouse cooperation/consolidation are summarized in Figure 2.3.

In any merger – whether it involves exchanges, clearinghouses, or both – willingness to sacrifice independence is a central issue. Unless mergers are negotiated from a position of

---

[2] Independent clearing agents that provide cross-border services to third parties (primarily participants rather than exchanges) are focused mainly on the OTC, rather than exchange-traded, marketplace.

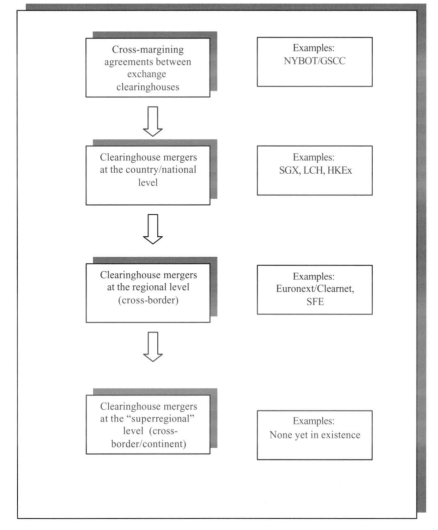

Figure 2.3   Clearinghouse cooperation/consolidation

strength, with both parties actively benefiting from a combination, one of the two is generally relegated to a "secondary" position – this can make it difficult to agree on a consolidation (particularly when mutual owners are involved). The loss of independence, particularly for an institution that may have been in business for many decades, or even centuries, can be wrenching. For some, however, there may be no alternative.

2.1.3 Alliances and cooperative agreements

In some cases large-scale mergers and acquisitions are not possible or desirable. The legal and regulatory complexities may be too great, exchange "personalities" too different, product and market coverage too similar, proposed cost savings too small, and so forth. When this happens, exchanges might still choose to form cooperative alliances that allow them to achieve very focused goals, such as:

- Extending product scope
- Improving access to member liquidity
- Increasing coverage of time zones/trading hours
- Accessing back-office services
- Sharing technology advances
- Overcoming regulatory barriers

Though alliances have been a characteristic of the exchange market since the 1980s, the speed at which new relationships are forming is accelerating. A sampling of alliances created over the past two decades includes:

- The CME and SGX trading link (via the *mutual offset system*) that allows exchange members to establish or cover positions on either exchange
- The LIFFE/TIFFE alliance that allows trading of the 3-month Euroyen contract on either exchange
- The LIFFE/TSE agreement that permits trading of the Japanese Government Bond (JGB) contract on either exchange
- The IPE/SGX alliance that permits trading of the Brent crude oil contract on either exchange
- The Globex alliance – which includes CME, Euronext, SGX, MEFF, BM&F, and MX – that allows trading and cross-margining privileges on all contracts (through the GLOBEX 2 electronic platform)
- The LIFFE and NASDAQ partnership that provides technical and product support for single stock futures (under the NASDAQ LIFFE Markets umbrella)
- The NYMEX and CME alliance that permits trading of energy "mini" contracts via the GLOBEX 2 platform
- The NYBOT and Cantor Fitzgerald joint venture (Cantor Financial Futures Exchange) centered on electronic trading of US Treasury futures
- The CME/Euronext "technology sharing" alliance that allows the two exchanges to use each other's trading/clearing platforms[3]
- The OneChicago joint venture between CME, CBOT, and CBOE that offers single stock futures through an all-electronic platform

These represent just a small "cross-section" of alliances – many others exist or are being contemplated. Though not all alliances work perfectly – witness the Alliance/CBOT/Eurex (a/c/e), which was restructured in 2002 after a divergence of views – additional combinations of traditional and nontraditional exchanges and services are likely to appear in the future. The logic behind such cooperative arrangements is often sound: not only are competitive threats reduced, product/market scope enhanced, and cost efficiencies increased, but capital investments in, or intellectual property related to, critical technology can be shared by several parties – all without the need for full-scale mergers.

---

[3] CME's GLOBEX 2 uses the Euronext-based NSC trading platform (originally developed by the Paris exchange), while Euronext has adapted CME's Clearing 21 platform.

2.2   ABANDONING OPEN-OUTCRY TRADING

Abandoning physical open-outcry trading in favor of pure electronic dealing means parting with many years of physical exchange experience in pricing, liquidity, and market-making. It requires more investment in technology and a revamp in the way members make markets, but can lead to greater customer efficiencies, transparency, and cost savings.

Open-outcry trading has been a useful and effective market pricing mechanism for many centuries, but it may ultimately be abandoned by the last "holdouts" in the industry. Indeed, as some exchanges have already discovered, there are compelling reasons for moving from open-outcry to electronic screen trading, including:

- Giving customers efficient trading and execution access
- Allowing market-makers to support activity on multiple exchanges, helping provide "transferable" pockets of liquidity as needed
- Lowering, and eventually eliminating, the costs associated with running physical infrastructure
- Helping guard against illegal activities, including front-running and noncompetitive orders
- Reducing manual operating errors
- Establishing remote trading locations that can be used for disaster recovery or business interruption

Perhaps the most visible sign of change in the exchange world has come with the closure of physical trading floors and the associated migration to purely automated, off-exchange, trading platforms. The abandonment of open-outcry trading – a colorful and exciting dimension of the financial world – is becoming a sign of the times. While not all exchanges have done away with their floors or open-outcry mechanisms – the IPE, LME, Chicago complex, NYMEX, and BM&F, among others, remain intact – most have recognized that in the world of advanced technologies and demanding customers, it makes sense to convert fully to an electronic platform. If clients and members can obtain the liquidity and price transparency that characterize trading through the largest open-outcry pits – more efficiently and cost-effectively – there may be no competitive advantage in operating on a physical basis.

Trading success is ultimately measured by depth of liquidity. The deeper the liquidity, the lower the cost of doing business. Supporters of open-outcry trading argue that local market-makers on the exchange floor are the ultimate source of liquidity, able to make two-way prices in all markets by being able to see and hear what is happening in the pit. Absent this physical contact, they believe real market-making may not always exist. They also note that it is the seasoned floor professionals, rather than the computerized interfaces and trading engines, that are most capable of executing complex orders (e.g. multiple option strategies). Supporters of electronic trading counter that technology and connectivity increase participation, expand volume, deepen liquidity, and lower costs. They note that electronic market-makers can supply liquidity on a "home exchange" as needed and, when things are slow, switch to other contracts on different exchanges to provide necessary volume and liquidity. Electronic trading draws in traders from across borders, giving markets greater breadth, depth, and, ultimately, transparency; it also permits more "around the clock" dealing – an important consideration in a global marketplace. Electronic platforms have already proven that they can provide the liquidity necessary for trading, in some cases even besting the physical exchanges (as noted earlier, Eurex became the market leader in Bund futures by taking most of LIFFE's market

Table 2.3   Exchange conversion from physical to pure electronic

Exchange	Location
BI	Milan
HKEx	Hong Kong
LIFFE (now part of Euronext)	London
MATIF (now part of Euronext)	Paris
MDEX	Kuala Lumpur
Mexder	Mexico City
MX	Montreal
OSE	Osaka
SFE	Sydney
SGX	Singapore
TGE	Tokyo
TIFFE*	Tokyo
TSE	Tokyo

*TIFFE never featured physical open-outcry trading on an exchange floor, but conducted business telephonically for more than 2 years before implementing an all-electronic platform.

share). Proponents of the electronic model also suggest that electronic trading can eliminate occasional problems that appear on exchange floors, including *collusion* (prearranging customer trades), *noncompetitive trading* (taking the other side of a customer trade without exposing it to the market), and *front-running* (trading ahead of a customer order).

Various exchanges that once operated physically have converted to electronic platforms that permit automated order entry, order routing, execution, and clearing; a sampling of exchanges that have closed their physical floors since the mid-1990s is summarized in Table 2.3 (of course some exchanges, such as the original DTB (now part of Eurex), have never even featured a trading floor: they commenced as, and remained, electronic conduits). Most exchanges have migrated from physical to electronic in multiyear phases in order to accustom members to a new operating environment. LIFFE, for instance, gravitated its contracts from the physical to the electronic over a period of nearly 24 months. In some cases, however, conversion has been rapid. For example, while MATIF (now part of Euronext Paris) had planned to convert its operations gradually, demand for electronic trading was so overwhelming that within a matter of weeks all trading had been migrated to screens.

The question of what will happen with some of the largest physical players – such as CME, CBOT, CBOE, LME, IPE, and NYMEX, among others – remains unanswered. To varying degrees, most of these physical players have evolved with the times – they started as paper-based pits, moved to telephonic pits, and have since added computerized order-routers to remain efficient and competitive[4] – but trading remains largely physical. To many observers the eventual closure of trading floors is inevitable – it is simply too inefficient and costly to operate a physical pit during "normal trading hours" and an electronic platform during "after hours" (or as a supplement to pit trading). Since markets are increasingly global, an exchange that does not have an electronic, after-hours capability is at a competitive disadvantage. In

---

[4] The CBOE is now said to receive 97% of its orders electronically, 37% of which are executed electronically against market-makers; a big dimension of its business is becoming electronic, yet the main trading function remains physical.

addition, physical execution is cumbersome compared to electronic execution. For instance, in a typical open-outcry environment:

1. A client calls a broker with an order.
2. The order is time-stamped.
3. A ticket is prepared and sent to the floor.
4. A floor order ticket is prepared (larger orders go directly to the broker booth).
5. The floor trader negotiates the price through bid/offer discussion or hand signals.
6. An agreed trade is written manually by the two traders.
7. The confirmation is passed back to the brokers and to the clearinghouse.
8. The clearinghouse clears and reconciles all trades at the end of the day.

By way of contrast, electronic mechanisms allow:

1. Direct trade input by the client or broker.
2. Instant electronic order matching through the exchange's host computer (which generally matches bids and offers by time/price/size/type priority rules).
3. Immediate electronic order confirmation.
4. Electronic transmission to the clearinghouse for end-of-day reconciliation.

This results in very fast and efficient processing.[5] Speed and efficiency also translate into cost savings; by abandoning many of the manually intensive tasks associated with execution and clearing, exchanges reduce their costs and provide clients with an even more compelling alternative.

It is possible that even the largest open-outcry forums believe a move to purely electronic trading is inevitable. Since many of the largest pit exchanges have already made significant investments in quite sophisticated electronic platforms (e.g. CME/GLOBEX 2, CBOT/eCBOT, NYMEX/ACCESS) and already conduct some amount of business through them,[6] they are already prepared to move to an all-electronic environment. While most initially created their platforms to support after-hours trading, many have expanded them to accommodate trading alongside the physical pits; in some cases daytime volumes on electronic platforms are becoming quite significant, even challenging physical activity (though not necessarily in the liquid benchmark contracts). For instance, when the CME introduced Eurodollar trading on GLOBEX 2 during daytime hours, a portion of its daily pit activity quickly shifted to the electronic version. In some cases contracts are traded exclusively on electronic platforms, despite the existence of physical pits (e.g. NYMEX's electricity contracts, CME's mini contracts, TGE's grain contracts, and so on). These facts suggest that open-outcry may eventually fade. As noted earlier, several physical exchanges have demutualized, converting from mutuals to corporations – meaning that the powerful floor membership constituencies, which at one time might have blocked all attempts to move off the floor, now lack the power to influence such strategic decisions. New exchanges that are in the "planning" stages, as well as those that might appear in the future, are unlikely to opt for a physical open-outcry presence – most are likely to move directly to the electronic model. The availability of proven front- and back-office technologies and the ability to link clients, intermediaries, and exchanges in the cash and derivative markets through electronic networks, are very compelling reasons to move from

---

[5] For example, the CME's GLOBEX 2 matches trades in less than 0.75 second (down from 2 seconds under the original GLOBEX platform); LIFFE indicates that 90% of trades flowing through LIFFE Connect are matched in less than 0.25 second.
[6] For instance, CME estimates 20% of its trading volume flows through GLOBEX 2.

the "planning stages" directly to the electronic model; if common clearing and settlement of cash and derivative products can be added to the mix, the reasons become even more attractive.

2.3 IMPLEMENTING NEW TECHNOLOGIES

Implementing new technologies means changing the way business is done, replacing manual methods of inputting, executing, clearing, settling, and communicating with automated ones. Though implementation is typically an expensive, multiyear proposition centered on the development of internal platforms or purchase of third-party systems, the advantages it generates through improved customer access and increased operating efficiencies are compelling.

New technology is at the heart of many of the changes under way at new and established exchanges. The benefits it brings are significant, and can include:

- Simple, yet powerful, trade entry that appeals to clients
- Improved routing, execution, matching, and clearing times
- Seamless front- to back-processing
- Increased capacity to develop new products in a shorter time frame
- Lower operational costs
- New sources of revenue (for those licensing their technology developments)
- Flexible exchange location (enabling relocation to less expensive centers and the creation of disaster recovery sites)

Technology is, perhaps, the single most important dimension of business development and transaction execution in the derivatives sector of the twenty-first century. Financial e-commerce in general, and derivatives e-commerce in particular, has moved steadily to the forefront over the past few years and has impacted exchanges and associated intermediaries. As large international banks began migrating aspects of their sales and trading capabilities online during the late 1990s, listed derivatives became one of the first to be offered through *electronic portals* (integrated research, pricing, and execution interfaces): the standardized nature of the contracts meant it was relatively simple to offer clients electronic trading access and then feed orders directly to exchanges. Using interfaces developed internally or by third-party vendors, intermediaries have been able to connect clients with exchanges, allowing clients to execute trades quickly and efficiently and receive daily risk/margin reporting. Many exchanges have come to realize the importance of properly supporting the new wave of e-commerce activity and have devoted resources to ensuring robust connectivity between clients, intermediaries, and exchange hubs.

Most exchanges have been receptive to electronic trading built on new technology. This is particularly true in Europe, where many forums developed as, or soon migrated to, electronic platforms; technology was thus part of their operating "mindset." For instance, OM, DTB (now part of Eurex), and MATIF (now part of Euronext) were all technology pioneers, using new architecture and models long before it became part of the "mainstream." Their success paved the way for others to purchase elements of proven technology or develop their own. As a result of new technologies, exchanges have been able to improve product creation and delivery, speed order flow, accelerate matching, execution, and clearing, lower execution costs, and strengthen reporting; these, as noted, are powerful advantages which can give electronic trading an edge over open-outcry trading. Exchanges unable to develop their own platforms can turn to those created by others; though they may not provide the precise functionality required straight "off the shelf," they can generally be adapted to an appropriate state (e.g. Euronext spent several years converting the CME's core Clearing 21 technology platform to better suit its needs). In fact, technology has become a new source of revenue for advanced exchanges, which license components of their platforms to others on a fee or royalty basis. The Eurex platform, for example, has been adopted by the CBOT, the NSC platform that forms one part of the Euronext infrastructure is used by the CME (as part of GLOBEX 2) as well as exchanges in France, Singapore, Brazil, and Canada, OM's CLICK, SECUR, and TORQUE platforms are used by over two dozen exchanges and clearinghouses (e.g. the HKEx, Austrian Derivatives Exchange, the Australian Stock Exchange, and so on), LIFFE's Connect platform forms part of TIFFE's operations, and so on. Most exchanges that offer technology services divide their exchange and technology operations into distinct subsidiaries in order to preserve independence and focus; for instance, OM's exchange business is distinct from the extensive technology business it conducts with other clearers and exchanges, Eurex's technology dealings are similarly separate from its core trading business, and so forth.

As indicated, many large exchanges have invested considerable sums in developing or purchasing new technologies in order to remain at the "leading edge" and help stem the competitive tide created by ECNs. From an access and execution standpoint, some have created standard "one size fits all" *application program interfaces* (APIs, software layers connecting network processes with client screens), while others have chosen more flexible approaches (typically in partnership with technology companies who have the requisite expertise to make flexible technical requirements a reality). For instance, as LIFFE developed its Connect platform, it joined with third parties in creating different components of the technology (e.g. PATS Systems, YES Trader, Easy Screen, and so on) and worked with the software community in developing APIs that could be customized and connected to a very broad range of clients. In the same way, routing, matching, and clearing technologies can be general or exchange-specific. Much of the functionality related to pricing algorithms, trade matching, post-trade reconciliation, margin computation, and so forth, is standard across exchanges – meaning these core components are, to a certain extent, fungible. Greater customization is needed primarily to accommodate the specific business of each exchange (e.g. individual types of products, internal/external communication and reporting flows, and so on).

The functionality of new technologies can be segregated into front-, middle- and back-office elements. Indeed, the creation of new technologies to expand exchange activity is not simply about executing futures and options trades, but applying it to all other front- and back-office applications. By extending the use of new technologies across the entire chain, a technology provider (whether independent or exchange-based) gets a greater return on development dollars invested. As noted in Chapter 1, a typical order flow chain in any exchange comprises several distinct segments – any, or all, of which can be automated. These include trade entry, acceptance, transmission, delivery, execution, reporting, and clearing/settlement.

- Front-office services are available for client interface and trade entry/execution. Comprehensive electronic platforms provide visibility into the structure of an exchange's order book and the range of bids/offers and volume
- Transmission and delivery stages that were once manual are fading as exchanges implement more efficient technological processes (this is increasingly true for open-outcry forums as well). Order routing itself is now very automated, with trade details conveyed electronically to matching engines (for electronic exchanges) or deck management systems (for physical exchanges)
- Middle-office services now provide for automated reporting, valuation, margin/position analysis, and risk analytics

- Back-office services emphasize automated clearing and settlement, position reconciliation, and trade confirmation. Some back-office modules provide controls that can save time and money (e.g. reducing errors by ensuring "out-trades" do not occur – if trades can only be matched electronically, there can be no disagreement or misinterpretation, as might be the case on the exchange floor).

Some platforms support specific segments, others the entire process. In some cases exchanges and their software partners have commenced with one component and then added others. For instance, LIFFE's Connect platform, which is now a fully automated system, started as a back-end processing platform; middle- and front-office capabilities were added over time.

Technology is truly useful when members, clients, and other exchanges can access it with ease. Accordingly, new technologies must emphasize robust and efficient network communication. Communication can be implemented in various forms. Some of the most common include:

- Direct connectivity, linking the exchange and members through APIs
- Third-party software/server links, linking exchanges and members through exchange API handlers and third-party software servers and front-end screens
- Application service provider (ASP) links, linking exchanges and members through ASP data centers and networks in order to outsource member software/hardware requirements

There is no single "correct" model for distributing technologies. Much depends on the sophistication of individual exchanges and members, their desire to preserve or outsource technology requirements, the amount they are willing to invest in applications, the degree to which they need customization, and so forth. The main point is that network distribution is essential and that various alternatives exist. Sample access templates are illustrated in Figure 2.4.

In addition to execution and efficiency benefits, technology can lower expenses by helping an exchange locate its operations in a "cheaper" environment. In fact, with proper technology physical location becomes almost irrelevant. APIs mask the location of central order books and clearing services, so the physical location of an exchange no longer means very much. Assuming no regulatory restrictions, an exchange platform can be located in New York or London, Detroit or Stuttgart. This means greater ability to operate where it is cheaper, reducing costs and enhancing profit margins. Proper use of technologies can also be important in minimizing the risk of disruption in the event of a catastrophe. Exchanges that operate on a physical basis risk closure if premises cannot be accessed for any reason – fire, earthquake or, as seen through the September 11, 2001 closure of the New York Stock Exchange, terrorism. Exchanges operating strictly on an electronic basis, with appropriate redundancies in their system architecture, can trade through these catastrophes without pause.

Exchange spending on new information technology (IT) initiatives has been considerable and is likely to remain so over the medium term. A Towers Group survey conducted during 2000 found that futures exchanges spent $1.2bn on IT initiatives in 2000, equal to a 30% annual compound growth rate over a 4-year period (the survey also noted that continued growth in spending is expected through the middle of the decade). (Iati, 2001, p. 1). The survey also found that a growing amount of exchange IT budgets is spent externally rather than internally, i.e. purchasing component tools rather than developing them in-house. Since it is very expensive and time-consuming for exchanges to independently build new technologies from scratch, acquiring the required platform from a third-party developer, or even forming alliances with others to spread costs, can be an attractive alternative (even Euronext, one of the market pioneers, operates its technology through a 50/50 joint venture with Atos, a French e-commerce technology firm).

Paying for these significant technology investments can be a considerable burden and generally occurs through one of three sources:

- Revenues, retained earnings/internal capital
- Government grants
- External capital

Once revenues from exchange operations have been used to cover operating costs, they can be allocated to technology investment. If an exchange can increase revenues while keeping costs under control, it has at its disposal funds for crucial technological investments. Grants from governmental agencies can also help defray the cost of investment. This type of approach is

Direct access

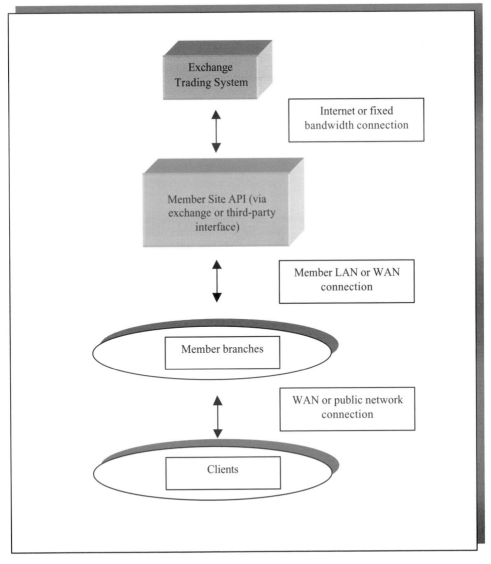

Figure 2.4   Exchange access templates

Third-party software/server access

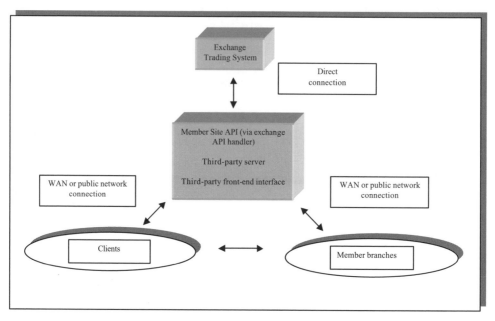

ASP access

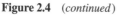
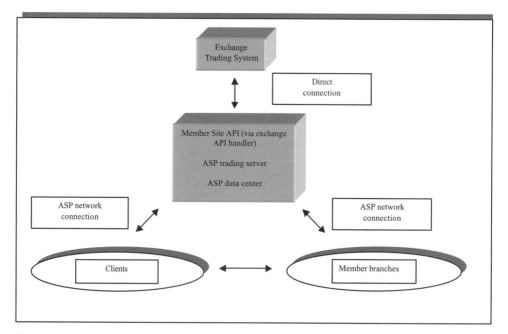

Figure 2.4   (*continued*)

somewhat rare, and noted primarily when government authorities in an emerging country are interested in promoting a viable national exchange; such grants might be "one time awards" to help an exchange create its technology platform, and are unlikely to be sustained in the medium term. External capital is an increasingly attractive funding method. Indeed, as noted earlier in the chapter, it is a central reason why some exchanges are converting from mutual to public corporate status; long-term capital provided by investors is well suited to long-term technology investment.

Though the costs of implementing these new technologies are obviously considerable so, too, are those associated with running physical open-outcry exchanges, where staff, buildings/physical plant, infrastructure, communications, and manual trade processing need to be funded. Exchanges thus face a trade-off: they can spend on technology and hopefully create a more efficient platform, or spend on expensive physical facilities without necessarily creating more efficiency. This simple trade-off ignores any increased volume generated by giving clients more flexible access at a cheaper price. Eurex has estimated that the cost of trading a Bund contract on an open-outcry basis is three times higher than doing so electronically; similarly, the SFE has indicated that when it converted from a physical to electronic environment in mid-1999, its costs declined by as much as 40%.

Technology thus emerges as one of the centerpieces of twenty-first-century listed derivatives, and exchanges must increasingly be technology leaders as well as business/financial leaders. Some exchanges have adopted a new mindset, realizing that future success in the marketplace will depend heavily on having a flexible and sophisticated platform. Indeed, it is possible that the unique product of the twenty-first-century exchange will be the platform rather the individual financial contracts. The opportunity (or threat, depending on one's view), is in the delivery mechanism rather than the specific futures and options. If the platform is robust, flexible, and efficient, it will attract users to the exchange and ensure that individual contracts have the liquidity to promote tight pricing. If this is true, those with a technological edge and vision should emerge as winners.

2.4 ENHANCING MARKET ACCESS AND PRODUCT CHOICE

Users want new products and access mechanisms in order to efficiently manage risks or take positions; enhancing products and access is thus an exchange priority. By creating better instruments and greater convenience, an exchange can strengthen activity and deepen liquidity. The ultimate goal is to provide enough choice and flexibility that those needing a derivative contract will turn to the listed market rather than the competing OTC or ECN markets.

In order to remain competitive in serving global customers, exchanges are enhancing and broadening product scope and improving access mechanisms and response times. The new environment increasingly features:

- Flexible global market access across exchanges, up to 24 hours a day
- Evolving product lines, where new instruments are developed or acquired, existing ones are refined, and irrelevant ones are abandoned
- Retail market penetration
- Information services

2.4.1 Market access

Ensuring timely and efficient access to products is a key goal for many exchanges. In a global and interlinked financial world participants want to deal in any listed contract whenever it is convenient for them to do so. Thus, if an investment company in the US wants to execute options contracts on the broad stock market indexes of the UK, Japan, and Germany, it should be able to do so through a single terminal/interface – at any time of the day or night. Connections should exist so that trades entered by the client through the interface are channeled to the FCM or broker, and from there to the relevant exchange platform, regardless of the time of day. Alternatively, if disintermediation forces continue to mount, the client might tap directly into the relevant exchanges. The client should not have to enter multiple trades into multiple systems, or pass orders verbally to one or more FCMs, and it should certainly not have to wait until official "market open." Technology exists to facilitate such work.

Though true 24-hour trading on multiple exchanges is not yet a universal reality, improved access – involving use of new technologies as well as formation of cross-exchange alliances and FCM portals – is drawing the world closer to "around the clock" trading on multiple exchanges. Computers, telecommunications, and networks already make it possible to access exchange liquidity from afar. Clients can often use interfaces to execute transactions remotely, even when an electronic exchange's "formal" trading hours are over (e.g. clients interested in trading Eurex's contracts can do so for up to 18 hours per day, those wanting to trade SFE's products can do so for up to 22 hours, and so on). Even certain physical exchanges with advanced technology allow clients to use electronic platforms to supplement and extend the trading day (e.g. NYMEX clients can use the ACCESS system to supplement pit trading activity during daytime hours and lengthen trading activity after hours).[7] Cross-exchange access is also vital in improving the client environment. Alliances permit client access to the products offered by participating exchanges,[8] meaning individual access points to each exchange no longer need to be considered. The Globex alliance serves as a case in point, as does MEFF's alliance with Eurex and Euronext on specified contracts. Consolidated portals offered by FCMs can provide similar functionality: the client simply enters a single order covering multiple exchanges into the FCM's portal, which then automatically accesses individual exchanges with order details. These types of advances greatly improve efficiencies for institutions that transact in multiple cross-border products, and should become the norm in the exchange world over the medium term.

2.4.2 Product choice

Realigning exchange products to meet the challenges of the new environment is critical. This most often takes one of three forms:

- Abandoning products that are no longer relevant or cannot compete efficiently with alternate risk management tools in the marketplace
- Remaining focused on a small core of products and adjusting them in order to deepen liquidity
- Broadening product scope – perhaps dramatically – in hopes of capturing different segments of the client market

---

[7] In contrast, an exchange like the LME is ripe for conversion to an electronic platform: it features a relatively short trading day, transacting only about 30% of its volume on the floor itself; the balance occurs off the exchange, primarily through telephonic contact – a process that could fit very well in an electronic environment.

[8] Consistent with applicable regulatory restrictions.

In some cases exchanges might simultaneously abandon ineffective products while introducing new ones. Indeed, exchanges that are not periodically retiring contracts that have "outlived their usefulness" are probably not operating as efficiently as possible. Market evolution demands that futures and options that are no longer needed be dropped so that unnecessary costs can be eliminated and new products introduced. For instance, once popular contracts such as CBOT's Government National Mortgage Association (GNMA) mortgage futures and NYMEX's silver futures were delisted once it became clear that they were no longer being used. Even as these exchanges abandoned certain products, however, they were actively developing new ones relevant to the changing times.

Some exchanges have retained their core base of instruments and simply improved them by "fine-tuning" features to more readily meet the demands of the client base (i.e. changing delivery terms, grades, locations, or denominations, creating price limits, introducing spread or basis contracts, and so on). This allows them to build on the base of liquidity that has already been established, and remain intently focused on what they do best. Exchanges such as TIFFE, MDEX, TOCOM, and HKEx, among others, have followed this route: each offers only a handful of contracts on select references, but most are very liquid.

For exchanges seeking to broaden their product offerings, one of four approaches, which we summarize in Figure 2.5, is generally necessary:

- Creating new products referencing an existing asset class
- Creating new products based on entirely new asset classes
- Introducing existing products to a new base of hedgers and speculators
- Expanding product choice through merger or acquisition

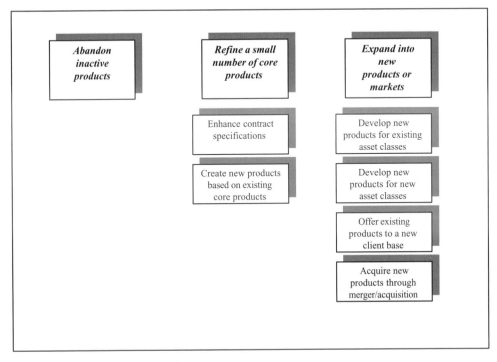

Figure 2.5 Product choice strategies

Some exchanges enhance their product scope by introducing new products on existing asset classes. For instance, during the early 1990s the *flex option* – or flexible exchange option, a standardized option contract with customizable features that allows it to look like an OTC derivative – was introduced on several exchanges, including CME and SFE. Flex options permit users to specify key items such as strike price, maturity date, and exercise style; by doing so they can match contracts and exposures more precisely and eliminate a greater amount of basis risk. *Low exercise price options* (or LEPOs, options with strikes set close to zero, so that they behave like a cash instrument, but with far greater leverage) and long-term options (with maturities extending out to 3 or 5 years) were also introduced in the late 1980s and early 1990s. Such instruments, which are available on equities, currencies, and interest rates, have found a ready base of users. Futures on single stocks serve as another example of a new product that extends an existing asset class. While investors, hedgers, and speculators have been able to deal in single equity options since the early 1970s, the ability to take similar positions through futures has developed more slowly (partly because of regulatory restrictions in certain countries). Stock futures give the long or short player much greater leverage than borrowing against a stock position or buying/selling options, meaning they are far more capital efficient (e.g. stock future margins are approximately 5%–15%, options 15%, and physical stock 50% or more); the leverage, of course, magnifies losses as well as gains. Creating a short position is much simpler with futures than stock (e.g. the short player simply sells the futures contract rather than finding a broker willing to lend the stock and then selling it in the market). And, like options, they can be closed out in advance of expiry, or settled in cash or physical. Single stock futures on large capital companies have proven quite popular, and various exchanges, such as SFE, SAFEX, and LIFFE, now list and trade them; in the US the OneChicago venture (which we describe at greater length in Chapter 32) was formed in 2001 to offer stock futures. In some cases exchanges are offering stock futures based on companies that are located in other marketplaces. For instance, LIFFE, through its joint venture with NASDAQ, lists single stock futures on various US stocks (thus acting as a direct competitor to OneChicago).

Swap futures serve as another example of the new contract/existing asset class approach to product expansion. While trading in OTC interest rate swaps commenced in the very early 1980s, equivalent swap futures contracts did not appear until the early 1990s when the CBOT launched its first swap future; options on swap futures took another decade to introduce. (Others, including SFE and LIFFE, have followed CBOT's lead by offering domestic swap contracts of their own.) Note that in some instances exchanges choose to expand product scope by offering existing asset classes/products traded on other exchanges through their own forums. For instance, NYMEX has introduced futures on the Eurotop equity indexes while OSE has done the same with the NASDAQ 100 and Dow Jones indexes; though the products are traded elsewhere, they have found additional "homes" on the two exchanges.

New products centered on existing asset classes need not be confined to traditional futures and options. Consider the *block trading facility* (BTF), a mechanism through which two parties agree to cross a large transaction away from the exchange – in order not to skew prices – and then register the resulting buy/sell with the exchange so that it passes through the clearinghouse. This "nontraditional" new product is designed to compete with the OTC market by allowing parties to enter into large, private transactions – though ones that still benefit from centralized clearing. Exchanges such as the SFE and OSE offer BTFs on a growing number of asset classes (e.g. equities, interest rates), and other forums are almost certain to introduce their own facilities in the future. In a similar light, some exchanges have introduced a new product mechanism in the form of a basis trading facility; this allows simultaneous execution of cash and futures trades on an underlying reference instrument, obviating the need to file separate orders in different markets. For example, the TSE offers a basis facility on Japanese Government Bonds.[9]

Some exchanges enhance product scope by creating new products on new asset classes; in this sense exchanges become true market pioneers, opening up entirely new asset classes for hedgers and speculators (equivalent OTC activity may, or may not, exist). For example, in the early 1980s the predecessor of MDEX created the world's first contracts on crude palm oil and palm olein. In the mid-1990s the CBOT began offering listed options on catastrophe indexes in the US; prior to the creation of the CBOT contract, the only way of obtaining risk protection against catastrophic events was through the insurance/reinsurance market. In the late 1990s the CME introduced contracts on the weather asset class (e.g. derivatives based on temperature indexes in various US cities) and in 2001 LIFFE created similar temperature contracts on several European cities. As global electricity deregulation started taking hold in the late 1990s several exchanges added contracts on this new asset class; NYMEX, OM (through UK Power Exchange), and SFE, among others, now offer electricity futures.

Some exchanges create new products by focusing on new users. For instance, various exchanges have started focusing on the long-neglected retail constituency. While a small number of contracts have been suitable for retail speculators for many years, most have only been "sized" for institutional participants (e.g. large contract size and tick value). Realizing that improved electronic access mechanisms can allow them to tap into the retail market on a cost-efficient basis, exchanges such as NYMEX, CME, BM&F, OSE, TSE, and TIFFE have created special *mini* contracts, with notionals and tick sizes that are attractive to individuals; this has opened up a brand new market. Since minis are such small contracts they are usually only traded electronically (even on physical exchanges). Though most minis have been targeted at equity indexes, where retail participation tends to be greatest, they are appearing in other asset classes – including energy, fixed income, and currencies. Another example of the "new user" approach can be found in various Asian exchanges, including HKEx and OSE, which now offer US and international stock index contracts to a new base of local investors, hedgers, and speculators.

Though some exchanges have expanded their product offerings "organically" – through natural product development – others, as noted earlier in the chapter, have done so through mergers, acquisitions, or alliances. LIFFE serves as a good example of "product growth through acquisition": after having built up its interest rate and currency product base in the 1980s, it acquired the LCE and LTOM in the 1990s, giving it commodity and UK equity option capabilities, then went on to form a single stock venture in global equities with NASDAQ (and finally agreed to be acquired by Euronext in 2001) – LIFFE thus features a very broad range of products and asset classes. Other examples abound: ICE/IPE have merged into a single entity which gives clients access to a broader range of energy-related OTC and listed products; NYMEX purchased COMEX in 1994 to add metals products to its already established energy platform; COMMEX and KLOFFE merged into MDEX in 2001 to give users a single platform for commodity and financial contracts; and so on. In a novel twist on product expansion through alliance, some exchanges are teaming up with ECNs to develop "co-branded" contracts that can be traded through electronic platforms. For instance, CME and ECN chemicals exchange CheMatch have created certain chemical futures that can be traded electronically and cleared through the CME's Clearing 21 platform.

---

[9] From a practical perspective basis trading capabilities must generally be confined to exchanges that already offer both the cash and derivative instruments (e.g. TSE, OSE, HKEx, SGX, SAFEX, BI, Euronext, among others); if cash and derivatives are handled by different exchanges then the likelihood of introducing an effective and efficient "cross-exchange" basis facility is likely to be much smaller.

While product expansion is often approached proactively, there are times when it arises as a defensive move – effectively carving out a new market niche when one has been lost. As noted in Chapter 1, the arrival of European Monetary Union in 1999 caused a number of exchanges to lose control of their benchmark bond and interest rate futures contracts as participants gravitated to the more liquid "single benchmark" contracts[10] – namely Eurex's Bund (along with Euronext's Bund, particularly when the Eurex contract gets *squeezed*).[11] Thus, MEFF's Bono, BI's BTP, and LIFFE's own Bund became marginalized. Forward-thinking exchanges have used market disruption as an opportunity to expand into new areas, such as equities. For instance, with liberalization of investment restrictions and elimination of euro bloc currency risk, pan-European equity investment and risk management have become far more significant. Exchanges such as Euronext Lisbon, MEFF, and BI have replaced their "dying" interest rate contracts with new "growth" equity contracts. Exchanges that fail to realign their products when needed are threatened with inactivity and, in the extreme, extinction.

In addition to traditional financial contracts, market information based on traded products has emerged as a product class of its own and is now being offered by many exchanges as a revenue generator. In a world of real-time risk information and position analytics, being able to feed such processes is vital and has been recognized as a potential source of profitability. Exchanges such as SGX and SFE have created separate information service departments that market data-related products on a fee-generating basis.

2.5   ENHANCING CLEARING AND SETTLEMENT SERVICES

Enhancing clearing and settlement services means giving end-users a more secure, efficient, and cost-effective process – thereby reinforcing one of the key advantages of the exchange-traded world. It also means turning such services into a source of revenues by offering them to third parties, including other exchanges and marketplaces.

The vital middle- and back-end of the listed sector has started to change just as dramatically as the more visible front-end. In a financial environment characterized by significant credit risks, the advantages of robust clearing processes become evident and desirable. Exchanges must therefore:

- Strengthen the clearing and settlement processes they already have, making sure they are as efficient and effective as possible
- Promote cross-margining arrangements so that clients can make better use of scarce margins
- Expand clearing services horizontally and/or vertically in order to develop new sources of revenue

Before expanding into new services or markets, clearers have to make sure they are operating as efficiently, cost-effectively, and securely as possible. They must employ leading-edge clearing technology (being able, for instance, to clear and settle new types of instruments or contracts with little or no reprogramming). They must also feature undoubted security and integrity. Participants turn to the exchange world, in large part, to minimize their credit risks;

---

[10] The "flip side" of losing a dozen local bond contracts in favor of one or two "superregional" bond contracts is, of course, enhanced liquidity: greater critical mass in a benchmark contract means tighter pricing. It also means a greater possibility of creating a true Eurodollar style curve, with a deep market on many contract dates at various points along the yield curve (this becomes a very important risk management tool for OTC swap participants, helping strengthen the ties between the two marketplaces).

[11] Relatively few bonds are deliverable into the Eurex Bund contract; this leads to occasional "squeezes" by market participants, resulting in price volatility. Such squeezes are very problematic for those trying to hedge positions.

clearinghouses must therefore continue to demonstrate that they are secure conduits by making sure adequate resources are on hand to cover counterparty default. These factors become even more important as volumes rise, product scope expands, and volatility increases. Improved settlement times are also important, as users want to know the status of their risk positions and margins on a real-time basis.

Cross-margining agreements, as noted earlier in the chapter, permit more efficient use of margin allocated to derivative positions on multiple exchanges;[12] more arrangements are likely to appear in the near term as they are a relatively simple way of creating client savings and attracting incremental business. Though cross-margining arrangements between stock index futures and options commenced in the 1980s, they have since spread into other areas. In recent years broad agreements have been arranged on various interest rate contracts (e.g. CME/CBOT and CME/LIFFE each have separate interest rate cross-margin arrangements) and between exchange and cash products (e.g. BOTCC and GSCC have a cross-margin arrangement covering Treasury futures held at BOTCC and Treasury cash/repo products held at GSCC; NYCC (clearing on behalf of Cantor Exchange) and GSCC have a similar arrangement in place).[13]

When core clearing is strong, exchange clearinghouses can expand services well beyond a single exchange or cross-margining arrangement. In fact, clearing functions emerge as an untapped source of revenues. Though only a few clearers – such as LCH, Clearnet, CME, BOTCC, OCC, NYMEX – have actively started offering clearing services to third parties, many are exploring opportunities through one of two models:

- *Horizontal services*: clearing of exchange products across different exchanges
- *Vertical services*: clearing of exchange and nonexchange products across different markets

Any clearing function expanding horizontally or vertically must have scalable and flexible technology architecture; in addition, services must be priced competitively (meaning clearers must already be operating in the most efficient way possible).

Horizontal clearing services are an obvious source of new revenues for large clearinghouses. Since established clearers already possess the structural, technological, and intellectual skills needed to clear contracts for their "parent" exchanges, they typically only need to overcome legal, regulatory, and technical hurdles in order to offer the same services to other exchanges. Once this happens, all participants stand to benefit: established clearers (and their parent exchanges) access a new source of revenue and lower their sunk costs, third-party host exchanges can offer their end-use customers better credit protection (and so attract a larger amount of business), and end-users can face the credit of a strong counterparty without worry. For instance, CME's clearinghouse clears trades for its traditional exchange customers as well as those dealing through MEFF[14] and OneChicago; BOTCC clears for NYBOT and BTEX, LCH clears for LIFFE, IPE and LME, and so forth.

Vertical clearing services emerge as another promising growth area. Rather than focusing strictly on exchange contract clearing, some are expanding their services to capture the cash, OTC derivative, and ECN markets. Many of the same structural mechanisms used for

---

[12] Through cross-margining participating clearinghouses examine the positions being cross-margined, compute the net of those positions, and then apply usual margins. Under this type of scheme collateral savings can be as high as 50–75%, meaning lower costs and greater financial flexibility. For instance, if a client has a long position of 100 contracts on Exchange 1 with a margin requirement of 5% and a short position of 60 contracts in the same underlying on Exchange 2 with the same margin requirement, it would have to post margins in the dollar equivalent amount of 5 contracts and 3 contracts, respectively, absent cross-margining. However, by participating in cross-margin programs only the net position, or 40 contracts, is margined – meaning the dollar equivalent of 2, rather than 8, contracts needs to be posted.

[13] From a practical perspective, collateral can either be held in a joint account so that each clearinghouse has access to the funds, or in two separate accounts (one at each clearinghouse) as long as there is prior agreement on how to share funds.

[14] For S&P index contracts only.

listed derivatives (e.g. initial/variation margins, security deposit/contribution to clearing funds, "know your customer," and so forth) can be offered to individual counterparties dealing in OTC derivatives. Third-party clearing services can also be extended to ECNs trading in cash or OTC derivatives. Since ECNs lack the security features of a true clearinghouse they must generally persuade users to accept the credit risk of the sponsoring institution(s) or contract with third-party escrow services (e.g. those that provide surety cover against counterparty default); however, most electronic escrow services are still regarded as burdensome and expensive, creating an opportunity for established clearinghouses. Cash clearing is one important dimension of vertical expansion. Certain cash trades can expose one counterparty to *delivery risk* – risk of default following delivery of cash or securities but prior to receipt of securities or cash; interposing a clearing party can reduce delivery risk and create a new source of clearinghouse revenue. The CME's Clearing 21 platform, LCH's EquityClear, BOTCC's Metaclear, and SGX's and HKEx's clearing platforms can all accommodate cash clearing. OTC derivative clearing is the second major dimension of vertical expansion; OTC credit risks can be very damaging and mechanisms to help mitigate such risks are increasingly in demand. LCH and Clearnet are examples of clearinghouses that can accommodate listed and OTC derivatives. As with horizontal services, the main requirements for offering vertical services include a satisfactory technology platform that can handle generic OTC and cash transaction records in real time and necessary regulatory approvals.[15]

As discussed earlier, the listed market may ultimately feature a handful of clearing entities. Consolidation may unite the fragmented efforts that currently exist, leading to lower costs, faster clearing times, more accurate risk and position reporting, and more efficient management of margins. Before a true "superregional" clearing sector emerges, however, hurdles will have to be overcome. Even after existing clearinghouses are convinced that consolidation might serve their interests, a host of technical, legal, and regulatory issues will have to be considered, including: analyzing cost savings, efficiencies, and administration; reconciling different regulatory approaches; resolving structural organization issues (e.g. mutual versus private, profit versus nonprofit); addressing potential monopoly issues; integrating technical platforms, and so forth.

2.6   REGULATORY CONSIDERATIONS

With transformation in the exchange-traded derivative sector comes the need for regulators to adapt – if not simultaneously, at least without too much delay. In general, regulators still appear to be engaged in a game of "catch up"; regulatory mechanisms do not necessarily permit efficient and logical review of exchange activities and risk becoming outpaced as exchange initiatives accelerate. Accordingly, the pressure for regulators to abandon "outdated" regulations and move to a new regime is building. In order to cope with these challenges, it is increasingly vital for regulators to impose a regimen of:

- Regulatory harmonization
- Regulatory parity
- Regulatory consolidation
- Regulatory cooperation

Regulatory harmonization – making certain that rules for exchanges are generally similar from country to country – must emerge in order to keep pace with growing cross-border activity

---

[15] For instance, as noted in Chapter 1, the CFTC, through the new CFMA, now permits US clearinghouses to clear exchange-traded and OTC instruments; in Europe and the UK regulators have permitted clearinghouses to handle multiple instruments for several years.

and intercountry mergers (e.g. ICE/IPE, Eurex, LIFFE/Euronext, SFE/NZFOE). For example, it makes little sense for British, Belgian, Portuguese, French, or Dutch authorities to regulate the "national components" of Euronext in different ways – such could be very disruptive to the smooth operation of the consolidated exchange. In Europe some harmonization has been accomplished through the Investor Services Directive, which removes barriers to securities and derivatives business in the European Union (EU) by creating a "passport" mechanism allowing banks and securities firms in EU member countries to branch into others (and so offer their services); the ISD eliminates local licensing requirements but does not address solicitation restrictions or broader "conduct of business" rules – it is but a first step in the deregulation process and must ultimately extend to exchanges and their products. Other countries and regions must follow suit.

Regulatory parity – creating a "level playing field," or equivalent rules, across similar marketplaces – is also important. Regulators must be fair and equal in treating marketplaces and instruments that perform the same function. For example, there should be general parity between exchange-traded and OTC derivatives, or else abuses/arbitrage may occur: users will simply gravitate to the marketplace with less, or more opaque, regulation. In addition, as more trading moves to purely electronic mechanisms, regulators should consider global standards that can be applied to activity, wherever it originates and however it is traded and cleared – this applies equally to traditional exchanges with electronic capabilities and newer ECNs.

Regulatory consolidation – combining different national regulators under a single "umbrella" – may ultimately strengthen the sector. In order to unify disparate regulatory views of exchanges and institutions, it is increasingly logical for countries to move toward single national regulatory authorities, or "superregulators." These authorities can ensure that fair, equal, and consistent treatment is applied across similar markets (e.g. exchange and OTC derivatives) and forums (e.g. traditional exchanges and ECNs). This avoids duplication or loopholes, and is especially important as financial instruments become easier to access (e.g. execution via the Internet and other network platforms), and as more retail products (e.g. minis) are made available to the general public – both are capable of causing considerable damage if not handled correctly. In some countries the idea of a national superregulator is not yet a reality. For instance, in the US the CFTC and SEC split responsibility for listed and OTC derivative markets, and the views and directives of the two regulators are not always synchronized. But in some countries "superregulators" already exist, making rules that are consistent across markets and forums. For instance, the UK's FSA has oversight over all financial activities in the country, as do "superregulators" in Korea, Australia, and Japan. If more consolidated national regulators emerge to monitor and guide the activities of financial institutions, markets, and instruments, greater efficiencies, consistency, and security should emerge.

Short of the establishment of "superregulators" a greater amount of *regulatory cooperation* – or assistance within, and across, national boundaries – is necessary. This can help ensure the integrity of the sector without overburdening it through multiple reviews or requests for information. For instance, regulators can share surveillance information on issues that cross boundaries and jointly discuss matters impacting financial instruments and markets that cross jurisdictions.

2.7   INSTITUTIONAL CONSIDERATIONS

Change of any kind can lead to disruption in the "status quo." With all the changes occurring in the listed derivatives market it comes as no surprise that many have been – and are being – impacted: some organizations and their employees have prospered while others have suffered, some have had to merge or combine with competitors while others have emerged as trailblazers. Indeed, there have already been certain "winners" and "losers" as a result of the changes we have discussed – and more are certain to emerge as the sector continues to transform:

- Winners
  - Exchanges capable of changing their structure and operations to become more commercial and "forward thinking"
  - Clearinghouses capable of using technology and alliances to create a broader web of "secure" vertical and horizontal business
  - Technology and software providers able to link exchanges with clearing firms, members, and end-users
  - Banks and investment banks able to bundle futures research and strategy into other professional advisory/sales activities
  - Clients able to take advantage of new products and access mechanisms
  - OTC derivative users that can turn to liquid listed markets to hedge or rebalance their positions (especially large international financial institutions)
- Losers
  - Exchanges incapable of altering corporate structure, refocusing on profitability, or employing new technologies
  - Employees at exchanges that have been acquired or merged into stronger organizations
  - Floor brokers and pit traders unwilling to change from open-outcry to electronic trading
  - Futures execution staff, including futures salespeople, at banks and investment banks
  - Traditional FCMs and futures brokers unable to add value in new ways
  - Clients unable, or unwilling, to use new access mechanisms

Those in the exchange community that have emerged as losers in the transformation process may be forced to adapt in order to survive; it is likely that inefficient or outdated exchanges, clearinghouses, FCMs, and intermediaries will close or be acquired by the leaders. There is even a risk that a small number of large, well-established exchanges – that choose not to adapt to the new environment – will cease to exist in the medium term.

The topics we have summarized in this chapter can be thought of as part of a cycle. Many exchanges, faced with the challenges covered in Chapter 1, are altering their corporate structures from member-owned forums to public, for-profit institutions to operate in a more commercial fashion and access external capital. They are also merging or forming alliances in order to operate more efficiently and introducing new value-added products/services to diversify revenues and increase market/product coverage. By doing so they hope to generate more activity, liquidity, and profitability (and market share, though only if this is consistent with profitability goals). Such profitability (together with external capital) can be invested in new technologies and product development that, again, permit greater market and product access – in turn expanding liquidity and profitability, and helping maximize shareholder value. This helps keep new and traditional competitors at bay. The cycle then repeats. All of this must be done, of course, in a secure and properly controlled environment, as this is one of the key advantages of the listed marketplace. Figure 2.6 summarizes the challenges, responses, and end goals facing the exchange-traded sector.

As noted in this chapter, many of the world's leading exchanges (as well as some of the newer listed exchanges and hybrid ECNs) are adapting quite well to the new market environment.

Many of the changes are radical, and basically dismantle, or redirect, decades of business process and structure. While we can only speculate, the ultimate "end-game" may actually be completely integrated regional markets that feature liquid cash, exchange, and OTC products that complement, and rely on, each other – products that are traded side by side in an electronic environment, and cleared through comprehensive clearinghouse structures. This "end-game" means overcoming many national and global regulatory and technology issues; it also demands a willingness by exchange leaders and OTC market-makers to bring their expertise together. In fact, these are such formidable "hurdles" that a truly integrated market may never really exist – but aspects of integration could emerge.

Based on the different forces at work in reshaping the exchange environment, it is interesting to hypothesize what the "ideal" exchange of the near future might look like. Obviously such an "ideal" is dependent on the needs of members, users, and intermediaries in different markets, and will take some time to refine and develop. Nevertheless, based on the discussion in this chapter, we can picture the "new" exchange as:

- A single legal entity, governed by a single regulator, that is:
  - Organized as a publicly held, "for profit" company
  - Able to trade standardized cross-border futures and options and "standard term" OTC contracts – at the lowest possible costs
  - Capable of trading contracts electronically, 24 hours per day
  - Able to support multiple technology interfaces into the front- and back-office processes of members
  - Linked into a strong, independent regional clearinghouse that supports cross-margining

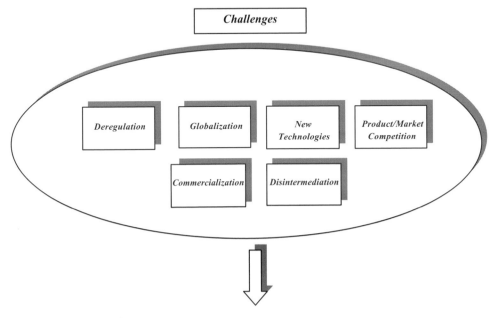

Figure 2.6 (*continued*)

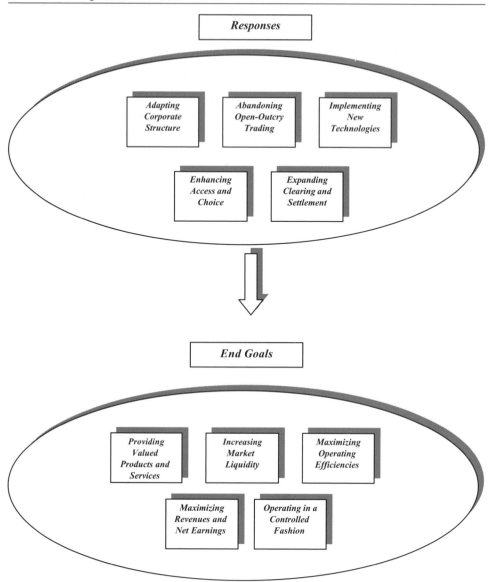

Figure 2.6   Challenges, responses and end goals

We can consider the same for the clearinghouse structure:

- A single legal entity, governed by a single regulator, operating on a regional or "superregional" basis, that is:
  - Independent of any exchange
  - Structured as a "for-profit" organization
  - Capable of clearing exchange-traded, OTC, and cash products

- Able to cross-margin with exchange/cash clearinghouses in other parts of the world in order to optimize client resources and lower costs
- Able to support multiple trading systems, interfaces, and protocols for seamless communication and processing
- Endowed with an undoubted financial guarantee/security position

Even if a full nexus of cash/exchange-traded and OTC instruments does not take place, futures and options should continue to penetrate the mainstream institutional and retail markets as electronic access improves and the utility of the products becomes better understood and appreciated. Though portions of the listed derivative market have been something of a "niche" in the past, this should change as the participation broadens and deepens. Exchanges that have been able to meet the challenges we have discussed – by changing their corporate structure, incorporating a culture of profit maximization, using new technologies, structuring alliances and mergers, and improving product performance, service, and access – should play a leading role in market growth. If the regulatory environment permits cross-border investment and market access, growth opportunities should continue to improve. In the next two parts of this book we discuss the overall structure and operation of some of the world's leading exchanges and some of its new entrants.

Part II
The Established Exchanges

Europe

Borsa Italiana (BI)

3.1 BACKGROUND

Though Borsa Italiana (BI) is a relatively recent creation, it traces its origins back several hundred years, to a time when Italian merchants traded shares in an informal marketplace. More recent history dates BI to 1997, when the Italian Stock Exchange, and its associated financial marketplaces, was privatized through a parliamentary decree; the new amalgamated exchange became operational in January 1998. BI is now the primary marketplace for listing and trading of Italian financial assets, including equities, fixed income securities, and listed futures and options. It is formally responsible for managing the listing and product development processes, maintaining orderly markets, and implementing technology initiatives – which together ensure liquid trading and transparent asset prices. From a practical perspective, BI operates through a number of units and subsidiaries, including those focused on equities and fixed income securities[1] (which are outside the scope of this book) and those dedicated to derivatives. Italy is thus one of several countries that have brought cash and derivative markets together under a single "umbrella" in order to promote synergies and efficiencies.

BI's derivative activities are conducted through two separate units:

- Italian Derivatives Market (IDEM), which is responsible for equity derivatives
- Italian Futures Market (MIF), which is responsible for fixed income derivatives

Equities have become a centerpiece of BI's derivative efforts, as the arrival of monetary union has decreased the need for dedicated trading in Italian government bonds and associated derivatives. Accordingly, BI has developed various new equity derivatives in recent years, and is introducing single stock futures. From a fixed income perspective MIF continues to list and trade 10- and 30-year Italian government bond (BTP) contracts and has added the short-term Euribor contract to MIF's listings. Volumes in the latter tend to be relatively low, however, as deeper Euribor liquidity can be found on LIFFE, Euronext, and Eurex. Though trading in Italian derivatives was conducted on a physical, open-outcry basis for many years, the exchange converted to an all-electronic platform in the late 1990s; this has improved efficiencies and access flexibilities.

BI is an exchange that has attempted to reposition and rescale its derivative operations in order to deal with the challenges of intense competition and a market environment that has caused some of its original products to become redundant. Considering the themes of Chapter 2, we note that BI:

- Has converted from a mutual, nonprofit organization to a profit-based corporation
- Has redesigned its product offerings by strengthening those where market opportunities are best (e.g. equity futures and options) and abandoning or de-emphasizing

---

[1] BI's cash equity/fixed income activities are conducted through the main MTA electronic share market, the Nuovo Mercato for small company listings, the Premi (or premium) market, the STAR and TAH "after hours" markets, the Ristretto (or restricted) market, the covered warrant market, and the MOT fixed income market.

those where competition is too great (and no specific competitive advantage can be delivered)
- Has incorporated new technology into its trading and execution efforts, abandoning its open-outcry operation in the process

3.2   CORPORATE STRUCTURE

BI is a "for profit" corporate entity that operates through a holding company. The holding company owns the cash and derivative exchange operations, as well as a 59% stake in the exchange clearinghouse (the remaining 41% is owned by six banks and one broker). From an internal business management perspective BI is organized by business units that focus on equity markets, fixed income markets, equity derivatives, fixed income derivatives, and new technologies.

3.3   TECHNOLOGY PLATFORM/INFRASTRUCTURE

BI has invested considerable time and effort since the mid-1990s in developing a technology platform that would allow it to migrate from physical to electronic trading. Much of BI's work was focused on in-house development of routing, execution, clearing, and settlement processes. Successful completion of these in-house efforts permitted the exchange to convert to an all-electronic environment at the end of the 1990s. In 2002, however, BI opted to convert its IDEM and MIF derivative trading processes to a customized version of OM's CLICK (see Chapter 10); the system became operational in April 2002. In addition to the customized CLICK platform, the exchange also features a proprietary margining system, Theoretical Intermarket Margin System (TIMS) that, like CME's SPAN, is used to compute margins on both a trade and portfolio basis. Derivatives executed through CLICK feed into TIMS during the clearing process.

3.4   CLEARING

All transactions executed through the BI, including derivatives via IDEM or the MIF, are cleared through the Cassa di Compensazione e Garanzia (CC&G), a joint stock clearinghouse founded in 1992 that is majority owned by BI. All IDEM and MIF exchange members must be clearing members in order to have trades cleared through CC&G; exchange members that are not clearing members must route trades through a clearing member. At the end of each trading day futures and options trades flow through BI's TIMS to determine contract margins; once margins have been determined trades are reregistered and CC&G becomes the legal counterparty. In addition to margins, CC&G's financial standing is supported by member equity and a guarantee fund.

3.5   PRODUCT OFFERINGS

As noted, BI's exchange-traded offerings are segregated by business division, with IDEM listing equity products and MIF listing fixed income products. Within equities (see Table 3.1), IDEM trades:

- Options on individual Italian stocks
- Futures and options on Italian indexes, including the MIB30 and MIDEX

Single stock futures will be introduced in the near term.

Table 3.1 IDEM equity derivatives

Reference	Futures	Options
Individual stocks	–	✓
MIB30 index*	✓	✓
MIDEX index	✓	–

*Also available as a mini.

Table 3.2 MIF fixed income derivatives

Reference	Futures	Futures options
Euribor (3 month)	✓	–
Italian government bonds (10-year BTP)	✓	✓
Italian government bonds (30-year BTP)	✓	–

MIF's fixed income contracts (see Table 3.2) include:

- Futures on short-term interest rates, including 3-month Euribor
- Futures and futures options on long-term interest rates, including 10- and 30-year Italian government bonds (BTPs)

3.6 REGULATION

BI's activities in general, and its derivative activities in particular, are overseen by the Banca D'Italia, the Italian central bank, and CONSOB, the Italian securities markets regulator. Futures and options traded via IDEM and MIF must adhere to specific regulatory rules put forth by CONSOB; the regulator periodically audits exchange compliance with regulations. BI maintains its own surveillance department to ensure adherence to appropriate regulations.

3.7 WEBSITE

The BI website provides details on contract specifications and data/price data sources: www.borsaitalia.com

4

Eurex

4.1 BACKGROUND

Eurex traces its origins back to late 1996 when Deutsche Borse (DB, parent of German futures exchange Deutsche Terminborse (DTB)) and the Swiss Exchange (parent company of the Swiss Options and Financial Futures Exchange (SOFFEX)) agreed to merge their operations. Though both exchanges had established effective electronic trading of financial derivatives in their respective home markets – SOFFEX was established in 1988, DTB in 1990 – they felt a combined entity would permit greater client access, liquidity, and cost efficiency. The merger of the two exchanges represented the first European cross-border exchange effort (predating the Euronext combination, discussed in Chapter 5, by several years). During 1997 DTB and SOFFEX worked on developing a combined trading and clearing platform to support their new operation and completed the project in May 1998. Once complete the exchange, which had by then been renamed Eurex, migrated its existing contracts to the new platform and started trading contracts previously handled through DTB and SOFFEX. Eurex expanded its product offerings in the early twenty-first century, introducing stock options on a broad range of European equities/indexes (including single stock, low exercise price options (LEPOs), and futures and options on various equity indexes). It also expanded outside its traditional futures and options domain by launching a Euro-Repo market, offering clients access to standard *repurchase agreement* (financing) contracts in an exchange setting.

The exchange has created a series of alliances over the past few years in order to maximize European and global market/product ties. For instance, in 1999 Eurex formed an alliance with the Helsinki Exchange (HEX) to list and trade HEX products via the Eurex platform. It also solidified a cross-product trading venture with the CBOT, known as Alliance/CBOT/Eurex, or a/c/e, to enable trading of Eurex and CBOT products on the same platform (subject to certain CFTC-related restrictions). While the early days of the a/c/e alliance appeared promising, the two exchanges were forced to restructure their cooperative venture in mid-2002 as it became clear that goals related to product development and technology-sharing were diverging. The new alliance now focuses on technical cooperation and cross-platform trading, but permits greater flexibility in the development of proprietary products (e.g. CBOT and Eurex are each developing new US$ and euro-based futures and options on their own, rather than in cooperation). Eurex also holds a significant minority stake in the electricity ECN EEX, discussed in Chapter 34.

In addition to product development and alliances, Eurex has actively promoted technology development. The exchange continually enhances its platform by releasing updated versions with new capabilities (e.g. the platform now has the capability to electronically accept basis (cash/futures), block and volatility trades, and to provide intraday risk/margin information) and expanding access through alternative mechanisms such as Bloomberg and the Internet. It has also used its technology development as a source of revenues, licensing components of its trading system to other exchanges.

By most measures Eurex is routinely one of the three most active exchanges in the world (as measured by turnover). This success has been made possible through a combination of product offerings (on many of Europe's key equity and fixed income benchmarks), global alliances, and technology. Considering the themes discussed in Chapter 2, Eurex has managed to cope with the changing environment by adapting its operations rather dramatically; the exchange:

- Is organized as a "for-profit" commercial company
- Has fully embraced the concept of mergers and alliances (despite the fact that the a/c/e alliance has not worked out as well as originally planned)
- Has migrated completely to an electronic environment and features leading-edge technology which it licenses to others
- Has promoted alternate access mechanisms through a variety of electronic platforms
- Has expanded its clearing services to handle OTC products
- Has actively developed new types of exchange-traded products

4.2   CORPORATE STRUCTURE

Eurex operates as a public "for profit" corporation through separate, but linked, subsidiaries, including Eurex Frankfurt (which handles all German-related products) and Eurex Zurich (which handles all Swiss-related products); Eurex effectively operates under the "one company, multiple exchange" structure (much like Euronext). The Swiss Exchange and DB each own 50% of Eurex Zurich, which owns 100% of Eurex Frankfurt; Eurex Frankfurt, in turn, is sole owner of Eurex Clearing AG.

From an internal business management perspective the exchange is managed by a single executive team that conducts business through separate divisions, including exchange operations (all exchange trading and product development) and technology services (development and marketing of exchange-based applications). The exchange's stated business model is to build liquidity through accessible trading networks and alliances.

4.3   TECHNOLOGY PLATFORM/INFRASTRUCTURE

Eurex features one of the most advanced technology platforms in the exchange world, with a single platform covering all stages of the process (from front-end entry and execution to back-end clearing and settlement). In fact, the system has been so successful that it has been licensed for use by other exchanges (and thus forms part of the exchange's revenue expansion strategy). Eurex's technology prowess is hardly surprising since both DTB and SOFFEX were created as electronic, rather than physical, exchanges, and thus had a long history of dealing with technology issues.

The exchange has implemented an advanced trading, routing, and matching system centered on the Eurex x-ceed front-end API introduced in September 1998. The front-end supports a broad range of products, including complex option strategies and spreads; as noted above, the system also accommodates basis, block, and volatility trades. All trades routed through the platform feed into the Eurex Clearing System used by the exchange's clearing arm, meaning the bulk of trade processing occurs in an entirely automated environment. Part of the exchange's success has been its willingness to embrace the "open API" approach, giving end-users, intermediaries, and clients complete flexibility in accessing exchange products and executing trades. Users can execute transactions through dedicated terminals, third-party information platforms, customized client interfaces, and so forth. Eurex currently operates a network of trading centers/hubs/access points that link members; these hubs are located in major centers such as Chicago, Helsinki, London, Madrid, and New York.

4.4 CLEARING

Eurex trades are cleared through Eurex Clearing AG, a wholly owned and guaranteed subsidiary of Eurex Frankfurt; any firm executing a transaction thus faces Eurex Clearing as its central counterparty. Clearing members have to be German or Swiss companies, or foreign firms with branches in Germany or Switzerland; in order to ensure exchange integrity, all clearing members are required to post initial and variation margins, and contribute to the exchange's guaranty fund. Though the bulk of Eurex Clearing's activity relates to exchange contracts, it began offering OTC clearing services in 2001; the exchange and clearinghouse expect to gain reasonable market share in OTC clearing over the medium term (once again supplementing revenues).

4.5 PRODUCT OFFERINGS

As a result of its geographic location, extensive European connections and alliances, Eurex has developed into one of the main pan-European forums for equity and fixed income derivative trading. Within the equity sector (see Table 4.1), Eurex offers:

- Options on individual German, Swiss, Nordic, Dutch, Italian, French, and US stocks
- Futures and options on global, pan-European, German, Swiss, and Nordic indexes and subindexes

Table 4.1 Eurex's equity derivatives

Reference	Futures	Options
German stocks	–	✓
Swiss stocks	–	✓
Nordic stocks	–	✓
Dutch stocks	–	✓
Italian stocks	–	✓
French stocks	–	✓
US stocks	–	✓
DJ Global Titan 50 index	✓	✓
DJ Stoxx 600 index	✓	✓
DJ Stoxx 600 Euro sector indexes	✓	✓
DJ Stoxx 50 index	✓	✓
DJ Stoxx 50 Euro index	✓	✓
DAX index	✓	✓
NEMAX index	✓	✓
SMI index	✓	✓
HEX 25 index	✓	✓

Table 4.2   Eurex's fixed income derivatives

Reference	Futures	Futures options
Euribor (1 month)	✓	✓
Euribor (3 month)	✓	–
German government bond (Schatz)	✓	✓
German government bond (Bobl)	✓	✓
German government bond (Bund)	✓	✓
German government bond (Buxl)	✓	–
Swiss government bond (Conf)	✓	–

In the fixed income sector (see Table 4.2), Eurex offers contracts on benchmark Euro and Swiss rates, including:

- Futures and futures options on short-term interest rates, including 1- and 3-month Euribor
- Futures and futures options on medium- and long-term Euro and Swiss interest rates, including the German and Swiss government bonds (i.e. Schatz, Bund, Bobl, Buxl and Conf)

4.6   REGULATION

Since Eurex is legally domiciled in Germany and Switzerland, and since no pan-European exchange licenses are yet available, it is regulated by authorities from both countries. The regulation of recognized exchanges in Germany is the responsibility of individual state governments. The state of Hesse is responsible for overseeing Eurex Frankfurt's German activities and making sure that the exchange complies with Exchange Supervisory Authority decrees, including those detailed under the German Stock Exchange Act. In addition, since derivative contracts come under the purview of the Federal Banking Supervisory Office, Eurex Frankfurt must adhere to regulations promulgated by the Banking Office; the Federal Authority for Financial Services Supervision also ensures that the exchange is not involved in manipulation of market prices. Eurex Zurich, in contrast, is regulated by the Swiss Banking Commission (EBK), which is responsible for establishing regulations for domestic financial markets, conduits, and institutions, and ensuring full compliance at all times. Both Eurex Frankfurt and Zurich maintain their own internal surveillance units to manage the self-regulation process.

4.7   WEBSITE

The Eurex website provides details on contract specifications and data/price data sources: www.eurexchange.com

5
Euronext

5.1 BACKGROUND

Euronext – a hybrid pan-European exchange that trades securities and listed derivatives, and provides clearing, settlement, listing, and information services – operates on a "one-company, multiple-exchange" basis. The exchange was originally created in 2000 through the merger of three long-established Continental European equity/derivative exchanges, including:

- Société des Bourses Françaises (SBF), owner of the Paris Stock Exchange and French derivatives exchange MATIF (and now known as Euronext Paris)
- The combined Belgian Stock Exchange and the Belgian Futures and Options Exchange, (now known as Euronext Brussels) and
- The combined Amsterdam Stock Exchange and Amsterdam Options Exchange (now known as Euronext Amsterdam)

Euronext's management operates under the belief that it can achieve greater liquidity and cost efficiencies combining pan-European securities and derivatives trading under a single "umbrella." To reinforce this operating philosophy it added two additional exchanges to the core group within 18 months of the original consolidation: in October 2001 Euronext purchased LIFFE, and in February 2002 it acquired Portugal's Bolsa de Valores de Lisboa e Porto (note that we discuss LIFFE's very significant operations separately in Chapter 7). More exchanges may be acquired in the medium term. In addition to outright acquisitions, Euronext has developed corporate alliances designed to expand its product/technology scope.[1] For instance, Euronext Paris (via the MATIF derivatives arm) was a founding member of the Globex alliance that includes the CME, SGX, BM&F, MX, and MEFF (as noted in Chapter 2, the alliance makes use of GLOBEX 2 which is based on Euronext's NSC systems). Euronext and CME also have a unique "technology-sharing" partnership that allows each exchange to use technology developed by the other (e.g. Euronext uses CME's Clearing 21 platform and CME uses the NSC execution platform). Euronext also provides comprehensive clearing and settlement services and has made considerable progress in offering "nonfinancial" services to its clients, including those based on technology and information.

The exchange, which operates strictly on an electronic basis, offers a broad range of financial and commodity-based derivatives (it also features trading in cash securities, funds, and warrants, though these are outside the scope of this book). Some of Euronext's contracts were developed by the original exchange partners (i.e. Paris, Brussels, Amsterdam, London, and Lisbon traded in various interest rate and equity index contracts prior to 2000), while others have been created since the consolidation (e.g. single stock futures were introduced after the merger).

---

[1] The exchange is also active in various equity alliances (i.e. one with the Luxembourg Stock Exchange), though such are outside the scope of this book.

Euronext has emerged as a "forward thinking" exchange that has transformed itself, quite radically, based on many of the themes discussed in Chapter 2. In particular, the exchange:

- Is organized as a public, "for-profit" commercial company
- Has fully embraced the concept of mergers and alliances
- Has migrated completely to an electronic environment and features leading-edge technology which it licenses to others
- Offers additional clearing and nontrading services to supplement its revenues
- Has been active in creating new types of futures and options products

5.2 CORPORATE STRUCTURE

Euronext's business crosses national boundaries and, since no pan-European exchange licenses exist, it operates on a corporate and legal basis through the individual exchanges that comprise the Euronext group. The company, which issued public equity in mid-2001, is legally separated into different operating subsidiaries, including Euronext Paris, Euronext Brussels, Euronext Amsterdam, and Euronext Lisbon. LIFFE is 100% owned by Euronext UK plc, itself 100% owned by the Euronext NV public holding company. Clearnet, the exchange's clearing operation, is a wholly owned subsidiary, while its technology unit, Atos-Euronext, is structured as a 50/50 joint venture with French technology firm Atos. From an internal business management perspective Euronext operates through a single executive team, with divisions focused on cash markets, derivative markets, clearing/netting, settlements, and listing/information services.

5.3 TECHNOLOGY PLATFORM/INFRASTRUCTURE

Euronext features one of the industry's most advanced technology platforms – though one that the exchange continues to enhance and refine. Ultimately, the exchange intends to operate through a single cash trading system, a single derivative trading system and a shared clearing and netting system.

The centerpiece of Euronext's technology architecture is the NSC trading engine, originally developed by Euronext Paris and Atos. The NSC system has proven so successful that it is used by more than a dozen other exchanges (including the stock exchanges of Warsaw, Brazil, and Toronto, several Globex alliance members (BM&F, MX, SGX, and CME), as well as four of the Euronext exchanges (LIFFE features its own Connect platform)). In derivatives, the exchange is consolidating its functionality into a new platform known as the Next Derivative System (NDS), which replaces much of the exchange's current architecture; when NDS is fully operational it will also be offered to the Globex alliance. Euronext's products can be accessed by local or remote members through the four primary gateways (Paris, Brussels, Amsterdam, Lisbon); cross-border access by foreign parties is also permissible and the platform supports a wide variety of proprietary and third-party APIs. As noted, Euronext's core clearing platform comes from its alliance with the CME, which it has adapted for its own use (including cash clearing, cross-margining and real-time netting).

5.4 CLEARING

Euronext clears contracts through Clearnet, a cash and derivatives clearing company that traces its origins back to 1990 (well before Euronext existed as an exchange). Following the Euronext

Table 5.1 Euronext's equity derivatives

Reference	Futures	Options
Individual stocks (A, B, P*, L)	✓	✓
AEX index/index light (A)	✓	✓
AMX index (A)	✓	✓
FTSE Eurotop 100 index (A)	✓	✓
Bel 20 index† (B)	✓	✓
DJ Euro Stoxx 50 (P, B)†	✓	–
CAC 40 index (P)	✓	✓
DJ Stoxx 50 (P)	✓	–
DJ Euro Stoxx sectors (P)	✓	–
DJ Stoxx sectors (P)	✓	–
PSI 20 index (L)	✓	✓

*Short- and long-term options only.
†Also available as a mini.

merger in 2000, the clearing systems of the three member exchanges were combined into a single legal entity that became known as Clearnet. The clearinghouse now clears and settles all traded products, including derivative contracts, equities, bonds, and other securities; it also accepts trades executed on other exchanges. Clearnet acts as legal counterparty on all transactions and is supported by member margins, a guarantee deposit fund, and equity. From a practical perspective, transactions flow through Clearnet and are settled either through global settlement agency Euroclear (or others, such as Clearstream).[2] In the medium term Euronext intends to expand its clearing activity to include coverage of more cash instruments and OTC derivatives.

5.5   PRODUCT OFFERINGS

Euronext offers exchange contracts in the equity, fixed income/currency, and commodity sectors. Not surprisingly, the group's individual exchanges have developed considerable depth in equities (see Table 5.1) and offer a large number of contracts on single stocks, national equity indexes, and pan-European indexes, including:

- Futures and options on individual Dutch, French, Belgian, and Portuguese companies
- Futures and options on national indexes, including AEX, Bel 20, CAC, and PSI, as well as pan-European indexes, including DJ Stoxx sectors

(The abbreviations A (Amsterdam), P (Paris), B (Brussels), and L (Lisbon) indicate the location of contract trading; as noted above, all of LIFFE's products are discussed separately in Chapter 7.)

Euronext offers a number of fixed income and currency contracts (see Table 5.2), including:

- Futures and options on US$/€ FX
- Futures on short-term interest rates, including 3 month Euribor, and long-term interest rates, including the 5-year and Notionnel government bond benchmarks

---

[2] Euronext maintains a significant interest in Euroclear. Euroclear, which merged with French settlement house Sicovam in 2001, is also merging with the Dutch and Belgian settlement houses to create a single settlement firm. When this occurs, Euronext has signed a memorandum of understanding that will let it take a majority stake in the combined Euroclear.

Table 5.2   Euronext's fixed income/currency derivatives

Reference	Futures	Options
US dollar/euro (A)	✓	✓
Euribor (3 month) (P)	✓	–
Government bond (Notionnel) (P)	✓	–
Government bond (5 year) (P)	✓	–

Table 5.3   Euronext's commodity derivatives

Reference	Futures	Options	Futures options
Potatoes (A)	✓	✓	–
Hogs (A)	✓	–	–
Rapeseed (P)	✓	–	✓
Wheat No. 2 (P)	✓	–	–
Corn (P)	✓	–	–
Wine (P)	✓	–	–
Sunflower (P)	✓	–	–

Euronext retains the most important commodity contracts originally developed and traded in Amsterdam and Paris (see Table 5.3), including:

• Futures and options on potatoes, hogs, rapeseed, wheat, corn, wine, and sunflower seeds

5.6   REGULATION

Since Euronext does not have the benefit of a pan-European exchange license, the individual exchanges that comprise the group are subject to local regulations imposed by each relevant national regulator. In early 2001, however, the national securities regulators and central banks of France, Netherlands, and Belgium (and, latterly, Portugal) signed a memorandum of understanding related to harmonization of rules applicable to the combined operation; this will also help form the basis of future regulatory integration in participating countries, an important step forward in ensuring uniform application of rules (as discussed in Chapter 2). Clearnet's activities are formally regulated by the French regulators, but the clearinghouse also works closely with regulators in the Netherlands and Belgium.

5.7   WEBSITE

The Euronext website provides details on contract specifications and data/price data sources: www.euronext.com

6

International Petroleum Exchange (IPE)

6.1 BACKGROUND

The International Petroleum Exchange of London Ltd (IPE) was founded as a mutual society in 1980 by several energy companies and futures firms interested in trading standardized energy products in an exchange setting. IPE commenced operations by listing a gas oil contract, and followed several years later with a contract on Brent crude oil – which ultimately became the second most actively traded energy benchmark in the world (after NYMEX's Light Sweet Crude futures[1]). During the latter part of the 1990s and into the new millennium IPE expanded into several new energy-related areas, including natural gas and electricity. It also negotiated a mutual offset alliance with SGX, allowing IPE Brent crude positions to be established or covered in the Singapore market (which has developed into Asia's regional energy hub). The IPE also permits *exchange for physicals* (EFPs), enabling customers to use futures to lock in a price and arrange for physical delivery.[2]

In early 2000 IPE members voted to demutualize the exchange in order to be able to operate more "commercially," access new sources of capital sources, and develop cross-exchange alliances; a new corporate holding company was established in February 2000 to acquire the exchange, thus separating ownership rights from trading rights. As part of its new commercial orientation IPE also focused on upgrading its trading systems, with an eventual goal of migrating its business partially, or totally, to an electronic environment. During its evaluation stages it entered into discussions with ICE which, as a "new" electronic exchange backed by energy companies and financial institutions, featured a robust technology platform that supported a broad suite of energy-related products. In early 2001 ICE offered to purchase IPE, and in April 2001 IPE shareholders approved the acquisition. The exchange now operates as a wholly owned subsidiary of ICE, retaining its name, branding, organization/management structure, and product offerings. Over the past few years IPE has only introduced two new products (e.g. natural gas and electricity futures) and has not created new clearing or technology services. However, its relationship with ICE largely obviates the need for such moves; as noted in Chapter 30, ICE features a broad range of customized and standardized OTC instruments and it is actively promoting leading-edge clearing services with the LCH (IPE's own clearer) and the Board of Trade Clearing Corporation (BOTCC).

IPE is an example of a marketplace that is attempting to become more competitive by exchanging its corporate independence (if not yet its management/organizational structure)

---

[1] Though IPE was the only exchange to offer a Brent crude futures contract for nearly 15 years, the new NYMEX Brent contract – introduced in 2001 – poses a significant competitive threat to the IPE's position. This is particularly true because NYMEX already lists the world's most active crude contract – on Light Sweet Crude – meaning that users can trade Brent/Light Sweet spreads through a single exchange.

[2] A counterparty might want to complement a physical transaction with a futures transaction and can advise its broker of its intent to execute an EFP (who must register the transaction with the IPE). For instance, if a refiner needs 1 million barrels of Brent it can buy 1000 IPE contracts. If a producer owns 1 million barrels it can agree to sell them to the buyer at the futures price. The refiner's long futures position will be "exchanged for physical" with the producer after they agree to the EFP and advise their brokers.

for the financial, business, and technological skills offered by another exchange. Considering the themes of Chapter 2, we note that IPE:

- Has altered its structure from a mutual society to a "for-profit" commercial company
- Has embraced the concept of cross-exchange alliances (e.g. its mutual offset program with SGX)
- Has commenced an active technology expansion and migration plan (dependent heavily on the platform of its new parent) that will eventually lead to abandonment of physical trading

6.2   CORPORATE STRUCTURE

IPE Holdings, created through the February 2000 demutualization of the exchange, owns 100% of the exchange. IPE Holdings, in turn, is majority-owned by ICE. As noted in Chapter 30, ICE is a privately held corporation controlled by various energy companies and financial institutions.

6.3   TECHNOLOGY PLATFORM/INFRASTRUCTURE

Prior to its acquisition by ICE, IPE had commenced an upgrade of its Electronic Trading System (ETS) – which allowed members (or clients registered as trade associates) to execute natural gas and electricity trades directly on-screen rather than through the floor of the exchange – to the new ETS II module. ETS II, which allows electronic execution of Brent crude and gas oil trades, was originally intended to supplement and lengthen the trading day (rather than replace the physical operation).

Following its acquisition, IPE agreed to invest $10mn in a new technology platform being developed by ICE; the system will ultimately accommodate all of IPE's contracts in a single platform. In fact, the new system is the centerpiece of IPE's ultimate goal of abandoning open-outcry trading. IPE management have indicated that over the medium term all trading will move from physical to electronic, but that migration will occur gradually so as not to disrupt the liquidity of the business (in fact, the exchange has already published a timetable that will allow for complete transition to an electronic environment over the coming years). As part of the process the exchange has contracted with third-party providers (e.g. EasyScreen) to develop tools and interfaces allowing seamless connection between clients, members, and the exchange. The new technology platform is also designed with electronic links directly into the LCH's clearing systems, helping promote the concept of straight-through-processing.

6.4   CLEARING

IPE trades are cleared through the LCH (which also clears trades for the LME, LIFFE, and LSE). LCH, which is 25% owned by IPE, LIFFE, LME, and LSE, and 75% owned by exchange members, is a recognized clearer under the Financial Services Authority (FSA) Act of 1986 and acts as central counterparty on all IPE trades.[3] LCH is contractually bound to ensure performance of trades registered by members; once LCH registers a trade at the end of a business day, it becomes the legal counterparty to that trade. The LCH requires clearing members to post initial and variation margins; clearing members settle margins with the LCH, and then

---

[3] As noted in Chapter 30, ICE and LCH have created a joint OTC energy derivative clearing service that also allows IPE positions to be factored into any cross-margining computation.

Table 6.1   IPE's energy derivatives

Reference	Futures	Options
Brent crude oil	✓	✓
Natural gas	✓	–
Gas oil	✓	–
Electricity	✓	–

settle margins with their own clients. Members must also contribute to a default fund (which amounted to nearly £300mn in 2002); this fund is supplemented by £100mn of insurance to protect against counterparty default.

Institutions can join LCH as clearing members (general or individual) or nonclearing members. Clearing members can clear their own trades, as well as trades of nonmembers, while nonclearing members can only clear their own trades. In order to become a clearing member a firm must meet certain minimum financial requirements and own a set number of exchange shares. All IPE floor members are members of the LCH, or have a clearing agreement with a floor member who is a member of the LCH.

6.5   PRODUCT OFFERINGS

Though the IPE features a small number of products (see Table 6.1), it has built strong liquidity in several of them and is now the second largest energy exchange in the world (after NYMEX). In particular, IPE's Brent contract, offsetable on SGX, serves as the price benchmark for two-thirds of the world's crude oil and is thus an extremely active derivative. IPE features:

• Futures and options on Brent crude, gas oil, natural gas, and electricity

6.6   REGULATION

IPE's activities are governed by the UK's FSA, the consolidated regulatory authority that formally came into existence in December 2001 through the Financial Services Markets Act 2000. Though the FSA has a broad remit to regulate financial activities in the UK, it is specifically responsible for regulating investment business, which is prohibited unless an entity is authorized or exempted. Recognized investment exchanges (RIEs), such as IPE, are exempted by the FSA. In order to qualify as an RIE, an exchange must demonstrate that it meets the FSA financial and regulatory requirements (e.g. those listed under the Financial Services Markets Act and the Companies Act), including protection of investors, fair/orderly trading mechanisms, trade, reporting, clearing and settlement facilities, and a general compliance structure. ICE, as the ultimate holding company of the IPE, is subject to regulations enforced by the SEC and the CFTC.

6.7   WEBSITE

The IPE website provides details on contract specifications and data/price data sources: www.ipe.co.uk

7
London International Financial Futures Exchange (LIFFE)

7.1 BACKGROUND

The London International Financial Futures Exchange (LIFFE) was formed in 1982 to offer financial futures and options in a newly deregulated operating environment (i.e. the UK had just abandoned its long-standing currency controls). The development of the exchange also coincided with London's attempts to enhance its role as a global financial center; though the country already featured established exchanges – including the LSE, LME, and IPE – it wanted to strengthen its position in financial instruments and markets. Though LIFFE's original focus was on interest rate and currency contracts, the exchange ultimately expanded via acquisition into equity options (through the 1992 purchase of the London Traded Options Market (LTOM)) and soft/agricultural commodities (through the 1996 purchase of the London Commodity Exchange (LCE)). LIFFE has also developed a series of exchange alliances over the years that have helped it increase its global presence. For instance, in July 1987 it entered into an agreement with the TSE to list the benchmark Japanese government bond (JGB), in April 1996 it entered into an arrangement with TIFFE to list and trade a fungible 3-month Euroyen contract, and in 2001 it joined with US stock exchange NASDAQ to create NASDAQ LIFFE markets, a platform to offer global single stock futures.

During the late 1990s LIFFE underwent several radical changes in order to "keep pace" with the changing environment; specifically, it abandoned open-outcry trading, demutualized the exchange, and issued shares to members. Though LIFFE had existed as an open-outcry exchange since its foundation, the exchange's membership voted to move away from open-outcry trading to fully automated trading through the LIFFE Connect platform in May 1998 in order to improve efficiencies. The process was completed in 2000, whereupon the trading floor was permanently closed. The exchange membership also voted to demutualize, becoming the first of London's derivative exchanges to do so.

In the midst of intense competition from Eurex, Euronext, and other forums at the end of the 1990s, LIFFE's own trading volumes suffered and its revenues stagnated. In mid-2001 the exchange became the focus of interest by various exchanges (including Euronext and the LSE), which were keen on acquiring LIFFE's operations. In October 2001 LIFFE's board of directors agreed to a £550mn purchase offer from Euronext (representing a 112% premium to LIFFE's share price). Under the terms of the acquisition LIFFE will ultimately become the nexus of Euronext's derivative activities, and London will become the hub of the combined exchange's European activities (see Chapter 5 for additional detail on Euronext).

LIFFE is an exchange that has attempted to cope with many of the structural changes in the marketplace and has generally been successful. Though the exchange has relinquished its independence to Euronext, it appears to have done so on terms that will allow it to remain an important, and somewhat independent, financial conduit. Considering the themes of Chapter 2, we note that LIFFE:

- Is organized as a "for-profit" commercial company
- Has fully embraced the concept of mergers and alliances (e.g. its own acquisitions of LTOM and LCE, its alliances with NASDAQ, TIFFE, TSE, and its own sale to Euronext)
- Has migrated completely to an electronic environment and features leading-edge technology which it licenses to others
- Offers additional clearing and nontrading services to supplement its revenues
- Has actively created new types of futures and options and is represented across a broad product spectrum

7.2   CORPORATE STRUCTURE

LIFFE was originally established as a mutually owned membership organization and retained that status until its conversion into a for-profit corporation, LIFFE Holdings plc, in February 1999. The shares were acquired by Euronext in late 2001. Though LIFFE is now part of Euronext, it retains its own branding, management, and technology.

From a business perspective LIFFE formally divides its operations into exchange-based services (focused on the development of core listed derivatives) and technology services (focused on technology services and e-commerce opportunities). In order to expand its technology initiative, LIFFE has created alliances/partnerships with Battery Ventures, Blackstone Group, and Cap Gemini Ernst & Young (some have since ended).

7.3   TECHNOLOGY PLATFORM/INFRASTRUCTURE

LIFFE has been aggressive in its development and use of technology. Though the exchange operated on a physical trading floor for more than 16 years, its successful creation of electronic trading, through the LIFFE Connect platform, led to the eventual migration from open-outcry to screen-based trading. LIFFE commenced electronic trading of its equity options in November 1998, and completed a full product migration just 2 years later.

LIFFE Connect is an anonymous, order-driven system. Customer trades are entered via API into an order router and flow to an exchange member for execution; the member electronically passes the order into the LIFFE Connect central limit order book (CLOB). Once received by the LIFFE Connect central processing system (which acts as a host) the order is considered firm (but can be changed at any time through an order amendment, which flows through the same process). Prices are visible, including those outside the best bid or offer. Once in the CLOB, the host matches the orders by price and time or pro rata (all orders and the best bid or offer have equal priority and are filled on a pro-rata basis). Preference is given to orders that match the best current bid or offer; time is the second priority. After execution the host confirms details to the Trade Registration System (TRS), which passes trades to the Clearing Processing System (CPS) for position maintenance, clearing, and daily data processing. Settlement prices are fed into the CPS and the clearinghouse.

LIFFE developed its platform in close cooperation with technology partners, independent software providers, and network service providers. This permitted the exchange to remain extremely flexible in offering its derivative products through different mechanisms, and has ultimately let users buy or build technology interfaces that are most suited to their needs. For instance, local users can trade through LIFFE's Easy network, while global users can do so through the Equant network, Internet service providers (ISPs), or proprietary networks (they can also trade via the order routing services offered by members).

7.4   CLEARING

LIFFE trades are cleared through the LCH – which, as noted in Chapter 6, also clears for the LME, IPE, and LSE; LCH is thus the central counterparty on all LIFFE derivative trades and is contractually bound to ensure performance of traders registered by members. When a trade is executed it is assigned to an account and registered with the LCH at the end of the business day; once registered, the LCH is legal counterparty to that trade. The LCH requires clearing members to post initial and variation margins and contribute to a default fund.

7.5   PRODUCT OFFERINGS

Though LIFFE commenced with a focus on interest rates and currencies, it ultimately became active across a broad spectrum of financial and nonfinancial contracts. The exchange currently offers futures and options on fixed income, equity and nonfinancial references. Within fixed income, its major offerings include (see Table 7.1):

- Futures and futures options on short-term interest rates, including Euribor, Euro Libor, Short Sterling, Euro Swiss Franc, Euroyen Tibor (in conjunction with TIFFE) and Euroyen Libor (note that the Euro Euribor and Short Sterling option contracts are also offered as a 1-year "mid-curve" structure)
- Futures and futures options on medium- and long-term interest rates, including long gilts (UK government bond), German Bunds and JGBs (in conjunction with TSE), as well as 2-, 5- and 10-year Euro swap rates (e.g. priced off the Euro swap curve)

Table 7.1   LIFFE's fixed income derivatives

Reference	Futures	Futures options
Euribor (3 month)*	✓	✓
Euro Libor (3 month)	✓	–
Short Sterling (3 month)*	✓	✓
Euro Swiss (3 month)	✓	✓
Tibor Euroyen (3 month)	✓	–
Libor Euroyen (3 month)	✓	–
UK government bond (long gilt)	✓	✓
German government bond (Bund)	✓	✓
Japanese government bond (10-year)	✓	–
2-year Swapnote	✓	–
5-year Swapnote	✓	–
10-year Swapnote	✓	–

*Also available as a 1-year mid-curve option.

Table 7.2   LIFFE's equity derivatives

Reference	Futures	Options
Universal stock futures	✓	–
Individual equity options	–	✓
FTSE 100 index*	✓	✓
FTSE 250 index	✓	–
FTSE Euro Stars index	✓	✓
FTSE Eurobloc 100 index	✓	✓
FTSE Eurotop 100 index	✓	✓
FTSE Europtop 300 index	✓	✓
FTSE Eurotop 300 (ex-UK)	✓	✓
MSCI Euro index	✓	✓
MSCI Pan-Euro index	✓	✓

*Available as mini futures and options.

Table 7.3   LIFFE's nonfinancial derivatives

Reference	Futures	Options
Cocoa	✓	✓
Robusta coffee	✓	✓
White sugar	✓	✓
Wheat	✓	✓
Barley	✓	✓
Potatoes	✓	✓
Biffex freight	✓	✓
Temperature*	✓	–

*Available on London, Paris, and Berlin.

LIFFE's equity products have expanded considerably in recent years and now cover the entire spectrum, from single stock futures and options to broad UK and pan-European indexes. The exchange currently lists (see Table 7.2):

- Futures and options on individual UK and international equities (in conjunction with NASDAQ)
- Futures and options on indexes, including various Financial Times Stock Exchange (FTSE) and Morgan Stanley Capital International (MSCI) UK and European indexes

LIFFE acquired its nonfinancial derivative capabilities through the purchase of the LCE and has preserved most of the original offerings. Since the acquisition it has also expanded into several new areas, including weather derivatives. The exchange lists (see Table 7.3):

- Futures and options on cocoa, robusta coffee, white sugar, wheat, barley, and potatoes
- Futures and options on the Baltic freight index (Biffex)
- Futures on weather (e.g. temperatures in London, Paris, and Berlin)

7.6   REGULATION

LIFFE's activities are governed by the UK's FSA, the consolidated regulatory authority that formally came into being in December 2001 through the Financial Services Markets Act 2000. Though the FSA has a broad remit to regulate financial activities in the UK, it is specifically responsible for regulating investment business, which is prohibited unless an entity is authorized or exempted; recognized investment exchanges (RIEs), such as LIFFE, are exempted by the FSA. In order to qualify as an RIE, an exchange must demonstrate that it meets the FSA financial and regulatory requirements (e.g. those listed under the Financial Services Markets Act and the Companies Act) including protection of investors, fair/orderly trading mechanisms, trade, reporting, clearing and settlement facilities, and general compliance structure. As noted in Chapter 5, Euronext, LIFFE's ultimate parent company, is regulated by national regulators of the Netherlands, France, Belgium, and Portugal.

7.7   WEBSITE

The LIFFE website provides details on contract specifications and data/price data sources: www.liffe.co.uk

8

London Metal Exchange (LME)

8.1 BACKGROUND

The London Metal Exchange (LME) was formally established in 1877 as a central marketplace for trading nonferrous metals – initially copper and tin – on a spot and futures basis (in fact, the exchange operated on an informal basis for several decades prior to its official establishment). Since that time the LME has emerged as the largest nonferrous metals trading exchange in the world. Its business is very global, with 90% of activity conducted by international participants (and 90% of its clearing members incorporated as foreign, or foreign-owned, entities). In addition to serving as a central forum for trading, the LME acts as the metals market "deliverer of last resort" – authorizing warehouses to store approved types of metal for use in meeting short-term supply squeezes. The exchange accepts delivery of more than 440 brands of metals from 65 different countries against its contracts.

Over the past few decades the LME has added new contracts (e.g. metal index futures, North American aluminum alloy futures) and upgraded the metal quality of its existing contracts; it has also abandoned those without a critical mass of liquidity (e.g. long-standing silver futures were delisted in 2002). The exchange has also successfully launched a unique "prompt date" trading concept (not found on any other futures exchange), which gives clients flexibility in establishing settlement dates on particular contracts – not unlike the OTC market. In particular, after initial 3-month contract dates have passed, prompt settlement dates are reduced to both monthly and weekly time periods. LME trading, which occurs primarily through physical open-outcry, is supplemented by a 24-hour "interoffice" telephonic market and a new electronic trading platform. Trading occurs by phone or electronically until the exchange's "ring" (pit) opens for one of several daily open-outcry sessions; ring sessions are followed by a "kerb" period, when informal trading takes place (the metal index contract is only traded during the kerb session). When the day's open-outcry sessions finish and settlement prices are determined, trading reverts to off-exchange phone/electronic format.

In 1987, after more than 100 years of operating as a member-owned mutual society, the exchange created a new company, London Metal Exchange Ltd, as a "company limited by guarantee" under the Companies Act. This was followed by exchange demutualization in January 2001. The creation of a new corporate structure coincided with LME's push into the world of technology. After soliciting proposals from various technology companies, the exchange contracted with OM's technology group to develop a new trading platform; the initial system was introduced in 2001 and has since been revised to give users enhanced flexibility.

The LME is responding to the changing environment by altering its organization and operating structure; despite a long and storied past, it has been willing to undertake some dramatic changes. Returning to the themes of Chapter 2, we note that LME:

- Has abandoned its mutual status and is now organized as a "for-profit" commercial company (though one that is still privately held by members)

- Has developed an electronic trading platform that currently supplements the trading day (and designed to assume the role currently played by the open-outcry ring membership, should that become necessary or desirable)
- Has actively sought to develop new types of products (e.g. North American aluminum alloy, "prompt date" trading), and refine those in its current roster

8.2   CORPORATE STRUCTURE

As noted, the LME existed as a member-owned mutual organization from its foundation until the new millennium. After obtaining member approval in September 2000, the exchange created a new corporate holding company (LME Holdings Ltd) in January 2001, which issued shares to existing members or cash payments in lieu of shares to those not wanting to retain an ownership interest. LME Holdings Ltd now owns London Metal Exchange Ltd, which owns the physical exchange. Though LME Holdings is not a public company, the change in corporate structure allows for future public capital raisings, if required.

8.3   TECHNOLOGY PLATFORM/INFRASTRUCTURE

Though the LME has operated through ring-based open-outcry for many decades, it began incorporating aspects of technology into its operations at the turn of the millennium. In 2000 exchange management requested from third-party technology firms proposals related to the development of an electronic platform that could be used to extend the trading day (and, ultimately, replace physical trading – though no date for abandoning open-outcry trading was, or has been, given). OM was awarded a contract to enhance a version of its CLICK trading platform. In 2001 the exchange launched the resulting LME Select system to support spot and "next nearby" futures trading on a member-to-member basis. Through the Select platform contracts are matched on a principal-to-principal basis; only LME broker clearing members can access the trading screens, meaning all electronic orders must flow through such members. The platform also supports standard margining and reporting functions and has electronic ties into LCH-supported clearing processes. An enhanced version, Select 2.0, was launched in late 2001 to give users greater execution flexibility.

8.4   CLEARING

LME trades are cleared through the LCH which, as noted earlier in Chapter 6, also clears for the IPE, LIFFE, and LSE; LCH is thus the central counterparty on all LME derivative trades and is contractually bound to ensure performance of traders registered by members. When a trade is executed it is assigned to an account and registered with the LCH at the end of the business day; once registered, the LCH is a legal counterparty to the trade. The LCH requires clearing members to post initial and variation margins and contribute to a default fund.

8.5   PRODUCT OFFERINGS

LME's trading is focused exclusively on nonferrous metals. The exchange offers (see Table 8.1):

- Futures and options on copper, aluminum, aluminum alloy, lead, zinc, nickel, and tin.
- Futures and options on the LMEX metals index comprising of the prices of the exchange's six main metals (aluminum, copper, zinc, tin, lead, nickel).

Table 8.1   LME's metal derivatives

Reference	Futures	Options
Aluminum (primary high grade)	✓	✓
Copper (Grade A)	✓	✓
Nickel (primary)	✓	✓
Lead (standard)	✓	✓
Tin	✓	✓
Zinc (special high grade)	✓	✓
Aluminum alloy	✓	✓
North American aluminum alloy	✓	–
LMEX index	✓	✓

As noted earlier, the exchange delisted silver futures and added North American aluminum alloy futures (its first ever regional listing) in 2002. The exchange has also regularly upgraded the quality of metals deliverable into its contracts; as new grades are mined or refining processes improved, the quality and purity of metal change and are reflected in contract upgrades.

8.6   REGULATION

LME's activities are governed by the UK's FSA. Though the FSA has a broad remit to regulate financial activities in the UK, it is specifically responsible for regulating investment business, which is prohibited unless an entity is authorized or exempted; recognized investment exchanges (RIEs), such as LME, are exempted by the FSA. In order to qualify as an RIE, an exchange must demonstrate that it meets the FSA financial and regulatory requirements (e.g. those listed under the Financial Services Markets Act and the Companies Act) including protection of investors, fair/orderly trading mechanisms, trade, reporting, clearing and settlement facilities, and general compliance structure.

8.7   WEBSITE

The LME website provides details on contract specifications and data/price data sources: www.lme.co.uk

9
Mercado Español de Futuros Financieros (MEFF)

9.1 BACKGROUND

Spain's Mercado Español de Futuros Financieros (MEFF) traces its origins to 1989, when exchange officials received approval from the Spanish Ministry of Finance to operate as an authorized financial futures exchange; trading through an all-electronic platform commenced later that same year. In 1991 MEFF Holding was created to combine the trading operations of the exchanges of Barcelona (MEFF Renta Fija) and Madrid (MEFF Renta Variable). Throughout the 1990s MEFF featured relatively active trading in Spanish equity and fixed income benchmark contracts. With the advent of the euro, however, activity in Spanish fixed income futures declined (i.e. business quickly gravitated to the German Bund contract offered by Eurex and Euronext), leading MEFF to create new equity products and form cross-exchange alliances. The exchange added individual stock futures and options, a mini version of its key IBEX index contract and, in order to attract a greater pan-European audience, S&P 350 European stock index contracts (offered in conjunction with CME, and cleared either through MEFF or the CME). MEFF also negotiated trading alliances in early 2002 with Eurex and Euronext that permit MEFF members to trade Eurex and Euronext equity contracts (e.g. DAX, DJ Eurostoxx 50, DJ Stoxx 50, CAC-40) and fixed income contracts (e.g. Bund, Bobl, Schatz, Notionnel, and Euribor). Through these cross-exchange alliances MEFF members have direct trading access to Eurex and Euronext liquidity through their own terminals and are not required to be members of the exchanges or their clearinghouses (Eurex AG or Clearnet). Similar access arrangements are being negotiated with other exchanges.

To promote greater efficiencies in the Spanish market the country's key exchanges were consolidated in 2001. Specifically, in October 2001 a new holding company was created to purchase the shareholdings of MEFF and exchanges focused on corporate and public debt trading. Though the combined entity, known as Grupo mF, is in its earliest stages of consolidated operation, it expects ultimately to create a single seamless trading and clearing platform for Spanish financial derivatives and debt (though not equities). Part of the consolidation is driven by MEFF's advanced technologies. Since the exchange was created as an all-electronic platform it has understood, for many years, the importance of technology in exchange operations; as noted below, MEFF's key system components are licensed for use by regional exchanges in Spain, Portugal, and Germany.

MEFF is an exchange that has attempted to reposition itself as an integrated, technology-savvy financial marketplace. Considering the themes of Chapter 2, we note that MEFF:

- Is organized as a "for-profit" commercial holding company
- Has successfully negotiated important alliances with Eurex and Euronext to ensure proper trading access to financial contracts that are important to MEFF members

- Has developed a successful technology platform that provides more efficient trading and a new source of revenue (e.g. license fees from other exchanges); it has also allowed it to bring together other elements of the Spanish debt markets
- Has been active in creating new products to fill the void left by the loss of its fixed income capabilities (e.g. new stock futures, S&P 350 index contracts)

9.2   CORPORATE STRUCTURE

As noted above, a new "for-profit" commercial holding company was created in October 2001 to hold the ownership interests of different components of the Spanish financial markets. In particular, MEFF AIAF SENAF Holding de Mercados Financieros SA owns the shares of the newly integrated companies, including MEFF Sociedad Holding de Productos Financieros (futures and options), AIAF (corporate debt) and SENAF (public debt). The exchange's trading, clearing, and technology units are all held under the MEFF Holding umbrella. From an internal business management perspective the exchange divides its operations into derivatives, public debt, corporate debt, and systems.

9.3   TECHNOLOGY PLATFORM/INFRASTRUCTURE

MEFF has been a pioneer in the area of trading and settlement technologies, having implemented an electronic trading platform prior to its opening in 1989. The exchange is completely electronic, and features an integrated trading, clearing, and settlement system known as MEFF S/MART. In addition to the S/MART front-end execution and trade-matching capabilities, the exchange created the MIBOS back-office system in 1994 to give clients real-time access to position and margin information, and the MEFNET fiber-optic network in 1995 to promote rapid communication between clearing members and the exchange (use of the dedicated network also permits faster access to position and risk control information). MEFF has supplemented its front- and back-office initiatives through the development of the TST trader support terminal, which gives exchange members access to pricing, position, and market information.

9.4   CLEARING

The MEFF Clearinghouse, a division of the exchange, acts as clearer and counterparty on all derivative trades executed on MEFF; the clearinghouse registers transactions at the end of each trading day, becoming counterparty to all buyers and sellers. It also computes and settles daily margins and settles contracts at expiry (note that in contrast to certain other exchanges, MEFF calculates margins on a gross, rather than net, basis). Clearing members are required to lodge initial and variation margins on a daily basis, and contribute to the exchange's guarantee fund.

9.5   PRODUCT OFFERINGS

Since much of the fixed income activity MEFF previously sponsored has disappeared with Spain's membership in the euro, the exchange's primary focus is on equity derivatives. Within the equity sector it lists (see Table 9.1):

- Futures and options on individual Spanish stocks
- Futures and options on national and pan-European indexes and subindexes, including the IBEX, S&P Europe 350 and S&P Europe 350 sectors

Table 9.1 MEFF's equity derivatives

Reference	Futures	Options
Individual stocks	✓	✓
IBEX 35 index*	✓	✓
S&P Europe 350 index	✓	✓
S&P Europe 350 index sectors	✓	✓

*Also available as a mini.

Table 9.2 MEFF's fixed income derivatives

Reference	Futures	Options
Spanish government bond (10-year)	✓	–

MEFF's sole fixed income offering is centered on (see Table 9.2):

• Futures on the 10-year Spanish government bond

As noted, MEFF members also have access to various fixed income and equity contracts on Eurex and Euronext.

9.6   REGULATION

MEFF's operations are authorized by the Spanish Ministry of Finance, and are overseen on a regular basis by the Spanish securities regulator, Comision Nacional del Mercado de Valores (CNMV). The Spanish Treasury and Financial Policy Department of the Bank of Spain provide additional oversight reviews. Grupo mF maintains its own surveillance and regulatory review department to ensure compliance with applicable regulations.

9.7   WEBSITE

The MEFF website provides details on contract specifications and data/price data sources: www.meff.es

10
OM/Stockholmsborsen (OM)

10.1 BACKGROUND

OM/Stockholmsborsen (OM) is a company that blends exchange trading and technology development: the group owns and operates exchanges and clearinghouses and also develops, uses, and licenses technology platforms. OM's exchange origins date back to 1985 when it was founded as the first electronic trading platform in Scandinavia. Though it initially listed only a small number of Nordic equity contracts, it soon added equity index options (e.g. the OMX index) and eventually expanded into various Scandinavian and pan-European equity and fixed income references. OM created its own clearinghouse in 1986, floated itself publicly in 1987, and created the OM London Exchange in 1989 (to trade Nordic derivatives in the London marketplace). In 1997 it acquired the Stockholm Stock Exchange (Stockholmsborsen) (which had converted to corporate status in 1993 and was seeking opportunities to expand its own operations); the acquisition was completed in early 1998, at which time OM combined all of its cash and derivative exchange operations – including those previously housed under OM Fixed Income Exchange – into a single unit. In the late 1990s OM purchased a majority interest in the Finnish Options Market SOM and formed the NOREX joint venture with the Copenhagen Stock Exchange to trade Danish and Swedish equities and derivatives. In an effort to expand its exchange operations outside of Scandinavia it offered to purchase LSE in 2000; the bid was unsuccessful, however, and the exchange eventually dropped its terms. In addition to traditional financial exchange activities, OM also owns two electronic trading platforms focused on integrated trading and clearing of power and gas: the UK Power Exchange (UKPX) and Canada's Natural Gas Exchange (NGX; OM originally held a 51% stake in NGX but acquired the balance in early 2001).[1]

OM introduced its first commercial trading system in 1989 and by 1991 early versions of its CLICK trading platform were being marketed to third-party customers. This paved the way for the creation of an integrated electronic trading, clearing, and settlement platform in 1995 and various other execution and settlement modules over the next few years (e.g. SECUR, SAXESS, and so forth). The flexibility and sophistication of OM systems soon attracted other customers, and by the start of the millennium OM's technology products were being used by more than 100 customers in 20 countries.[2]

OM is a true hybrid operation that has combined its exchange operations with technology in order to diversify revenues and remain on the leading edge of trading system technology – for its own benefit and the benefit of others. Considering the themes of Chapter 2, we note that OM:

---

[1] OM was also partial (then sole) owner of Jiway, a pioneering electronic stock exchange platform developed with Morgan Stanley, until 2002; however, in late 2002 OM closed down the operation as a result of insufficient activity.

[2] OM counts many of the world's largest exchanges as its customers; over the years it has created systems platforms for the American Stock Exchange, Minneapolis Grain Exchange, Nordpool, BOTCC, NASDAQ, all of the Scandinavian stock exchanges, and so on; in fact, several of the derivative exchanges discussed in this book, including BI, LME, KOFEX, ISE, BTEX, HKEx, and SFE rely on OM-based trading, clearing, and/or settlement technologies. To give an indication of OM's technology penetration, as of 2002 CLICK and SAXESS were used by 20 global exchanges and SECUR was utilized by 10 clearing organizations – far more than any other third-party exchange vendor.

- Is organized as a "for-profit" commercial company and has floated its shares publicly in order to raise capital
- Has fully embraced the concept of mergers and alliances (e.g. its own acquisitions of Stockholmsborsen, its NOREX alliance with the Copenhagen Stock Exchange, and so on)
- Has always existed as an electronic trading platform, and continues to develop leading-edge technology which it licenses to others
- Offers additional clearing and nontrading services to supplement its revenues
- Has actively developed new types of futures and options products and trading platforms (e.g. UKPX, NGX, OM London Exchange)

10.2   CORPORATE STRUCTURE

OM AB is a public company listed and traded on Stockholmsborsen. From a corporate ownership perspective, OM AB is sole owner of Stockholmsborsen, which is sole owner of the OM London Exchange. From a business perspective, OM operates through various business subsidiaries, including Division Transaction, which manages Stockholmsborsen (OM's Nordic equity, fixed income, and listed derivatives exchange) and OM London Exchange. The group's technology services are supplied through various wholly owned units, including Broker Services (which provides system solutions and back-office services for financial institutions), Energy Market Solutions (which provides technology for deregulating energy markets and also operates the NGX and UKPX exchanges), Financial Market Solutions (which supplies systems for exchanges, clearinghouses, banks, and brokers), and Global Services (which provides systems for exchanges and clearinghouses).

10.3   TECHNOLOGY PLATFORM/INFRASTRUCTURE

As indicated, OM has been one of the most active players in developing and offering exchange and clearing technology to third parties; in fact, it is the single largest supplier of exchange and clearing technologies in the market. The company spends a considerable amount of its revenues and cash flow on technology and research development (the payoff has been worthwhile, as earnings from technology outpaced those from exchange operations for the first time in 2001). Its flagship products include CLICK (derivatives trading system), SAXESS (equity trading system), SECUR (derivatives clearing system), OneWorld (settlements system) and Exigo CSD (central settlement and depository system).

Not surprisingly, OM uses the same modules in its own trading operations; OM, OM London Exchange, UKPX, and NGX all make use of different OM-based technologies. CLICK serves as the primary front-end derivative trading system for OM's derivative exchanges, while SAXESS is the primary system for cash trading. SECUR is the primary clearing system and Exigo CSD is the core settlements process (though one that is in the process of being upgraded and replaced). OM's suite of products allow for straight-through-processing based on electronic trade entry, execution/matching, clearing, settlement, and reporting.

10.4   CLEARING

Trades executed through OM-related companies (including Stockholmsborsen and OM London Exchange) are cleared through the Stockholm and London operations of Stockholmsborsen, which has been authorized as an official clearer by Swedish regulators. Stockholmsborsen requires all clearing members to post initial and variation margins, and has obtained extra loss coverage from an AAA-rated insurer in order to ensure exchange integrity. In addition to clearing standardized futures and options contracts Stockholmsborsen also provides "Tailor-Made Clearing" (TMC) clearing services for OTC derivative contracts through the SECUR platform, and has established clearing links for exchanges in Oslo and Helsinki; these arrangements generate additional revenues for the OM Group. UKPX, which clears its own power contracts, now offers third-party clearing services for OTC power and gas transactions.

10.5   PRODUCT OFFERINGS

OM, through Stockholmsborsen, OM London Exchange, and UKPX, features a broad range of standardized derivative contracts. In the equity sector the exchange lists and trades (see Table 10.1):

- Futures and options on Swedish, Danish, and Norwegian companies
- Futures and options on major Nordic indexes, including the Swedish OMX and Danish KFX

In the fixed income sector, OM lists and trades (see Table 10.2):

- Futures and futures options on short-term interest rates, including 6-month Treasury bills, Stibor (Stockholm interbank offer rate) forward rate agreements, and STINA (Stockholm Tomnext interbank agreement) swaps
- Futures and futures options on medium- and long-term interest rates, including 2-, 5- and 10-year Swedish government bonds, Nordbanken hypotek (mortgage) bonds, Stadshypotek (mortgage) bonds, SBAB bonds, and 10-year swaps

Table 10.1   OM's equity derivatives

Reference	Futures	Options
Individual stocks	✓	✓
OMX index	✓	✓
KFX index*	✓	✓

*Available as a futures option contract.

Table 10.2   OM's fixed income derivatives

Reference	Futures	Futures options
Treasury bills (6 month)	✓	–
Stibor FRAs	✓	–
STINA swaps	✓	–
Swedish government bonds (2 year)	✓	✓
Swedish government bonds (5 year)	✓	✓
Swedish government bonds (10 year)	✓	✓
Nordbanken hypotek bonds	✓	–
Stadshypotek bonds	✓	–
SBAB bonds	✓	–
10-year swaps	✓	–

Table 10.3   OM's commodity derivatives

Reference	Futures	Futures options
NBSK pulp	✓	✓
UK base load power*	✓	–
UK peak load power*	✓	–

*Via UKPX.

In the commodity sector OM and UKPX list several commodity-related contracts (NGX, the natural gas exchange, trades primarily on a spot and short-term forward basis, and does not yet feature standard gas futures and options). The OM exchanges list (see Table 10.3):

- Futures and futures options on NBSK pulp
- Futures on UK base and peak load electricity

10.6   REGULATION

OM's exchange activities are subject to the regulations of Sweden, UK, and Canada. Stockholmsborsen's trading is regulated by the Swedish Financial Supervisory Authority, which has authorized, and supervises, all domestic exchange activities; Stockholmsborsen is one of three Swedish exchanges authorized to operate under the Securities Exchange and Clearing Operations Act. OM London Exchange's business is overseen by the UK's FSA (as described in Chapter 6); the exchange is one of the country's seven registered investment exchanges (RIEs). UKPX's activities also fall under the purview of the FSA. In Canada, NGX's trading business is regulated by the Alberta Securities Commission.

10.7   WEBSITE

The OM website provides details on contract specifications and data/price data sources: www.omgroup.com

North America

11
Chicago Board of Trade (CBOT)

11.1 BACKGROUND

The Chicago Board of Trade (CBOT) was established in 1848 as an open-outcry marketplace to trade in wheat, corn, and oats. The exchange focused exclusively on commodity contracts until the mid-1970s, when volatility in the financial markets sparked the need for new financial risk management instruments. In 1975 the CBOT introduced its first financial futures contract, on Government National Mortgage Association (GNMA) mortgage-backed securities (a contract it has since discontinued), and steadily added new products over time. For instance, in 1982 the exchange introduced options on futures, in October 1997 it commenced trading in Dow Jones Industrial Average (DJIA) futures, based on the widely followed DJIA index, and in 2000 it developed US agency note futures linked to increasingly popular and liquid agency benchmarks (i.e. Federal National Mortgage Agency (FNMA) and Federal Home Loan Mortgage Corporation (FHLMC)).

Over the years the CBOT has participated actively in acquisitions and alliances. For example, in 1986 it acquired the MidAmerica Commodity Exchange (MACE); though MACE operates as a separate legal entity, CBOT is the sole equity owner.[1] In addition, in order to broaden its international product and market scope, it joined with Eurex in October 1999 in the creation of alliance/CBOT/Eurex (a/c/e), permitting members to trade each exchange's contracts through the a/c/e electronic platform. Despite rather ambitious plans to develop and trade new products around the globe, the two exchanges redefined their cooperation in mid-2002 when it became clear that each had different expectations. The a/c/e alliance now provides for cooperation but greater flexibility, and does not bind either exchange to specific product or technology development. CBOT is also one of three key partners in the OneChicago joint venture created in 2001 to trade US single stock futures (see Chapter 32 for additional detail).

Despite its physical trading character, CBOT has been a strong proponent of electronic trading for years, becoming one of the first major exchanges to integrate technology in its operations. In 1994 CBOT created the "Project A" electronic platform, which has since been replaced by the more sophisticated eCBOT trading system (note that the exchange has also contributed important technologies to a/c/e). Though CBOT continues to trade the majority of its contracts physically, it has employed technology throughout its operations in order to increase efficiencies.

CBOT is a successful exchange that continues to transform and expand its operations; in fact, it has pioneered some of the key structural transformations of the exchange-traded sector that many others are now employing (e.g. technology, alliances, select new products). Considering the themes of Chapter 2, we note that CME:

- Is still organized as a mutual, nonprofit company but has made allowances for a change in corporate structure should that prove advisable (i.e. it has filed a shelf registration with the SEC)

---

[1] We do not consider MACE's structure or products in this text.

- Has been an active proponent of acquisitions and alliances as a means of expanding business breadth and depth (e.g. MACE, a/c/e, OneChicago)
- Retains an open-outcry focus, but has incorporated new technologies where possible and necessary
- Has actively developed new types of products and is represented across a broad spectrum of products

11.2 CORPORATE STRUCTURE

Unlike various other large exchanges, the CBOT continues to operate as a member-owned, nonprofit, nonstock company. Despite its mutual status, the CBOT has submitted to the SEC an extensive reorganization proposal that its membership can adopt at any time through an affirmative vote. The key features of the restructuring call for:

- Creation of a new for-profit holding company, CBOT Holdings, which will own the exchange (which will remain a nonstock, for-profit subsidiary)
- Elimination of the member "petition process" in favor of more rapid and efficient stockholder voting
- Combination of all of CBOT's electronic trading businesses (including those held by the third-party Ceres partnership) under the eCBOT umbrella

Until, and if, the restructuring proposal is adopted, CBOT will continue to operate in its long-established, member-owned fashion.

11.3 TECHNOLOGY PLATFORM/INFRASTRUCTURE

As indicated above, CBOT was a relatively early promoter of trading technology, primarily as a way of increasing trading floor efficiencies and extending trading hour coverage. CBOT features electronic capabilities in its domestic operations and through a/c/e (the a/c/e platform, which became operational in August 2000, is based on a modified version of Eurex's own technology platform).[2]

In its domestic operations, CBOT uses the proprietary OrderDirect API and routing network, which allows members to link their proprietary or vendor order systems to the exchange's routing network. In early 2000 the exchange also introduced the Electronic Open-Outcry system, giving FCMs the ability to electronically manage business on or off the floor. The process is based on the creation and use of an *electronic ticket* ("e-ticket") that is updated and circulated in real time as new pieces of information in the transaction flow are created. For instance, an e-ticket can be created when a customer enters an order off the floor (e.g. via the Internet), an off-floor FCM enters it into an order entry system, or a floor FCM enters it into a mobile entry device. When the order is executed in the pit, the price is added to the e-ticket and returned electronically to the FCM and customer, and also sent to the clearinghouse for matching and clearing. Though most products on the CBOT are traded via open-outcry and technology is used as a supplement, certain contracts (such as DJIA minis) trade only on an electronic basis. As noted, portions of CBOT's electronic trading are operated by the Ceres partnership, but will ultimately combined under the eCBOT umbrella.

---

[2] The initial version of a/c/e technology proved quite successful, but further revisions were needed for the second release; due to financial constraints, CBOT opted not to fund development on the new release, forcing Eurex to proceed on its own.

Table 11.1 CBOT's fixed income derivatives

Reference	Futures	Futures options
US Treasury bonds[*†]	✓	✓
US Treasury notes (2 year)[†]	✓	✓
US Treasury notes (5 year)[†]	✓	✓
US Treasury notes (10 year)[*†]	✓	✓
Agency notes (5 year)	✓	–
Agency notes (10 year)	✓	–
30-day Federal Funds	✓	–
Eurodollar (3 month)[*]	✓	–
Eurodollar (3 month, deferred)[‡]	✓	–
Municipal bonds	✓	–
Inflation T-bonds	✓	✓
Inflation T-note (long term)	✓	✓
Inflation T-note (medium term)	✓	✓
5-year swaps	✓	✓
10-year swaps	✓	✓

[*] Also available as mini.
[†] Also available as a flex option.
[‡] Only available as mini.

11.4   CLEARING

All trades executed on the CBOT (and MACE) are cleared by the Board of Trade Clearing Corp (BOTCC), an independent clearinghouse owned by members of the CBOT and MACE. BOTCC acts as guarantor to clearing members on all trades, reconciles accounts, and adjusts clearing member margins; all clearing is done on a real-time basis, through BOTCC's technology links (built around OM's SECUR platform). In order to ensure trade integrity, BOTCC is backed by member margins, a $100mn insurance policy and a $200mn credit line.

Although BOTCC exists primarily to clear CBOT and MACE trades, it is under no obligation to do so and can clear contracts for other exchanges. In fact, in order to diversify and expand its revenues the clearinghouse clears contracts for various other exchanges, including ICE (for OTC power contracts), Commodities Management Exchange (for metals contracts), Merchants Exchange of St Louis (for commodity contracts), and so forth. (BOTCC's third-party clearing services are available through its MetaClear product, a comprehensive suite of clearing links, tools, and reports that provide for real-time clearing, risk, margin, and position management.)

11.5   PRODUCT OFFERINGS

CBOT offers futures and options in the fixed income, equity, agricultural, and metals sectors. Within the fixed income world the exchange lists (see Table 11.1):

- Futures on short-term interest rates, including Eurodollar (e.g Libor) and Federal Funds
- Futures, futures options and flex options on medium- and long-term interest rates, including 2-, 5-, 10- and 30-year Treasuries,[3] 5- and 10-year agencies, and 5- and 10-year interest rate swaps

---

[3] The 30-year Treasury futures contract may ultimately be abandoned as the US Government is no longer issuing long-dated debt and supply will begin to decline as bonds mature. With decreasing supply, the possibility of deliverable contract squeezes increases, making hedges and positions more difficult to manage.

Table 11.2   CBOT's equity derivatives

Reference	Futures	Options
DJ Industrial Average*	✓	✓

*Also available as mini.

Table 11.3   CBOT's agricultural derivatives

Reference	Futures	Options
Corn	✓	✓
Soybeans	✓	✓
Soybean oil	✓	✓
Soybean meal	✓	✓
Wheat	✓	✓
Oats	✓	✓
Rough rice	✓	✓
DJ AIG Commodity index	✓	–
CBOT X-Funds	✓	–

Table 11.4   CBOT's metal derivatives

Reference	Futures	Options
Gold*	✓	–
Silver†	✓	–

*Only available as mini.
†Also available as mini.

Flex options, which permit customization of strike price, expiry and exercise style, are available on select references.

In the equity sector CBOT offers (see Table 11.2):

- Futures and options on the DJIA

(As noted earlier, the exchange is also a participant in the OneChicago single stock futures venture, though such trades do not flow through the CBOT itself.)

Within agricultural commodities, its original market focus, CBOT lists (see Table 11.3):

- Futures and options on corn, the soybean complex, wheat, oats, and rice
- Futures and options on commodity indexes, including the DJ AIG index and various CBOT cross-funds

Within metals, the exchange lists and trades (see Table 11.4):

- Futures contracts on gold and silver

11.6   REGULATION

The CBOT is a self-regulatory organization (SRO) that oversees its own operations based on guidelines and regulations set forth by the CFTC and the NFA. The CFTC is an independent government agency established in 1974 to administer the federal commodity laws. CFTC has authority over futures, options, and leveraged contracts involving commodities and indexes of securities. It is responsible for reviewing terms/conditions of national markets/contracts, ensuring that contracts meet normal market flows and conducting daily surveillance. CFTC works closely with, and audits, the NFA.

11.7   WEBSITE

The CBOT website provides details on contract specifications and data/price data sources: www.cbot.com

12
Chicago Board Options Exchange (CBOE)

12.1 BACKGROUND

The Chicago Board Options Exchange (CBOE) was created in 1973 as an open-outcry forum to trade standardized option contracts on single stocks. Though the exchange was established under the auspices of the CBOT (see Chapter 11), it has always been managed and regulated independently. Prior to the early 1970s stock options dealing was ad hoc and informal, with no guarantee that pricing for buyers or sellers was equitable. As the demand for standard contracts with transparent pricing grew, CBOE introduced call options on 16 large US stocks. Between 1973 and 1977 the exchange added calls on more stocks and in 1977 it expanded into put options. Competing efforts on other exchanges (e.g. the Midwest Stock Exchange (MSE), American Stock Exchange, Pacific Stock Exchange and ISE), led the SEC to place a moratorium on new option listings for 3 years while it investigated activity in the marketplace. The SEC eventually lifted the ban in 1980, and the CBOE (and others) responded by adding new stocks, series, and strike prices. By 2002 CBOE listed options on over 1500 stocks.

CBOE's efforts have not been limited to single stocks; over the years the exchange has gradually expanded into equity index options, long-term options, and interest rate options. For instance, in 1983 it introduced the first standardized index options contracts on the Standard & Poor's (S&P) 100 index, in June 1989 it added options on various US Treasury securities (in order to diversify away from a pure equity focus, and take advantage of growing activity in US Treasury trading), and in 1990 it created long-term options with maturities extending to 3 years (dubbed "LEAPS"). During the 1990s it also introduced *sector options* (e.g. on banks, automobiles, telecoms, and so forth), international index options (e.g. on Mexican, Japanese, Israeli stock indexes) and subindex options (e.g. on special indexes, such as Barra Growth and Barra Value).

In 1993 it brought the exchange-traded and OTC worlds closer together by creating flexible exchange options ("Flex," options), contracts that permit a certain amount of customization (e.g. on expiry, strike price, exercise type, and settlement basis); early Flex options were available on the S&P 100, S&P 500 and Russell 2000 indexes, and have since been expanded to other references. One of its key contract introductions came in 1997 when it started trading options on the bellwether DJIA (the introduction coincided with CBOT's rollout of DJIA futures). NASDAQ mini options and I-shares (index contracts that trade like stocks) followed in 2000. In order to expand business domestically, CBOE has acquired other exchanges, including the MSE and a majority stake in the Cincinnati Stock Exchange (CSE, which it then decided to resell in 2002). It is also a partner with the other two Chicago exchanges in the OneChicago single stock futures joint venture (CBOE holds a 41.6% stake). Unlike its Chicago counterparts, however, it has not negotiated international alliances to attract a larger foreign customer base or cross-trade across multiple time zones.

Though CBOE remains an open-outcry forum, it has made considerable progress in introducing systems to facilitate trading and execution; though it seems unlikely the exchange will shift to a pure electronic platform in the near term, it appears committed to implementing relevant technology processes to speed trading and settlement.

The CBOE is an exchange that successfully developed new equity-related products over an extended period of time, so becoming a market leader in its sector. Despite a small expansion into Treasury options the exchange is essentially an equity forum and its fortunes will continue to rise and fall based on interest and activity in the equity markets. Considering the themes of Chapter 2, we note that CBOE:

- Has embraced the concept of domestic mergers and alliances (e.g. its own acquisition of MSE, its partnership with the Chicago exchanges in OneChicago)
- Has incorporated aspects of new technology into its trading and execution efforts
- Has been extremely active in pioneering new equity-related option products

12.2 CORPORATE STRUCTURE

The CBOE is structured as a mutual, nonprofit organization that is owned by its clearing members. The CBOE has not yet contemplated a conversion to corporate "for profit" status.

12.3 TECHNOLOGY PLATFORM/INFRASTRUCTURE

CBOE features a broad-based technology platform that is designed to enhance, rather than replace, its traditional floor execution – which it believes gives customers the best possible price discovery. The technology platform is centered on several different components, including the CBOEdirect module, introduced in October 2002, that replicates trading floor activity on-screen and allows order matching and execution; CBOEdirect essentially expands the trading day by allowing market activity prior to official exchange opening. CBOEdirect builds on the exchange's Public Automated Routing (PAR) system, a PC-based touch-screen order routing and execution system with "electronic trading cards" that are filled with appropriate information at different stages in the process (exchange officials estimate that 25% of customer orders flow through PAR). When a trade is executed, PAR sends an electronic "fill" report to the customer and the option price reporting authority. CBOE also uses the EBOOK platform, a fully automated public customer order book which sorts and files orders in price/time sequence; approximately one-third of CBOE's public customer orders are executed via EBOOK. Those routed through EBOOK are immediately represented in the marketplace; if they are market orders they are automatically executed. The exchange also offers retail customers access to its Retail Automatic Execution System (RAES), a platform that enables small customer orders to be automatically filled at the prevailing bid or offer and reported back to the customer immediately. In mid-2002 the exchange created a Large Order Utility (LOU) module, which permits instant execution and confirmation of large orders directly on the floor of the exchange.

12.4 CLEARING

All options trades executed on the CBOE are cleared through the Options Clearing Corporation (OCC), which becomes counterparty to all transactions that are registered at the end of the trading day. OCC was created in 1972, as a corporation equally owned by the five US exchanges that actively trade listed stock options; CBOE is thus a 20% owner of the OCC. In order to provide appropriate safeguards, the OCC reviews the financial standing of all members, sets appropriate

Table 12.1 CBOE's equity derivatives

Reference	Futures	Options
Single stocks*†	–	✓
DJIA index*	–	✓
DIAMONDS index	–	✓
DJ Transportation index*	–	✓
DJ Utility index	–	✓
DJ Equity REIT index	–	✓
DJ Internet Commerce index	–	✓
S&P 100 index*‡	–	✓
I-shares index	–	✓
S&P 500 index*	–	✓
S&P 600 index	–	✓
NASDAQ 100 index§	–	✓
NASDAQ 100 index tracker	–	✓
GSTI Composite index	–	✓
NYSE Composite index	–	✓
Russell 2000 index	–	✓
Morgan Stanley (MS) Multinational index	–	✓
MS Retail index	–	✓
MS Biotech index	–	✓
MS Oil services index	–	✓
Gold index	–	✓
Internet index*	–	✓
Oil index	–	✓
Mexico index	–	✓
Technology index	–	✓
Goldman Sachs (GS) Hardware index	–	✓
GS Internet index	–	✓
GS Multimedia network index	–	✓
GS Semiconductor index	–	✓
GS Software index	–	✓
GS Services index	–	✓
GS Composite index	–	✓

*Also available as LEAPS.
†Also available as a flex option.
‡Also available as European exercise.
§Also available as a mini or mini LEAP.

position limits, takes margins, and requires all clearing members to contribute to a clearing fund.

12.5 PRODUCT OFFERINGS

Though the CBOE commenced its operations with a strict focus on "vanilla" single stock options, it has expanded its product line to include long-term and flexible options, as well as options on indexes, subindexes, and interest rates. CBOE's single stock options are American style, physical settlement contracts, while its index options are American or European style, cash settlement contracts. Within equities, the exchange lists (see Table 12.1):

- Options on single stocks (1500+), indexes, and subindexes
- Long-term and flexible options on select references (e.g. LEAPS and Flex options)

Table 12.2   CBOE's fixed income derivatives

Reference	Futures	Options
US Treasury bills (13 week)	–	✓
US Treasury notes (5 year)	–	✓
US Treasury notes (10 year)	–	✓
US Treasury bonds	–	✓

In the fixed income sector CBOE began listing interest rate options in 1989 and now features (see Table 12.2):

- Options on short-term interest rates, including 13-week US Treasury bills
- Options on medium- and long-term interest rates, including 5- and 10-year US Treasury notes, and 30-year US Treasury bonds[1]

12.6   REGULATION

The CBOE is an SRO that oversees its own operations based on guidelines and regulations set forth by the SEC, rather than the CFTC. Unlike exchanges that deal in futures as well as options, CBOE's strict option focus means that it falls under the jurisdiction of the SEC. The SEC is an independent government agency charged with overseeing the US securities markets, including its institutions, marketplaces, and securities.

12.7   WEBSITE

The CBOE website provides details on contract specifications and data/price data sources: www.cboe.com

---

[1] As noted in the previous chapter, the decision by the US Treasury not to issue 30-year bonds may cause the CBOE to ultimately delist its 30-year US Treasury options contract.

Chicago Mercantile Exchange (CME)

13.1 BACKGROUND

The Chicago Mercantile Exchange (CME) traces its origins to the Chicago Butter and Egg Board, a mutual organization established in 1898 to trade spot and futures contracts on eggs and dairy; in 1919, after the exchange's product scope was widened to include live cattle, feeder cattle, and pork bellies, the exchange changed its name to the CME. The CME remained an agricultural marketplace until the early 1970s, when growing financial volatility fuelled by deregulation led the exchange to develop futures contracts on increasingly volatile currencies such as the yen, pound, and Swiss franc. A broad range of financial futures and options followed during the 1980s and 1990s – contracts that have, in some cases, become bellwethers (e.g. S&P 500 index futures, Eurodollar futures). In the late 1990s and early 2000s the exchange continued its creative product development, designing equity and currency "minis," weather and cross-currency derivatives, and so forth.

Over the years the CME has supplemented its product development with alliances, joint ventures and other partnerships, and now features cooperative arrangements that let it execute or clear across multiple exchanges and time zones. For instance, CME and SGX (when it was still operating as SIMEX) created a mutual offset system permitting members to establish or close out contracts on either exchange. CME was also a founding member of the Globex alliance that allows members to access products traded on other alliance exchanges (as noted earlier in the text, the other Globex partners include Eurex, SGX, MEFF, MX, and BM&F). The exchange has also entered into a partnership with MEFF to allow European S&P index contracts traded through MEFF's electronic platform to be cleared through the CME, and is developing interest rate and equity products jointly with the TSE (it already jointly lists/trades Japanese government bond contracts). CME, along with its Chicago partners, is a member of the OneChicago stock futures venture that became operational in 2002. Recognizing the growing importance of ECN platforms, the exchange has also entered into select electronic ventures (e.g. it created co-branded chemical futures with B2B exchange ChemMatch in late 2001).

CME has been at the forefront of cross-margining[1] in order to improve use of member margins across exchanges. For instance, the exchange has entered into separate cross-margining agreements with:

- LCH and LIFFE covering short-term interest rate contracts
- OCC and NYCC covering a broad range of US financial and commodity contracts, and
- BOTCC covering short-term US interest rate contracts

The CME, one of the largest physical open-outcry exchanges in the world, has also been one of the most active developers and users of technology (even licensing its software to other

---

[1] Under a typical CME cross-margining arrangement the participating clearinghouses hold a joint lien and security interests in the positions of the client and receive proportional shares in the event of liquidation.

exchanges). It uses technology to increase operating efficiencies, permit after-hours trading, and allow trading of mini contracts (minis are not traded on an open-outcry basis as a result of their small size). From a structural perspective, the CME became the first US exchange to demutualize, converting to "for-profit" corporate status in November 2000. Shares in the exchange were granted to the CME's members without a public listing (though the exchange filed a registration statement with the SEC in June 2002 related to a future IPO).

The CME serves as a good example of an exchange that has adapted its strategies to ensure that it remains one of the leading forums in the new market environment. Returning to the themes of Chapter 2, we note that CME:

- Is organized as a "for-profit" commercial company and has registered with the SEC for a future flotation of its shares
- Has been a driving force in alliances and joint ventures in order to broaden its market penetration (e.g. the Globex alliance, agreements with MEFF and TSE on joint product development and trading, OneChicago, cross-margining arrangements, and so on)
- Has developed an extensive electronic platform for use in its own operations and for sale to others (despite the fact that it remains one of the largest open-outcry forums in the world)
- Offers additional clearing and nontrading services to supplement its revenues
- Has actively developed new types of futures and options products and is represented across a broad product spectrum

13.2   CORPORATE STRUCTURE

The CME operates as a "for-profit" corporation, known as CME Inc., with transferable shares held by members. In December 2001 the CME created a holding company, CME Holdings Inc., so that future ventures and alliances can be housed under a single corporate umbrella. CME Holdings is 100% owner of CME Inc.

13.3   TECHNOLOGY PLATFORM/INFRASTRUCTURE

As noted above, CME has been one of the technology pioneers and innovators of the exchange-traded world. Its centerpiece, the GLOBEX 2 platform, has been in use since the early 1990s, though it has been through various revisions and improvements since that time. The GLOBEX 2 platform is used for trading after-hours, trading of all mini contracts and trading of GLOBEX 2 alliance partner products; a new module, dubbed "Eagle," permits efficient electronic execution of calendar spreads. GLOBEX 2 features a trade-matching engine that allows orders flowing into the exchange (through an interface or the Trade Order Processing System (TOPS)) to be automatically matched by price and time; once matched, members and the clearinghouse receive electronic confirmations. Clients can access the GLOBEX 2 platform through APIs developed by third parties, FCMs or introducing brokers, or the GLOBEX 2 Trader interface (which can be used via network or direct connection). In addition to front-end execution, the exchange has also integrated technology into its floor operations. For instance, trades can be routed electronically to the CME Universal Broker Station (CUBS), located in the pit, for subsequent execution. Trades can also be transmitted to brokers in the pit through handheld wireless technology.

In addition to GLOBEX 2, CME developed the Standard Portfolio Analysis of Risk (SPAN) system that has become the "industry standard" mechanism for determining margins on single and compound positions, complex strategies, spreads, portfolios, and so forth. SPAN was originally developed in 1988 (and has been revised several times since) and has been licensed to many exchanges around the world.

13.4 CLEARING

All trades executed through the CME are cleared through the CME clearinghouse, a division (rather than separate subsidiary) of the exchange; the division thus acts as a central counterparty on all transactions, assuming the role of intermediary once all trades flowing from the exchange have been reconciled. In order to ensure exchange integrity, all clearing members are required to post appropriate margins and contribute to the exchange's deposit guarantee fund. In addition to standard margining through the SPAN system, the clearinghouse also operates the "Concentration Margining Program" that allows the exchange to take greater margins when a client amasses a very large position in a given contract.

13.5 PRODUCT OFFERINGS

The CME features one of the broadest product ranges in the exchange-traded sector, with liquid contracts covering fixed income/currencies, equities, and commodities.

Within currencies and fixed income the exchange offers (see Table 13.1):

- Futures and options on short-term interest rates, including Euroyen, Eurodollars, and US Treasury bills
- Futures on the 10-year Japanese government bond (in conjunction with TSE)

Table 13.1 CME's fixed income/currency derivatives

Reference	Futures	Options
Australian dollar	✓	✓
Brazilian real	✓	✓
British pound	✓	✓
Canadian dollar	✓	✓
Euro*	✓	✓
Euro/pound	✓	–
Euro/yen	✓	–
Euro/Swiss franc	✓	–
Japanese yen*	✓	✓
Mexican peso	✓	✓
New Zealand dollar	✓	✓
Russian rouble	✓	✓
South African rand	✓	✓
Swiss franc	✓	✓
US Treasury bill (3 month)	✓	✓
Euroyen Libor (3 month)	✓	–
Eurodollars (1 month)	✓	✓
Eurodollars (3 month)	✓	✓
Japanese government bond (10 year)	✓	–

*Also available as a mini future.

Table 13.2   CME's equity derivatives

Reference	Futures	Options
Fortune e-50 index	✓	✓
GSCI	✓	✓
NASDAQ 100 index*	✓	✓
Nikkei 225 index	✓	✓
Russell 2000 index*	✓	✓
S&P 500/Barra Growth index	✓	✓
S&P 500/Barra Value index	✓	✓
S&P 500 index*	✓	✓
S&P 400 Midcap index	✓	✓

*Also available as a mini future.

Table 13.3   CME's commodity derivatives

Reference	Futures	Options
Butter	✓	✓
Butter (spot)	✓	✓
Cheese (spot)	✓	✓
Milk (Class III)	✓	✓
Milk (Class IV)	✓	✓
Milk (nonfat dry, spot)	✓	✓
Feeder cattle	✓	✓
Pork bellies (frozen)	✓	✓
Lean hogs	✓	✓
Live cattle	✓	✓
Lumber (random length)	✓	✓
Benzene*	✓	–
Mixed xylenes*	✓	–
Temperature (heating degrees)†	✓	–
Temperature (cooling degrees)†	✓	–
Quarterly bankruptcy index	✓	✓

*Co-branded and traded through ChemMatch.
†Available on various US cities.

- Futures and options on the US$ against the Australian dollar, New Zealand dollar, Canadian dollar, British sterling, euro, Swiss franc, and Japanese yen, along with relevant euro cross-rates. In the emerging bloc it features contracts on the Brazilian real, Mexican peso, Russian rouble and South African rand

Within the equity sector the CME lists (see Table 13.2):

- Futures and options on key US indexes, including the NASDAQ 100, Russell 2000, S&P 500, S&P 400 and several S&P subindexes
- Futures and options on the Japanese Nikkei 225 index

The CME also features a range of nonfinancial products, including (see Table 13.3):

- Futures and options on dairy (butter, cheese, and milk) and meat (live and feeder cattle and pork bellies)

- Futures on hard commodities, including lumber, benzene, and xylenes
- Futures on other nonfinancial commodity references, including US temperature and quarterly bankruptcies

13.6   REGULATION

The CME is an SRO that oversees its own operations based on guidelines and regulations set forth by the CFTC and the NFA. The CFTC is an independent government agency established in 1974 to administer the federal commodity laws. CFTC has authority over futures, options, and leveraged contracts involving commodities and indexes of securities. It is responsible for reviewing terms/conditions of national markets/contracts, ensuring that contracts meet normal market flows, and conducting daily surveillance. CFTC works closely with, and audits, the NFA.

13.7   WEBSITE

The CME website provides details on contract specifications and data/price data sources: www.cme.com

14
Montreal Exchange (MX)

14.1 BACKGROUND

The Montreal Exchange (MX) traces its origins back to 1832 when informal trading of stocks began at the Exchange Coffee House in Montreal. This informal trading continued until 1874, when the "coffee house participants" decided to establish a more robust marketplace, which became known as the Montreal Stock Exchange (MSE). The MSE remained essentially unchanged for the better part of a century, trading Canadian stocks and government securities on an open-outcry basis. In 1974 MSE merged with the nationally focused Canadian Stock Exchange (CSE), and a year later it became the first Canadian marketplace to offer stock options. During the late 1970s and early 1980s the exchange created new derivatives, and in 1982 renamed itself MX in order to reflect the decreasing importance of stock trading, and increasing importance of derivative trading, in its operations. From the 1990s into the millennium MX introduced various new financial contracts, including futures and options on Canadian bankers acceptances (the country's benchmark short-term interest rate) and 5- and 10-year government bonds, long-term options on single stocks and indexes, futures on single stocks and equity sectors,[1] and futures on overnight repos. In a critical structural step designed to establish a single pool of liquidity within the Canadian financial derivatives market, the exchanges of Montreal, Alberta, British Columbia, Ontario, and Quebec signed a Memorandum of Agreement (MOA) in March 1999, agreeing to conduct all financially based exchange derivative business through a single location – namely MX; the exchange can thus be regarded as the central Canadian marketplace for financial derivatives (note that regional commodity futures exchanges focused on agricultural contracts still exist (e.g. Winnipeg Commodity Exchange (WCE)).

Though MX operated through a physical trading floor until the new millennium, it was an "early adopter" of technology. For instance, the exchange created its first automated platform, the Montreal Registered Representative Order Routing System, in 1983, and established an electronic link with the Boston Stock Exchange (BSE) in 1984 (it has since expanded its relationship with the BSE, creating the Boston Options Exchange (BOX) to electronically trade single stock and index futures and options using MX-developed technologies).[2] A new platform, Exchange Trading Access (ETA), was introduced in 1996, permitting domestic and foreign customers to electronically access exchange products. The exchange followed with its Système Automatique Montreal (SAM) platform in September 2000, a front-to-back system that allowed it to migrate all operations to an electronic environment. In fact, the exchange began shifting its products to SAM in late 2000 and completed the process in late 2001; once completed, MX closed down its physical trading floor.

MX is an exchange that is making considerable progress in coping with many of the structural changes in the marketplace – to the point where it can rightly be regarded as Canada's main derivatives exchange. Returning to the themes of Chapter 2, we note that MX:

---

[1] MX was the first North American exchange to introduce single stock futures.
[2] The BOX venture also includes Interactive Brokers, Crédit Suisse First Boston, JP Morgan Chase, Citigroup, and UBS as partners.

- Is organized as a "for-profit" commercial company
- Has fully embraced the concept of mergers and alliances (e.g. its own acquisition of CSE, its assumption of all financial derivative trading from other Canadian exchanges, its venture with BOX, and so on)
- Has migrated completely to an all-electronic environment and features leading-edge technology which it licenses to others
- Offers additional clearing and nontrading services to supplement its revenues
- Has actively developed new types of futures and options products and is represented across a broad product spectrum

14.2   CORPORATE STRUCTURE

MX existed as a mutual organization from its founding until September 2000, at which time the MX's legal entity parent, Bourse de Montréal Inc., was demutualized and incorporated as a "for profit" entity. Bourse de Montréal wholly owns MX, as well as the Canadian Derivatives Clearing Corp (CDCC, as discussed below); the firm's interest in CDCC increased from 50 to 100% in 2001.

14.3   TECHNOLOGY PLATFORM/INFRASTRUCTURE

As indicated above, MX introduced the SAM platform in 2000 and migrated all trading to the new electronic environment in late 2001. SAM features a trading engine that is built on NSC architecture (originally developed by the French exchanges and now used by Euronext and others). Through the MMTP API firms can connect to SAM and enter orders that are routed and automatically matched in a central order book (through NSC-driven technologies); executed trades are then passed electronically to the CDCC clearinghouse. In an important legal ruling, MX obtained clearance from the CFTC in 2002 to permit US broker-dealers and FCMs to access SAM directly from terminals located in the US; the exchange expects additional cross-border activity as a result of the ruling. The SAM application has proven so successful that it has been sold to third parties, including the BOX venture noted above.

14.4   CLEARING

All trades flowing through MX are cleared through the CDCC, a wholly owned subsidiary of Bourse de Montréal. CDCC was originally founded in the mid-1970s as TransCanada Options Inc., a nonprofit clearing entity used by all of the Canadian exchanges (including MX). Following the approval of the MOA, which made MX the sole Canadian financial derivatives exchange, MX became sole owner of CDCC. CDCC now acts as the central clearinghouse for all Canadian financial derivatives and also provides clearing services to others, on a commercial, third-party basis (e.g. WCE and the WCE Clearing Corp are clients of the CDCC). Though CDCC is wholly owned by MX, it operates independently and features its own board of directors and management organization.

At the conclusion of each trading day, transactions executed on MX through the SAM platform flow into CDCC where they are reconciled and settled; at that point CDCC becomes counterparty to all member trades. In order to ensure exchange integrity, members are required to post initial and variation margins and contribute to a guarantee fund.

Table 14.1   MX's equity derivatives

Reference	Futures	Options
Individual stocks	✓	✓
S&P Canada 60 index	✓	✓
S&P/TSX 60 index fund	–	✓
Sector indexes	✓	–

Table 14.2   MX's fixed income derivatives

Reference	Futures	Options	Futures options
Overnight repo	✓	–	–
Canadian BAs (1 month)	✓	–	–
Canadian BAs (3 month)	✓	–	✓
Canadian government bond (5 year)	✓	–	–
Canadian government bond (10 year)	✓	✓	✓

14.5   PRODUCT OFFERINGS

MX features fixed income and equity derivatives centered on many of Canada's key benchmark rates and indexes. Within the equity sector, the exchange lists and trades (see Table 14.1):

• Futures and options on major Canadian companies
• Futures and options on Canadian indexes and sectors (including technology, energy, financials, and gold)

(Note that MX also lists sponsored equity derivatives that are marketed and traded through financial institution sponsors; for instance, *equity warrants* launched by Citibank and Société Générale on Canadian equity references are traded via MX.)

In the fixed income sector MX lists and trades (see Table 14.2):

• Futures, options, and futures options on short-term interest rates, including 1- and 3-month Canadian bankers' acceptances (BAs) and overnight repo rates
• Futures, options, and futures option on medium- and long-term interest rates, including 5- and 10-year government of Canada bonds

14.6   REGULATION

MX is regulated by the Commission des Valeurs Mobilières du Québec (CVMQ) and must meet financial requirements set forth by the CVMQ in order to retain its authorization. In addition, CVMQ requires MX to operate as an SRO, policing the activities of its own membership.

14.7   WEBSITE

The MX website provides details on contract specifications and data/price data sources: www.m-x.ca

15

New York Board of Trade (NYBOT)

15.1 BACKGROUND

Although the New York Board of Trade (NYBOT) is a relatively recent creation – having been formally established in 1998 – its constituent parts trace their histories back to nineteenth-century New York. Specifically:

- The New York Cotton Exchange (NYCE), one part of NYBOT, was created in 1870 to trade cotton futures. Its clearinghouse, the NYCE Clearing Association, was formally constituted in 1915 (eventually changing its name to the Commodity Clearing Corporation (CCC))
- The Coffee Exchange (CE), a second part of NYBOT, was established in 1882 to trade coffee on a spot and futures basis; it added sugar contracts in 1925 and renamed itself the New York Coffee and Sugar Exchange (NYCSE) at that time
- In the same year a third part of NYBOT, the New York Cocoa Exchange (NYCoE), started trading cocoa contracts
- In 1979 the New York Futures Exchange (NYFE) was created to trade in NYSE index futures

In 1979 the NYCSE and NYCoE merged to become the Coffee, Sugar and Cocoa Exchange (CSCE); over the next few years CSCE added several new contracts to its operations, including milk futures and options. NYCE, attempting to diversify away from cotton, created the Financial Exchange (FINEX) division to trade currency futures; over the years FINEX has become widely known for its active cross-rate contracts. NYFE, likewise, introduced new contracts in the 1980s and 1990s, including futures on the benchmark Commodity Research Board (CRB's) commodity index. In 1994 NYCE purchased NYFE, and in 1998 CSCE and NYCE merged their operations into the newly named NYBOT, a physical, open-outcry forum trading financial and commodity contracts. NYBOT now acts as a holding company for the individual exchanges and their divisions (the original CCC, which remained a central clearinghouse for the NYCE, was renamed the New York Clearing Corp (NYCC) and now clears all NYBOT contracts). In order to continue product expansion – and to take advantage of the growing move toward e-commerce – NYBOT and bond broker Cantor Fitzgerald created the Cantor Financial Futures Exchange (CFFE) in 2000; CFFE is a full-time, electronic market for US Treasury and agency futures.

NYBOT serves as an example of an exchange that is trying to remain viable through mergers, alliances, and product development. Though it has made progress in establishing a broad product base through exchange consolidation, it faces considerable challenges related to expanding its market share/presence and implementing new technologies. Considering the themes of Chapter 2, we note that NYBOT:

- Has been an active proponent of mergers and acquisitions for many years (e.g. NYCE/NYFE, CSCE/NYCE)
- Has been able to develop new electronically focused ventures (e.g. CFFE)

- Has started to embrace technology in its operations
- Has been quite active in developing new types of futures and options products and is represented across a broad product spectrum

15.2   CORPORATE STRUCTURE

NYBOT is organized as a nonprofit mutual company that is owned by its members. NYBOT acts as the parent company of CSCE and NYCE and their divisions (e.g. NYFE, FINEX), as well as the NYCC clearing operation. Though NYBOT owns NYCC, the clearing arm operates independently and appoints its own board directors and managers.

15.3   TECHNOLOGY PLATFORM/INFRASTRUCTURE

NYBOT still operates primarily as an open-outcry exchange with a physical trading floor, though it is attempting to introduce elements of technology into its processes in order to improve efficiencies.[1] Specifically, NYBOT has created a new Electronic Order Routing System (EORS) and an Order Book Management System (OBMS), which together permit real-time trade matching, execution, and processing. The OBMS works with EORS, letting FCMs send orders over the Internet (or alternate network connection) to a session manager on the floor, who can then instantly route details to the floor trader. All orders are processed via NYBOT's Trade Input Processing System (TIPS), which matches trades on an ongoing basis and allocates them to clearing members; once allocated they are sent electronically to the NYCC for clearing. In addition to exchange-based entry, execution, and clearing, NYBOT has developed an Electronic Commodity Operations Processing System (ECOPS), which eliminates much of the manually intensive paper process that characterizes coffee and cocoa trading.

15.4   CLEARING

As noted above, NYCC has assumed the role as central clearinghouse for all transactions executed through NYBOT subsidiaries/divisions (i.e. CSCE, NYCE, NYFE, FINEX, as well as those flowing through CFFE). Trades processed and allocated through the exchange's technology platform and assigned to individual clearing members are settled at the end of each day, at which point NYCC becomes legal counterparty. In order to ensure exchange integrity, the NYCC places minimum financial standards on all clearing members, limits the amount of exposure granted to each, requires that initial and variation margins be posted according to set time frames, and requires contribution to the NYCC Guaranty Fund.

15.5   PRODUCT OFFERINGS

Given the amalgamation of exchanges that comprise NYBOT, it comes as no surprise that the exchange features a large number of contracts across the commodity, currency, and equity sectors. Within the commodity area, NYBOT lists and trades (see Table 15.1):

---

[1] Technology underlying the CFFE venture is distinct from that used by NYBOT and is based on components created by eSpeed, a B2B technology specialist.

Table 15.1   NYBOT's commodity derivatives

Reference	Futures	Futures options
Coffee "C"*	✓	✓
Sugar No. 11	✓	✓
Sugar No. 14	✓	–
Cocoa	✓	✓
Cotton No. 2	✓	✓
FC Orange Juice 1	✓	✓
FC Orange Juice 2	✓	–
FC Orange Juice differential	✓	–
S&P Commodity index	✓	✓
CM index	✓	✓
CRB/Bridge index	✓	✓

*Also available as a mini.

Table 15.2   NYBOT's currency derivatives

Reference	Futures	Futures options
Australian dollar/Japanese yen	✓	✓
Australian dollar/NZ dollar	✓	✓
Australian dollar/Canadian dollar	✓	✓
Canadian dollar/Japanese yen	✓	✓
British sterling/Japanese yen	✓	✓
British sterling/Swiss franc	✓	✓
Euro/British sterling	✓	✓
Euro/Canadian dollar	✓	✓
Euro/Japanese yen	✓	✓
Euro/Norwegian kroner	✓	✓
Euro/Swedish kroner	✓	✓
Euro/Swiss franc	✓	✓
Euro/Australian dollar	✓	✓
Swiss franc/Japanese yen	✓	✓
Euro/US dollar*	✓	✓
Australian dollar/US dollar	✓	✓
British sterling/US dollar	✓	✓
NZ dollar/US dollar	✓	✓
US dollar/Canadian dollar	✓	✓
US dollar/British sterling	✓	✓
US dollar/South African rand	✓	✓
US dollar/Swiss franc	✓	✓
US dollar/Swedish kroner	✓	✓
US dollar/Norwegian kroner	✓	✓
US dollar index	✓	✓

*Available in large and small contract size.

- Futures and futures options on coffee, sugar, cocoa, cotton, and frozen concentrated (FC) orange juice
- Futures and futures options on commodity index contracts, including the S&P Commodity index, Commercial Markets index (CMI) and CRB/Bridge index

Table 15.3 NYBOT's equity derivatives

Reference	Futures	Futures options
NYSE Composite index*	✓	✓
Russell 1000 index	✓	✓

*Available in large, regular and mini contract size.

Within the currency sector, the FINEX division operating out of New York and Dublin offers a large number of cross-rate contracts, including (see Table 15.2):

- Futures and futures options on euro, US dollar bloc, and Asia Pacific FX rates
- Futures and futures options on the US dollar currency index

In the equity index sector, NYBOT lists (see Table 15.3):

- Futures and futures options on the NYSE Composite index and Russell 1000 index

15.6 REGULATION

NYBOT is an SRO that oversees its own operations based on guidelines and regulations set forth by the CFTC and the NFA. The CFTC is an independent government agency established in 1974 to administer the federal commodity laws. CFTC has authority over futures, options, and leveraged contracts involving commodities and indexes of securities. It is responsible for reviewing terms/conditions of national markets/contracts, ensuring that contracts meet normal market flows and conducting daily surveillance. CFTC works closely with, and audits, the NFA.

15.7 WEBSITE

The NYBOT website provides details on contract specifications and data/price data sources: www.nybot.com

16

New York Mercantile Exchange (NYMEX)

16.1 BACKGROUND

The New York Mercantile Exchange (NYMEX) was established in 1872 as the Butter and Cheese Exchange of New York (subsequently renamed the Butter, Cheese and Egg Exchange of the City of New York). In order to attract a broader range of grocers and merchants, the exchange was renamed NYMEX in 1882, but maintained its agricultural commodity focus for most of the next century. With the onset of financial and energy sector volatility in the 1970s and 1980s, however, NYMEX decided to expand into energy contracts. In 1978 NYMEX developed a heating oil contract, in 1983 it launched light sweet crude oil futures (which ultimately became the most actively traded energy contract in the world), and in 1984 it created gasoline futures. New contracts on natural gas, electricity, and Brent crude followed during the 1990s and into the new millennium. Over the years NYMEX has become the largest exchange for energy trading, outpacing the long-established IPE.[1] Note that as the exchange achieved a critical mass of business in energy products during the 1980s and 1990s, it systematically abandoned its original soft commodity contracts.

While NYMEX was still trading its original agricultural contracts, a second New York-based exchange, the Commodity Exchange of New York (COMEX), offered clients standard contracts on copper, silver, tin, rubber, silk, and hides; COMEX was, itself, the product of a 1933 amalgamation of the National Metal Exchange, the National Raw Silk Exchange, the New York Hide Exchange, and the Rubber Exchange of New York. As turnover in silk, rubber, and hides dwindled over ensuing decades, COMEX narrowed its focus to metals; when the US Government's ban on private ownership of gold was lifted in 1974, COMEX introduced gold futures and established itself as a key metals exchange.

During the early 1990s NYMEX decided to reduce its reliance on the energy sector by expanding product scope. In August 1994 the exchange agreed to acquire COMEX's operations and COMEX now operates as a wholly owned subsidiary of NYMEX. In early 2001 the exchange also began trading equity derivatives on the FTSE Eurotop 100 and 300 indexes and in mid-2002 it joined with the CME in introducing fractional energy contracts (e.g. energy "e-minNYs") through the CME GLOBEX 2 platform; the contracts, which are cleared through NYMEX, are modeled on CME's own minis. Though NYMEX is still organized as a physical, open-outcry exchange, it has adopted new technologies aggressively and now permits simultaneous electronic and physical trading (some instruments, such as power futures and options, can only be traded electronically, through the exchange's ACCESS system).

---

[1] The introduction of NYMEX's Brent contract is regarded as an important milestone, as IPE's Brent contracts have been NYMEX's primary competition; if NYMEX is able to gain a reasonable market share of Brent through its own contracts, it will facilitate popular Brent-WTI basis trading.

NYMEX is an exchange that is adapting its business strategies to make certain that it remains one of the leading energy and metals traders in the new market environment. Returning to the themes discussed in Chapter 2, we note that NYMEX:

- Remains organized as a mutually owned, "nonprofit" company, but has filed a registration statement with the SEC regarding future demutualization (the timing of such demutualization is still uncertain)
- Has been an active participant in acquisitions and alliances in order to diversify its business lines (e.g. the COMEX acquisition, the CME alliance on energy mini contracts)
- Has developed a robust electronic platform that is supplementing, and in some cases replacing, open-outcry trading
- Offers additional OTC clearing services to supplement its revenues
- Has actively developed new types of futures and options products

16.2   CORPORATE STRUCTURE

NYMEX is structured as a nonprofit, mutual organization that is owned by its members. However, the exchange has filed registration documents with the SEC that allow for demutualization and conversion to "for profit" corporate status, should the exchange and its members decide to do so. NYMEX's clearing function is organized as a division, rather than subsidiary, of the exchange. COMEX is organized as a separate, wholly owned subsidiary of NYMEX and is expected to remain so after any demutualization; COMEX is sole owner of the COMEX Clearing Association (CCA), its clearinghouse subsidiary.

16.3   TECHNOLOGY PLATFORM/INFRASTRUCTURE

NYMEX began creating its ACCESS technology platform in 1993, hoping to create a system that would permit efficient, off-hours trading in its key contracts. ACCESS now serves as a comprehensive trade entry, routing, matching, and execution system, with communication links to back-office processes and third-party clearing platforms. The exchange upgraded ACCESS at frequent intervals during the 1990s and, by the end of the decade, featured a comprehensive platform suitable for trading in all of the exchange's products. As part of its continuous upgrades, the exchange replaced its clearing subsystem in 1999 with CME's Clearing 21 platform; the new platform provides greater efficiencies and automation, and a stronger link between trade execution and clearing. In November 1999 NYMEX commenced daytime trading of contracts on ACCESS alongside its physical pits, giving clients a 22-hour daily electronic trading window. ACCESS terminals are operational in various countries, including Australia, China, and the UK, giving customers easier access to exchange products and pricing.

16.4   CLEARING

NYMEX energy and equity contracts are cleared through NYMEX's own clearing division, which acts as a central counterparty on all trades. COMEX metal contracts, in contrast, are cleared through the CCA[2] (though CCA's clearing operations will eventually be merged with

---

[2] It should be noted that a COMEX clearing member defaulted on contracts in 1985, but the margins lodged were sufficient to cover the loss; no call on the CCA guarantee fund was required.

NYMEX's to create a seamless platform). To ensure exchange integrity, NYMEX and CCA place minimum capital requirements and position limits on all clearing members, require posting of appropriate margins and contribution to relevant guarantee funds. Further "safety nets" exist in the event of clearing member default, including exchange seizure of defaulting member assets, call on the exchange's surplus (e.g. retained earnings) and a further call on funds of other clearing members based on their level of participation.

NYMEX introduced OTC clearing services in 2002 in order to expand its business scope and supplement its revenues. Under the new facility OTC brokers and trade counterparties submit certain types of approved OTC energy transactions to NYMEX (e.g. oil swaps, natural gas forwards, and so forth, on liquid and recognizable benchmarks such as light sweet crude oil or Henry Hub gas) where they are cleared centrally; trade counterparties thus face NYMEX as their counterparty on credit-sensitive OTC transactions.

16.5   PRODUCT OFFERINGS

NYMEX features an extensive range of energy and metals contracts through its two divisions. Through the energy division the exchange lists and trades (see Table 16.1):

- Futures and futures options on crude oil, heating oil, natural gas, gasoline, propane (and relevant basis, e.g. Brent/Light Sweet Crude)
- Futures on coal
- Futures and futures options on electricity
- Futures options on *crack spreads* (e.g. differential between crude oil and a refined product such as gasoline or heating oil)

Table 16.1   NYMEX's energy derivatives

Reference	Futures	Futures options
Brent Crude Oil	✓	✓
Brent Crude Oil calendar spreads	–	✓
Brent/Light Sweet Crude basis spreads	–	✓
Central Appalachian Coal	✓	–
Crack spreads*	–	✓
Heating Oil	✓	✓
Heating Oil calendar spreads	–	✓
Henry Hub Natural Gas	✓	✓
Natural Gas calendar spreads	–	✓
Light Sweet Crude Oil[†]	✓	✓
Light Sweet Crude calendar spreads	–	✓
NY Harbor Unleaded Gasoline	✓	✓
NY Harbor Gasoline calendar spreads	–	✓
Propane	✓	–
Electricity (California–Oregon border)	✓	✓
Electricity (Palo Verde)	✓	✓
Electricity (Cinergy)	✓	✓
Electricity (Entergy)	✓	✓
Electricity (Pennsylvania/Jersey/Maryland)	✓	–

*Available on heating oil/crude and gasoline/crude.
[†]Available as a mini through the CME alliance.

Table 16.2   NYMEX's metal derivatives

Reference	Futures	Futures options
Aluminum	✓	✓
Copper	✓	✓
Gold	✓	✓
Palladium	✓	–
Platinum	✓	✓
Silver	✓	✓

Table 16.3   NYMEX's equity derivatives

Reference	Futures	Options
FTSE Eurotop 100 index	✓	–
FTSE Eurotop 300 index	✓	–

- Futures options on calendar spreads

Metals contracts traded on the COMEX division include (see Table 16.2):

- Futures and futures options on gold, silver, platinum, palladium, aluminum, and copper

In its most recent asset class expansion NYMEX has introduced equity derivatives through the COMEX division, including (see Table 16.3):

- Futures on the FTSE Eurotop 300 and 100 indexes

16.6   REGULATION

NYMEX is an SRO that oversees its own operations based on guidelines and regulations set forth by the CFTC and the NFA. The CFTC is an independent government agency established in 1974 to administer the federal commodity laws. CFTC has authority over futures, options, and leveraged contracts involving commodities and indexes of securities. It is responsible for reviewing terms/conditions of national markets/contracts, ensuring that contracts meet normal market flows, and conducting daily surveillance. CFTC works closely with, and audits, the NFA.

16.7   WEBSITE

The NYMEX website provides details on contract specifications and data/price data sources: www.nymex.com

Asia-Pacific

Hong Kong Exchanges and Clearing (HKEx)

17.1 BACKGROUND

Hong Kong, a Special Administrative Region (SAR) of China, has featured a futures exchange since 1976, when financial institutions created the mutual, open-outcry Hong Kong Futures Exchange (HKFE). HKFE pioneered regional equity and fixed income futures and options, and its contracts on the local Hang Seng index (HSI) soon became a barometer for activity in the non-Japanese Asian equity markets. HKFE's listed derivative efforts were supplemented by those of the Stock Exchange of Hong Kong (SEHK), the territory's central stock marketplace, which started a very successful covered equity warrant program in the 1980s, and followed with listed stock options in the 1990s. SEHK traces its origins to 1891, when the Association of Stockbrokers in Hong Kong was created as a central forum for stock trading; the association renamed itself the Hong Kong Stock Exchange (HKSE) in 1914 and expanded through the acquisition of a second exchange in 1947. As the regional economy started growing in the 1960s several new local exchanges were created, including the Far East Exchange (1969), Kam Ngan Stock Exchange (1971), and Kowloon Stock Exchange (1972); these were combined with the HKSE in 1980 to form the new SEHK.

In early 1999 Hong Kong's Financial Secretary reflected on the need for the SAR's exchanges to operate more efficiently and competitively, and proposed a merger of Hong Kong's stock, futures, and clearing forums. The goal was to bring the cash and derivative markets closer together, eliminate duplicative clearing and execution processes, and reduce staff and management ranks. The merger of the two exchanges and their clearing functions, into a new entity known as Hong Kong Exchanges and Clearing Ltd (HKEx), was formally approved by the government in October 1999 and became effective in March 2000. In order to build on the momentum fostered by the consolidation, HKEx converted from a mutual to a commercial, publicly quoted company in June 2000 and, by the end of that year, had abandoned open-outcry trading in favor of electronic trading.

HKEx now serves as Hong Kong's sole cash, futures, and options exchange. The equity products division (incorporating the former SEHK) trades cash equity and single stock options (and is responsible for negotiating and operating the SAR's international stock trading program in conjunction with several global exchanges), while the derivative products unit (the former HKFE) handles all derivatives trading (except single stock options, though plans call for their eventual transfer into the derivative unit). In order to expand its product and business scope HKEx introduced DJIA index futures trading in May 2002 and purchased a minority (16%) stake in the Internet bond trading platform BondsinAsia; it also established a joint venture with technology provider Wilco to offer securities processing services in the region.

HKEx is an exchange that has actively restructured its operations in order to compete successfully in the new environment; its strategies have been bold and may serve as a model for other Asian (and global) exchanges seeking to remain viable and competitive. Considering the themes of Chapter 2, we note that HKEx:

- Has merged its cash and derivative operations into a single unit
- Has demutualized its exchange operations and floated itself publicly
- Has embraced the concept of mergers and alliances (e.g. its own SEHK/HKFE merger, its partnership with Wilco, and so on)
- Has incorporated aspects of new technology into its execution and clearing, to the point where it has abandoned physical trading
- Is offering third-party services, such as clearing and settlement and securities processing
- Has introduced new futures and options products

17.2 CORPORATE STRUCTURE

The merger and reorganization of the Hong Kong exchanges resulted in the creation of the publicly listed HKEx holding company. HKEx owns SEHK, HKFE, and HK Securities Clearing Co. (HKSCC), which continue to operate as separate legal entities. From a business perspective, HKEx operates through four divisions: exchanges (which include the equity and derivative units mentioned above), clearing and settlement, electronic business, and information services/information technology.

17.3 TECHNOLOGY PLATFORM/INFRASTRUCTURE

Though the individual exchanges comprising HKEx were originally designed as open-outcry forums, both had a long history of dealing with technology. In fact, SEHK and HKFE had gradually automated aspects of their operations over the years, particularly in back-end processing. As a result, migration to an all-electronic environment, in a relatively short time frame, proved feasible.

Following closure of the two trading floors in 2000, the consolidated exchange adopted the Hong Kong Futures Automated Trading System (ATS) for futures and options trading (equities and other cash products are traded through the third-generation AMS/3 automated order matching and execution system). ATS is an open system that allows direct trade entry and execution by clearing members, and can also accommodate Internet trading and straight-through-processing. Since the merger the platform has been upgraded to accommodate electronic order matching and execution, along with electronic settlement through either the Central Clearing and Settlement System (CCASS/3) and the Derivative Clearing and Settlement System (DCASS/3).

17.4 CLEARING

All HKEx exchange products are cleared through the HKSCC, a separately capitalized subsidiary within the HKEx group. HKSCC, which requires members trading in derivatives to post appropriate margins and contribute to the exchange guarantee fund, acts as central counterparty on all transactions. The clearinghouse is heavily reliant on technology, receiving automated trade information from middle-office process through CCASS/3 and DCASS/3. In order to generate additional revenue, HKEx has commenced work on offering third-party clearing services. Under the proposal HKSCC will act as central counterparty on other types of transactions, including OTC derivatives.

Table 17.1 HKEx's fixed income derivatives

Reference	Futures	Options
HIBOR (1 month)	✓	–
HIBOR (3 month)	✓	–
Exchange Fund note (3 year)	✓	–

Table 17.2 HKEx's equity derivatives

Reference	Futures	Options	Futures options
Individual stocks	✓	✓	✓
DJIA index	✓	–	–
Hang Seng index*	✓	✓	–
MSCI China Free index	✓	–	–

*Also available as a mini.

17.5 PRODUCT OFFERINGS

HKEx features fixed income and equity contracts based on the territory's primary financial references (as well as certain international indexes); some instruments were created during the HKFE era, while others represent new products created after the consolidation. As part of its ongoing review process, the exchange has abandoned products that are no longer viable (e.g. Hang Seng subindex futures) or adjusted them to meet market demands (e.g. increasing the size of its short-term interest rate contracts by a factor of five). Within the fixed income sector, the exchange trades (see Table 17.1):

- Futures on short-term interest rates, including 1- and 3-month Hong Kong Interbank Offer Rate (HIBOR)
- Futures on medium-term interest rates based on the 3-year Exchange Fund note (EFN)

Given the close link between SEHK and HKFE in the equity sector, HKEx has expanded its equity offerings in recent years and now lists and trades (see Table 17.2):

- Futures, options, and futures options on individual Chinese and international stocks
- Futures and options on Chinese and international stock indexes

17.6 REGULATION

The SAR's primary financial regulator, the Hong Kong Securities and Futures Commission (SFC), regulates HKEx's activities. All matters related to the exchange are overseen by the SFC, which conducts periodic audits and investigations to ensure compliance with policies. HKEx maintains its own self-regulatory surveillance unit to make certain it complies with appropriate reporting and rules.

17.7 WEBSITE

The HKEx website provides details on contract specifications and data/price data sources: www.hkex.com

Osaka Securities Exchange (OSE)

18.1 BACKGROUND

The Osaka Securities Exchange (OSE) traces its origins back to 1878 when it was founded as a "for profit" corporation (then known as the Osaka Stock Exchange) to trade in Japanese stocks. The exchange, and its core trading business, remained relatively unchanged until the war period of the early 1940s, after which it became part of a unified exchange. In 1948 OSE was reestablished under the Securities and Exchange Law (SEL), and restarted operations in 1949 as a mutually owned, nonprofit company. OSE's focus for the next four decades remained exclusively on stock and bond trading; derivative contracts did not become part of its operations until June 1987, when the exchange launched the Osaka Stock Futures 50 (OSF 50), a physical delivery futures contract on 50 large Japanese stocks. In May 1988 the SEL was amended to permit the creation and trading of cash-settled stock index futures and options. Shortly thereafter OSE launched the key Nikkei 225 index futures contract (several months after SIMEX, now SGX, had introduced its own Nikkei 225 contract) and followed with Nikkei 225 options the following year. Since this period represented an important time of Japanese economic expansion and stock market growth, the OSE contract quickly became one of the most actively traded in the world; only after Japan's economy retreated in the early to mid-1990s did the contract lose some momentum. It is worth noting that the OSE's cash and derivative trading capabilities did not arise from the amalgamation of previously existing cash and derivative exchanges (as in the cases of HKEx, SGX, and MDEX, among others). Rather, the exchange added derivative capabilities to its existing securities trading operations over an extended period of time; it comes as no surprise, then, that securities trading continues to dominate exchange operations (the same can be said for the TSE, discussed in Chapter 24). Though OSE's futures and options contracts were always traded electronically/telephonically, securities were traded on an open-outcry basis on the floor of the exchange; indeed, even after stock trading switched to an electronic platform in 1991, the OSE preserved its trading floor. In late 1997, however, the trading floor was closed, and all dealings now occur electronically.

From a competitive standpoint the OSE faces challenges on two fronts: domestically it competes for business with the TSE, which lists Japanese equity and index contracts of its own (e.g. single stocks, sectors, Topix index); and, internationally, it competes with exchanges such as SGX and CME, which do a considerable amount of business in Nikkei contracts. In order to meet these competitive challenges, and to keep pace with changing customer requirements, OSE has expanded its product offerings over the years – though always preserving a strict equity focus. For instance, in the early 1990s the exchange created new derivatives on the Nikkei 300 index and subindexes (e.g. technology, financials, and consumer goods, though all were subsequently delisted due to inactivity). In mid-1997, following deregulation measures allowing trade in single stock options, the OSE introduced options on 20 stocks, and has since expanded to well over 100. The OSE, like many other global exchanges, has also sought to build new international alliances. In 2000 and 2001, for example, the exchange entered into negotiations with NADAQ,[1] Dow Jones, MSCI, and FTSE to create OSE-traded futures on the NASDAQ 100, DJIA, MSCI Japan index and FTSE Japan index; contracts on all four indexes were introduced in 2002 (note that the listing of DJIA and NASDAQ futures represents the first time international equity index contracts have been tradable in Japan). In May 2002 the exchange also introduced a block trading facility (BTF) to accommodate large, off-exchange transactions; the development of the BTF is seen as an important mechanism to stem the loss of business to other exchanges and markets.

The OSE is an exchange that is attempting to realign its derivative operations in order to compete more effectively with local, regional, and international competitors. Since it is both a cash and derivative trading venture, it cannot necessarily devote all of its resources to reshaping its derivative business and this may ultimately slow progress. Considering the themes of Chapter 2, we note that OSE:

- Is organized as a "for-profit" commercial company
- Has embraced cooperative ventures in order to expand its product lines (e.g. its arrangements with Dow Jones, NASDAQ, FTSE, and MSCI on new contracts)
- Has migrated to an electronic environment and continues to upgrade its technology platform
- Has been reasonably active in creating new types of futures and options products and is expanding outside the Japanese marketplace for the first time in its history

18.2 CORPORATE STRUCTURE

As noted above, the OSE converted from a "for profit" corporation to a nonprofit mutual in 1948. In 2001, however, the exchange membership voted to revert to its original state, and in April 2001 once again became a joint stock corporation. From an internal business perspective OSE operates through divisions centered on securities trading, derivatives, information and technology, and clearing.

18.3 TECHNOLOGY PLATFORM/INFRASTRUCTURE

Over the past few years the OSE has moved its trading from a mix of floor, telephonic, and computerized trading to a consolidated electronic environment. In July 1999 it completed a multiyear technology conversion and all trading now occurs through the OSE Trading System (the core trading platform used for trade execution and matching), the J-Net System (for negotiated transactions and cross-trading) and the OSE Clearing System (for clearing and settlement of all transactions); prices are disseminated via the Electronic Information Service. These four modules effectively permit electronic straight-through-processing for listed derivatives (as well as stock and bond transactions). In 2002 the exchange announced that it would commence a multiyear project to upgrade its clearing system in order to support the new international index contracts introduced in mid-2002.

18.4 CLEARING

From its founding until 1999 the OSE acted as settlement agent, rather than principal, on all derivative and securities transactions; this meant the exchange brought individual

---

[1] The OSE and NASDAQ also have a venture known as NASDAQ Japan Markets that is designed to list the stock of small, or new, Japanese companies.

Table 18.1   OSE's equity derivatives

Reference	Futures	Options
Individual stocks		✓
Nikkei 225 index	✓	✓
Nikkei 300 index	✓	✓
MSCI Japan index	✓	–
FTSE Japan index	✓	–
DJIA index	✓	–
NASDAQ 100 index	✓	–

counterparties together but allowed them to face one another directly. In November 1999 the exchange converted to a structure more characteristic of a typical clearinghouse, with the OSE Clearing Administration Department becoming counterparty on all futures and options transactions registered with the department at the end of the trading day. The OSE licensed SPAN from the CME in 1999, and the Clearing Administration Department uses it to compute margins on trades, strategies, and portfolios. In order to protect itself against losses arising from member default, the OSE requires clearing members to post margins on all transactions and contribute to a special deposit fund.

18.5   PRODUCT OFFERINGS

Given its long history in stock trading, the OSE lists derivatives based on stocks and stock indexes. Specifically, the exchange features (see Table 18.1):

- Options on individual Japanese stocks
- Futures and options on local and international indexes

18.6   REGULATION

The OSE is regulated by several different authorities and also maintains certain self-regulatory powers, which it administers through the OSE Self-Regulation Department. Financial contracts, including those listed on the OSE, fall under the regulations of the SEL (commodity contracts, in contrast, are governed by the Commodity Exchange Law). The SEL, which has been amended several times in recent years to allow for new products and trading mechanisms, specifies the minimum standards that must be maintained in order to ensure client and market integrity; audits of these rules are conducted on a regular basis. The Ministry of Finance and the Japan Securities Dealers Association (JSDA, a self-regulating body acting under the auspices of the SEL) provide further regulatory oversight.

18.7   WEBSITE

The OSE website provides details on contract specifications and data/price data sources: www.ose.or.jp

Singapore Exchange (SGX)

19.1 BACKGROUND

The Singapore Exchange (SGX) was created in December 1999 through the merger of Singapore's two primary exchanges,[1] the Stock Exchange of Singapore (SES) and the Singapore International Monetary Exchange (SIMEX). SES was originally created in May 1973 to trade in Singaporean and select Malaysian stocks; SIMEX was established in September 1984 to trade financial futures. SGX was the first Asian exchange outside of Japan to combine cash and derivative operations (and was soon followed by others, including HKEx and MDEX). The SGX consolidation was motivated by the opportunity to increase efficiencies, lower costs, and bring the cash and derivative markets closer together (so enhancing liquidity). Though SIMEX and SES had both existed as member-owned mutuals, the new exchange group was established as a corporate, "for profit" organization. Approximately one year later, in November 2000, SGX floated itself publicly, becoming the first Asian exchange to list and trade its shares. The combined exchange continues to operate on both a physical and electronic basis; all equity trading occurs electronically, while derivative trading occurs physically and electronically.

Though SGX operates as a combined entity, it maintains a dual focus on cash products (which it defines to include equities, warrants, equity options, exchange-traded funds, and bonds) and local/international derivatives; our focus in this chapter is on the latter. While SGX has enjoyed a long and successful track record in international derivatives trading (e.g. Nikkei 225, Eurodollars, Brent crude, and so on), its local/regional trading effort is still relatively new. Starting in 2000 the exchange began introducing regional contracts, including futures/options on Singaporean stocks, the MSCI Taiwan, Hong Kong, and Singapore indexes, the Straits Times index (STI) and 3-month and 5-year Singapore dollar interest rates. It is also launching a new contract on the price of dynamic random access memory (DRAM) microchips, the first of its kind in the exchange world. While SGX has developed new products, it has also abandoned those lacking in client interest and liquidity; for instance, over the past few years the exchange has delisted contracts on gold, fuel oil, and currencies.

SGX has created alliances and partnerships in order to expand its product scope and market presence. For instance, SIMEX and the CME pioneered the mutual offset system (MOS) in 1984, allowing positions to be taken or closed out in either exchange; the success of the SIMEX/CME MOS on Eurodollars led the exchange to create similar arrangements with other marketplaces, and it now features MOS agreements with:

- CME, for Eurodollars
- IPE, for Brent crude oil
- TIFFE, for Tibor Euroyen, and
- TSE, for JGBs

---

[1] Singapore also features the Singapore Commodity Exchange (SICOM), a smaller forum that deals in commodity futures on rubber and coffee.

SGX is also a partner in the Globex alliance (see Chapter 13 for detail) and has been at the forefront in developing indexes/products with other exchanges (e.g. Indian index futures with the National Stock Exchange of India (NSEI), exchange-traded funds with the American Stock Exchange (ASE), Middle East Crude Oil (MECO) futures with TOCOM, and so forth); it has also expanded into securities processing/settlement through a joint venture with DBS Vickers.

SGX is an exchange that has changed its operating structure dramatically in order to remain a regional, indeed global, leader. It has been largely successful in its efforts and serves as an interesting model for other exchanges seeking to remain competitive. Returning to the themes of Chapter 2 we note that SGX:

- Is organized as a "for-profit" commercial company and has floated its shares publicly in order to raise capital
- Has fully embraced the concept of mergers and alliances (e.g. its own consolidation of SIMEX and SES, its participation in the Globex alliance, its ventures with ASE, NSEI, and TOCOM, its multiple MOS arrangements, and so forth)
- Has migrated heavily to an electronic environment and features leading-edge technology which it licenses to others
- Offers additional clearing and nontrading services to supplement its revenues
- Has been active in creating new types of futures and options products and lists a broad range of international, regional, and local contracts

19.2   CORPORATE STRUCTURE

SGX is a "for-profit" corporation with shares held by the investing public. The exchange operates through five distinct subsidiaries: Singapore Exchange Securities Trading (the former SES), Singapore Exchange Derivatives Trading (the former SIMEX), Singapore Exchange Derivatives Clearing (SGX DC, the derivatives clearinghouse), the Central Depository Pte (CDP, the securities clearinghouse) and the Singapore Exchange IT Solutions Pte (the back-office systems and technology licensing services).

19.3   TECHNOLOGY PLATFORM/INFRASTRUCTURE

As noted, SGX operates as a hybrid open-outcry/electronic exchange, with equity trading occurring on-screen[2] and derivative trading occurring both physically and electronically. Electronic trading via SGX does not exist solely for after-hours execution – it can also be used during the trading day.

Despite the fact that SGX trades a portion of its contracts physically, it still features one of the most advanced technology platforms in the industry. When the SGX combined its operations it renewed its focus on electronic, open-access trading, clearing, and settlement. All trading occurs through the SGX Electronic Trading System (ETS), a platform based on Euronext's NSC architecture (which effectively replaced the exchange's previous Automated Trading System (ATS)). ETS can be accessed directly by members (clients of clearing members can also apply for direct access); the exchange permits open connectivity between members and customers through a variety of hosts, including member APIs, third-party software applications,

---

[2] The equity trading division uses separate technology based on the SGXAxess platform.

the Internet, and financial information providers (e.g. Bloomberg). In fact, SGX actively promotes flexible interfaces and works with third-party developers to create links into ETS; it is also working to accommodate cross-trading by other Globex members. ETS is linked to various other modules, including the Clearing Operations and Risk Evaluation system (CORE), implemented in 2001, that handles clearing functions and permits intraday risk monitoring and margin management, and the Trade Allocation and Register System, a real-time trade-matching system. All trade information is conveyed electronically to members through the Trade Dissemination System (TDS). Though SGX's platform is leading-edge in many respects, the exchange is reviewing the possibility of combining all cash and derivative execution and clearing functions in a single platform.

19.4   CLEARING

All derivative trades executed on SGX are cleared through SGX DC, a clearing subsidiary wholly owned by the exchange (securities trades are cleared through CDP). SGX DC becomes legal counterparty on all derivative transactions flowing through the exchange, and requires clearing members to post margins and contribute to the exchange's guarantee fund. SGX DC uses the CORE platform to clear trades and also administers the MOS 21 platform (based on CME's Clearing 21 system) for instantaneous acceptance/rejection of trades – this reduces overnight out-trades.

19.5   PRODUCT OFFERINGS

SGX features one of the broadest contract listings in the world, with products covering international, regional, and domestic references in the fixed income, equity, and commodity sectors. Within the fixed income market, SGX lists (see Table 19.1):

- Futures and options on short-term interest rates, including 3-month Eurodollars, Euroyen (both Tibor and Libor), and Singapore dollar swap offer rate (SOR)
- Futures and options on medium- and long-term interest rates, including 10-year JGBs and 5-year Singapore government bonds (note that the JGB contract was increased in notional size in 2002 to make it equal to, and potentially fungible with, the TSE's own contract)

In the equity sector SGX has expanded its product scope considerably since 2000 by introducing a range of contracts based on regional indexes. The exchange now lists and trades (see Table 19.2):

Table 19.1   SGX's fixed income derivatives

Reference	Futures	Options
Singapore dollar swap offer rate (3 month)	✓	–
Eurodollars (3 month)	✓	–
Tibor Euroyen (3 month)	✓	✓
Libor Euroyen (3 month)	✓	✓
Japanese government bonds (10 year)	✓	✓
Singapore government bonds (5 year)	✓	–

Table 19.2   SGX's equity derivatives

Reference	Futures	Options	Futures Options
Single stocks	✓	✓	–
Nikkei 225 index	✓	–	✓
Nikkei 300 index	✓	–	–
MSCI Hong Kong index	✓	–	–
MSCI Japan index	✓	–	–
MSCI Singapore index	✓	–	–
MSCI Taiwan index	✓	✓	–
S&P CNX Nifty India index	✓	–	–
Straits Times index	✓	–	–

Table 19.3   SGX's commodity derivatives

Reference	Futures	Options
Brent crude oil	✓	–
MECO crude oil	✓	–
DRAM microchips	✓	–

- Futures and options on individual Singaporean stocks (as noted above, single stock options are still traded through the equity unit of SGX, though are expected to be migrated to the derivative unit in time)
- Futures, options, and futures options on regional and international stock indexes

Prior to the exchange consolidation, SIMEX featured a number of energy-related contracts, including those related to fuel oil and gas oil; those have been abandoned in favor of (see Table 19.3):

- Futures on Brent crude oil (MOS with IPE) and a new MECO contract developed jointly with TOCOM
- Futures on dynamic random access memory microchips

19.6   REGULATION

The consolidated equity and derivative trading operations of SGX are regulated by Singapore's primary financial regulator, the Monetary Authority of Singapore (MAS); following the Barings scandal of 1995 (when unauthorized trading of SIMEX (and other) contracts through a Singaporean subsidiary of British merchant bank Barings caused large losses), MAS was given even greater enforcement powers and required SIMEX to strengthen its own internal controls. Regulatory legislation applicable to listed contracts is contained in the Futures Trading Act (FTA); exchanges dealing in financial contracts (rather than soft commodities) must be approved under the FTA.

19.7   WEBSITE

The SGX website provides details on contract specifications and data/price data sources: www.sgx.com

20

Sydney Futures Exchange (SFE)

20.1 BACKGROUND

The Sydney Futures Exchange (SFE) was originally established in 1960 as the Sydney Greasy Wool Exchange, a mutually owned forum for trading futures on various classes of wool; over ensuing decades it added various other contracts to its product base, but always maintained a strict agricultural commodity focus. However, as Sydney became an increasingly important regional financial center during the 1980s and 1990s, the exchange introduced contracts on Australia's main financial benchmarks, and gradually became known as a true financial derivatives exchange. Though the SFE traded on a physical, open-outcry basis for several decades, it introduced new technologies during the early to mid-1990s that allowed it to gradually migrate to an electronic environment; physical trading was abandoned completely in 1999. The SFE exists today as a publicly traded, electronic financial/commodity exchange, having demutualized and floated shares on the Australian Stock Exchange (ASX) in 2002.

In 1992 the exchange expanded its geographic and product horizons by acquiring the New Zealand Futures and Options Exchange (NZFOE, which traces its roots back to 1953); NZFOE now operates as a wholly owned subsidiary of SFE, retaining its own marketing, branding, and management, but utilizing SFE's general product expertise and technology. In 2000 the SFE consolidated its market position in the clearing sector by acquiring debt securities clearer Austraclear; the new consolidated platform clears listed and OTC derivatives, debt securities, and repurchase agreements. It is important to note that the SFE does not control all listed derivatives activity in the region; the ASX, as the country's central stock market, is responsible for trading standardized single stock options on the main Australian blue-chip companies (discussions between the SFE and ASX about a possible combination of all products (or at least derivative products) have not yielded results due to regulatory issues).

Over the years SFE has introduced various new products, including EFPs and BTFs, electricity futures (in conjunction with electricity firm Transpower), cattle futures, A$/US$ FX futures, swap futures, and overnight options; following the success of overnight options (which were introduced in 1993), the exchange created intraday options, valid only for a current exchange session. Since the start of the millennium SFE has also actively pursued discussions with various regional exchanges about ventures that would allow cross-product trading/cooperation; for instance, it has signed memoranda of understanding with HKEx, OSE, and TIFFE regarding product development, clearing, and technology ventures.

The SFE is an exchange that has responded well to the changing marketplace, transforming itself almost completely over a relatively short 2-year period and becoming a regional leader in many areas. Returning to the themes of Chapter 2, we note that SFE:

- Is organized as a "for-profit" commercial company and has floated its shares publicly in order to raise capital

- Has fully embraced the concept of mergers and alliances (e.g. its own acquisitions of NZFOE and Austraclear, its joint venture with Transpower, and its regional exchange cooperation agreements)
- Has migrated completely to an electronic environment and closed down its trading floor
- Offers additional clearing and nontrading services to supplement its revenues
- Has actively developed new types of futures and options products and is represented across a broad product spectrum

20.2   CORPORATE STRUCTURE

SFE converted from a mutual, nonprofit organization to a public company, SFE Corp Ltd, prior to its public flotation. Following corporatization the exchange holding company was initially listed on the exempt Austock market and followed with a full listing on the ASX in April 2002; the investing public can now buy and sell shares in SFE Corp. SFE Corp owns SFE Clearing Corp (SFECC, derivatives clearing), Austraclear (securities clearing), SFE Ltd (the main Sydney exchange), and NZFOE (the New Zealand exchange). From a business organization perspective the SFE is divided into SFE Trading (all derivative trading activities) and SFE Clearing (all cash and derivative clearing activities).

20.3   TECHNOLOGY PLATFORM/INFRASTRUCTURE

The SFE has emphasized technology in its operations since the early 1990s, and reached its goal of providing members (and authorized clients of full members) with fully automated access to its markets, 24 hours per day, by the end of the decade. The exchange's primary platform, SYCOM IV, has been through various upgrades and enhancements since its original development; it serves as the "backbone" for trade routing and execution (handling all SFE and NZFOE trades) and can be accessed through various means, including:

- From a member API through the SFE interface and into a routing hub
- Through an SFE workstation equipped with an SFE interface, or
- Through the Internet, and then via an SFE broker into the SFE interface

SYCOM links directly into the SFECC for trade clearing and settling; as noted below, SFE's clearing system is now based on OM's SECUR platform (and a new, integrated clearing platform is in the process of development). Though the SFE's platform already permits efficient and secure trading, further upgrades are planned in order to speed execution times. It should be noted that the CFTC and other global regulators have approved SYCOM terminals for use in the US (and other countries).

20.4   CLEARING

The SFE created the SFE Clearinghouse in 1991 to clear futures and options contracts; as noted above, the exchange acquired Austraclear in late 2000 to form the new SFE Clearing Corp (SFECC). SFECC acts as counterparty on all SFE and NZFOE transactions through its Central Counterparty Clearing facility (which accommodates exchange futures and options, bonds, repurchase agreements, and OTC derivatives). Within the exchange product sector, margins and special guarantee deposits provide adequate assurance of performance in the event of counterparty default.

SFE has also introduced a remote clearing facility for nonresident members who do not want to replicate clearing infrastructure within Australia. For instance, remote clearing members can use their own APIs, or the OM SECUR interface, to link directly into the SFECC. Institutions dealing directly in A$-denominated securities and contracts can link into the SFECC through the Fintracs interface. SFE's original clearing systems were replaced in December 2001 with OM's SECUR platform; in addition, the exchange announced in 2002 that OM will develop the new Central Securities Depository System to replace Austraclear's original Fintracs platform.

20.5   PRODUCT OFFERINGS

The SFE, directly and through the NZFOE, features contracts on equity, fixed income and commodity references. Within the equity sector, SFE lists (see Table 20.1):

- Futures and options on individual Australian and New Zealand stocks
- Futures and futures options on major market indexes, including the SPI 200 in Australia and NZSE 10 in New Zealand

As noted above, the ASX, rather than the SFE, lists and trades individual equity options (including standard options, flex options, and long-term options); the same is not true in New Zealand – the New Zealand Stock Exchange has given all equity option trading rights directly to the NZFOE.

In the fixed income sector, the SFE lists (see Table 20.2):

Table 20.1   SFE's equity derivatives

Reference	Futures	Options	Futures options
Individual stocks (Aus)	✓	–	–
Individual stocks (NZ)*	–	✓	–
SPI 200 index	✓	–	✓
NZSE 10* index	✓	–	✓

*Traded via the NZFOE.

Table 20.2   SFE's fixed income/currency derivatives

Reference	Futures	Futures options
Bank bill (90 day) (Aus)	✓	✓
Bank bill (90 day) (NZ)*	✓	✓
Commonwealth government bond (3 year) (Aus)	✓	✓
NZ government bond (3 year) (NZ)*	✓	✓
Commonwealth government bond (10 year) (Aus)	✓	✓
NZ government bond (10 year) (NZ)*	✓	✓
3-year swaps (Aus)	✓	–
10-year swaps (Aus)	✓	–
Australian dollar/US dollar (Aus)	✓	–

*Traded via the NZFOE.

Table 20.3   SFE's commodity derivatives

Reference	Futures	Futures options
Wool (fine)	✓	–
Wool (broad)	✓	–
Wool (greasy)	✓	✓
Cattle	✓	–
Electricity (NSW – base)	✓	–
Electricity (NSE – peak)	✓	–
Electricity (Victoria – base)	✓	–
Electricity (Victoria – peak)	✓	–
Electricity (South Australia – base)	✓	–
Electricity (South Australia – peak)	✓	–
Electricity (Queensland – base)	✓	–
Electricity (Queensland – peak)	✓	–
Electricity (North Island – base)*	✓	–
Electricity (North Island – peak)*	✓	–

*Traded via the NZFOE.

- Futures and futures options on short-term interest rates, including 90-day Australian and New Zealand bank bill rates
- Futures and futures options on medium- and long-term interest rates, including 3- and 10-year Australian and New Zealand government bonds, and 3- and 10-year interest rate swaps
- Futures on the Australian dollar/US dollar FX rate

In the commodity sector the exchange features (see Table 20.3):

- Futures and futures options on wool (i.e. fine, broad, and greasy wool indexes) and cattle
- Futures on Australian and New Zealand electricity (both base load and peak period, on a cash settlement basis)

20.6   REGULATION

The SFE is regulated by the Australian Securities and Investment Commission (ASIC) and the Reserve Bank of Australia (RBA), Australia's two primary financial regulators. The ASIC is responsible for administering the Corporations Law and the Securities Law (which are broad legal frameworks intended to control activities related to instruments, participants, and marketplaces); the RBA, in contrast, is responsible for overseeing the activities of financial institutions and conduits in the local marketplace. The regulatory authorities have also granted the SFE (and other exchanges) self-regulatory status and guidelines.

20.7   WEBSITE

The SFE website provides details on contract specifications and data/price data sources: www.sfe.com.au

21
Tokyo Commodity Exchange (TOCOM)

21.1 BACKGROUND

The Tokyo Commodity Exchange (TOCOM) was established in 1984 to serve as a central trading forum for futures on metals, energy, and other hard commodities. In fact, TOCOM was created through the merger of several long-established Japanese commodity exchanges, including the Tokyo Textile Exchange (TTE, founded in 1951), Tokyo Rubber Exchange (TRE, 1952) and Tokyo Gold Exchange (TGEx, 1982); the consolidation was driven by the need to create cost efficiencies, product diversification, and deeper liquidity in benchmark contracts. TOCOM trades on both an electronic and physical basis: the exchange's metals and energy contracts are traded via an electronic platform, while its rubber contract is traded in the traditional "Itayose" open-outcry method on the floor of the exchange (however, eventual migration to a completely electronic environment is expected).

In recent years TOCOM has delisted certain inactive contracts (e.g. wool and cotton yarn futures were abandoned in 1999) and introduced several new ones – primarily in the critical energy sector. Japan is a major importer and consumer of energy products for its industrial base, and requires contracts that meet its specific requirements; accordingly, the exchange has developed energy futures based on references impacting Japanese imports and exports. For instance, gasoline and kerosene futures, introduced in 1999, reference refined indexes applicable to the Japanese market, while crude oil futures, launched in September 2001, relate to the Middle East crude oil (MECO) price (an average of Oman and Dubai crude) to which many Japanese importers are exposed. The exchange has also developed the TOCOM Asian Petroleum Index (API), referencing a basket of crudes used in the Asian market; it hopes ultimately to list and trade contracts on the API. In early 2002 TOCOM and SGX announced a joint effort to launch a MECO contract on SGX (denominated in US dollar/barrel rather than yen/kiloliter to make it more accessible to international participants); the SGX contract is now operational, and both exchanges have expressed interest in making the contracts fungible at a future time. TOCOM is also planning new contracts on gas oil and TRS 20 rubber.

TOCOM is an exchange that has successfully combined different marketplaces and realigned its product offerings to become more relevant in the current environment. However, it still faces considerable challenges, including those related to corporate structure, technology, revenue diversification, global alliances, and clearing services. Considering the themes of Chapter 2, we note that TOCOM:

- Has embraced the concept of mergers and alliances (e.g. its own consolidations of TTE, TGEx, and TRE)
- Has migrated partially to an electronic environment
- Has actively developed new types of futures and options products (particularly in the sensitive and important energy sector)

21.2   CORPORATE STRUCTURE

TOCOM is organized as a nonprofit, mutual organization that is owned by exchange members. Unlike other Japanese exchanges, including TSE and OSE, TOCOM has opted not to convert to a corporate entity.

21.3   TECHNOLOGY PLATFORM/INFRASTRUCTURE

As noted, a portion of TOCOM's trading occurs through an electronic trading platform, and full migration to an electronic environment is expected in the medium term. The exchange uses a basic platform, developed during the early 1990s, that is capable of handling trade entry, order routing, order matching, clearing, and settlement. Though the platform has been upgraded in recent years, the overall architecture is somewhat outdated. As a result, exchange management decided in 2002 to upgrade its entire front- and back-office systems functionality and expects to have a new open architecture platform in place in 2003 (including a new clearing and settlement module that will reduce clearing times).

21.4   CLEARING

Unlike Japan's financial exchanges, the country's commodity exchanges, including TOCOM, do not feature centralized clearing units. Thus, TOCOM acts as an agent between buying and selling members executing trades. At the end of each trading day the exchange revalues all open positions and accepts funds from those showing a loss and forwards them to those showing a gain. In the event of counterparty default the exchange draws on special deposits lodged by members; the exchange, however, is not a legal counterparty to the transactions and is not liable to cover defaulted trades.

21.5   PRODUCT OFFERINGS

TOCOM lists a range of futures contracts on commodities that cross "traditional" boundaries, including metals, energy, and other hard commodities. The exchange only lists and trades futures and has no near-term plans to offer options. Its primary contracts include (see Table 21.1):

Table 21.1   TOCOM's commodity derivatives

Reference	Futures	Options
Gold	✓	–
Silver	✓	–
Platinum	✓	–
Palladium	✓	–
Aluminum	✓	–
Gasoline	✓	–
Kerosene	✓	–
MECO Crude Oil	✓	–
Rubber (RSS 3)	✓	–

- Futures on metals, including gold, silver, platinum, palladium, and aluminum
- Futures on energy products, including gasoline, kerosene, and crude oil
- Futures on rubber

21.6 REGULATION

TOCOM is authorized to operate under the revised Commodity Exchange Law (CEL), which sets performance and safety requirements for all commodity exchanges and ensures that investors are afforded appropriate protection. In addition to the rules of the CEL, TOCOM's overall operations are regulated the Ministry of Economy, Trade, and Industry (METI), which is broadly responsible for Japan's trade and industrial marketplaces and related forums and products.

21.7 WEBSITE

The TOCOM website provides details on contract specifications and data/price data sources: www.tocom.or.jp

Tokyo Grain Exchange (TGE)

22.1 BACKGROUND

The Tokyo Grain Exchange (TGE) traces its origins to 1874, the start of official rice futures trading in Japan (informal trading actually started more than a century before that date). In 1893, as market liberalization took greater hold, the TGE expanded into futures trading in cotton, sugar, and raw silk and its business grew steadily until the early 1940s. The exchange ceased operations during the war, as rationing of commodities meant there was little need for a commodity-based futures exchange. In 1950, however, a new Commodity Exchange Law (CEL) was passed, allowing the resumption of commodity trading. TGE restarted its operations and soon began developing new products, including futures on red beans, soybeans, and potato starch (all in 1952), and US soybeans (1961). While TGE concentrated its efforts on grains the Tokyo Sugar Exchange (TSEx), founded in 1952, offered customers contracts on raw and refined sugar. In 1993, in an attempt to rationalize operations and build a broader product base, the TGE and TSEx merged into a new exchange, retaining the well-established TGE name. A further consolidation followed in April 1995 when the Hokkaido Grain Exchange (HGE, a regionally focused grain trading forum) was merged into TGE; the consolidation reduced expenses and, more importantly, helped build liquidity by eliminating duplicative contracts. Throughout the 1990s and into the millennium, the "new" TGE focused heavily on the creation of new products to meet growing customer demand, introducing futures on corn, arabica and robusta coffees, soybean meal, nongenetically modified organism (non-GMO) soybeans, and options on raw sugar and corn futures. Though TGE operated as an open-outcry forum for many decades it successfully transitioned to an all-electronic environment in the late 1980s – earlier, in fact, than other Japanese exchanges; in April 1988 TGE became the first Japanese exchange to convert to a fully electronic platform (TSEx followed with its own fully automated system in 1991).

TGE serves as a good example of an exchange that is making adjustments to its structure and operations in order to continue competing effectively. Though it remains a mutually owned exchange without much revenue diversification, it has made important strides in mergers, product development, and technology. Returning to the themes of Chapter 2, we note that TGE:

- Has embraced mergers and acquisitions (e.g. its own combinations with TSEx and HGE)
- Has a fully electronic platform (and was the first in Japan to abandon open-outcry trading)
- Has actively created new types of futures and options products (though ones that remain tied to its core competencies)

22.2 CORPORATE STRUCTURE

The TGE was originally established as a nonprofit, mutual organization. Though other Japanese exchanges created as mutuals have since converted into "for profit" corporate entities, TGE has opted to remain a mutual and has no specific plans for altering its structure.

22.3   TECHNOLOGY PLATFORM/INFRASTRUCTURE

As noted, TGE was the first Japanese exchange to fully employ technology in its operations, closing its physical trading floor well before other exchanges (e.g. TSE and OSE) did so. The TGE currently features two separate trading platforms, one for futures and a second for options on futures. The futures platform is a "session trading" mechanism with a single price display that only operates during set hours; all futures trades executed by members must flow through the system. The options platform, in contrast, is a "continuous trading" mechanism with multiple prices that can be used at any time. Both modules feed electronically into back-office settlement and reporting processes.

22.4   CLEARING

Unlike other Japanese financial exchanges, the country's commodity exchanges do not feature centralized clearing (e.g. there is no clearinghouse assuming the role of counterparty on every trade). Rather, the TGE acts as an intermediary between buying and selling members executing trades. At the end of each trading day the TGE revalues open positions, accepting funds from those showing a loss and forwarding them to those showing a gain. In the event of counterparty default the exchange draws on special deposits lodged by members; the exchange, however, is not a legal counterparty to the transactions and is not liable to cover defaulted trades. (Note that the exchange requires clearing members to segregate customer funds into separate accounts for added protection.)

22.5   PRODUCT OFFERINGS

TGE's product offerings are focused exclusively on the commodity sector, where it lists and trades (see Table 22.1):

- Futures and futures options on grains, including corn, red beans, and soybeans (US, non-GMO, and meal)
- Futures on arabica and robusta coffees
- Futures and futures options on raw and refined sugar

Table 22.1   TGE's commodity derivatives

Reference	Futures	Futures options
Corn	✓	✓
Soybean meal	✓	–
US soybean	✓	✓
Non-GMO soybean	✓	–
Red bean	✓	–
Arabica coffee	✓	–
Robusta coffee	✓	–
Raw sugar	✓	✓
Refined sugar	✓	–

22.6   REGULATION

The TGE's activities fall under the jurisdiction of the revised CEL, which dictates the operating requirements to which commodity exchanges must adhere, and ensures that exchange participants are afforded appropriate protection. Various divisions within the Ministry of Agriculture, Forestry, and Fisheries (MAFF), which is responsible for the Japanese agricultural marketplace and related forums and products, also review TGE's operations on a periodic basis.

22.7   WEBSITE

The TGE website provides details on contract specifications and data/price data sources: www.tge.or.jp

Tokyo International Financial Futures Exchange (TIFFE)

23.1 BACKGROUND

The Tokyo International Financial Futures Exchange (TIFFE) is one of Japan's newest exchanges, having been created in April 1989 to trade fixed income and currency derivatives. The exchange commenced operations telephonically, rather than on-exchange, before adopting a fully automated trading platform in early 1991 – making it one of the country's first exchanges to convert to electronic trading. Since its creation TIFFE has maintained a relatively narrow focus, specializing in short-term interest rate and currency contracts; equity and long-term interest rate derivatives are the domain of the TSE and OSE, while commodity derivatives are traded by TOCOM and TGE (among others). Despite its relatively narrow product focus, TIFFE has enhanced its business by offering innovative calendar and basis spread contracts. For instance, in 1991 it created options on its benchmark 3-month Tibor Euroyen futures contract, in 1992 it introduced a contract on 12-month Euroyen (which it ultimately delisted), in 1994 it increased option strikes and series on 3-month Euroyen, in 1998 it introduced Euroyen calendar spreads, and a year later it created a new 3-month Libor Euroyen contract; it followed with Libor/Tibor spread contracts in 2001.

In late 1995 TIFFE expanded its market presence by forging a link with LIFFE to lengthen the trading day and share contract liquidity. The LIFFE–TIFFE link allows clients to trade LIFFE Euroyen futures in London and pass them to TIFFE at the close of the LIFFE business day; once on TIFFE, they are counted as part of TIFFE's volume and open interest. The linkage, which became operational in April 1996, has helped increase outstanding Euroyen volume on both exchanges. Note that the relationship that developed between the two exchanges led TIFFE's management to select LIFFE's Connect trading platform when it needed to upgrade its technology. To further expand its market presence and create products of regional benefit, TIFFE signed memoranda of understanding with KOFEX and SFE in 2001 regarding cross-exchange membership, joint product development, and market surveillance and shared technologies.

TIFFE is an exchange that is trying to expand its operations while remaining focused on its core expertise. While it has made progress in creating new products that play to its strengths and revamping its technology platform based on the architecture of a proven leader (e.g. LIFFE's Connect), it remains mutually owned and has not expanded its revenue base outside of its core business – it is very heavily reliant on activity in Euroyen contracts. Considering the themes of Chapter 2, we note that TIFFE:

- Has created a strong alliance with a global exchange (LIFFE) and is negotiating others (e.g. KOFEX, SFE)
- Has migrated completely to an electronic environment and now features leading-edge technology
- Has been active in creating new types of futures and options products (albeit ones that are heavily related to its core Euroyen base)

23.2   CORPORATE STRUCTURE

TIFFE is organized as a mutual, nonprofit organization; clearing members own all outstanding shares in the exchange. Unlike other Japanese exchanges, including OSE and TSE, TIFFE has elected not to change its corporate status.

23.3   TECHNOLOGY PLATFORM/INFRASTRUCTURE

As noted, TIFFE introduced its first technology platform (FACTS, or Fully Automated Computer Trading System) in 1991 and enhanced it at various intervals over the next decade (e.g. in 1996 it installed new terminals to support the TIFFE/LIFFE linkage and added CME's SPAN risk portfolio calculator, in 1999 it created a new API allowing simpler connection between its trading engine and member systems, and so forth). In 2001 the exchange decided to overhaul its trading technology and selected LIFFE's Connect platform as the centerpiece of its new efforts. Connect is well suited to TIFFE's business because it can handle the complex, multi-leg transactions that characterize TIFFE's business with relative ease. As part of the process the exchange also decided to upgrade its clearing system through the efforts of Fujitsu Corporation, a Japanese technology company. The Connect and Fujitsu platforms are meant to be operational in 2003, at which time FACTS will be retired.

23.4   CLEARING

All contracts traded on TIFFE (including those initiated on LIFFE and transferred to TIFFE at the end of the trading day) are cleared through TIFFE's clearing division; accordingly, the exchange acts as counterparty on all trades that are reregistered at the close of business. In addition to margins posted on every contract, TIFFE protects itself from possible client default losses through a special fund supported by mandatory contributions from clearing members. Though TIFFE currently only clears its own contracts, it is exploring the possibility of offering third-party clearing services to other exchanges as well as the OTC market. A March 2002 amendment to the Financial Futures Trading Law (FFTL) (as well as the CEL) permits exchanges and marketplaces to elect either internal or external clearing, opening up the possibility of new business opportunities for those capable of delivering such services.

23.5   PRODUCT OFFERINGS

As indicated above, TIFFE remains very focused on the short-end of the Japanese fixed income market. The exchange lists (see Table 23.1):

Table 23.1   TIFFE's fixed income/currency derivatives

Reference	Futures	Options
Tibor Euroyen (3 month)	✓	✓
Libor Euroyen (3 month)	✓	–
Euroyen (3 month) calendar spread	✓	–
Libor-Tibor Euroyen spread	✓	–
US dollar/Japanese yen	✓	–

- Futures and options on short-term interest rates, including 3-month Tibor and Libor Euroyen, Tibor–Libor spreads, Euroyen calendar spreads
- Futures on US dollar/Japanese yen FX rates

23.6   REGULATION

TIFFE falls under the jurisdiction of the Japanese FFTL (in contrast to financial products traded via the OSE and TSE, which are governed by the Securities and Exchange Law). The FFTL, which covers all activity in deposit and currency contracts, requires that trading be specifically conducted via TIFFE, through a financial futures trading company licensed by the Ministry of Finance as a general or clearing member. The Ministry and the JSDA provide further regulatory oversight.

23.7   WEBSITE

The TIFFE website provides details on contract specifications and data/price data sources: www.tiffe.or.jp

24

Tokyo Stock Exchange (TSE)

24.1 BACKGROUND

The Tokyo Stock Exchange (TSE) was founded in 1878 as a profit-making corporation to promote trading of Japanese stocks and other securities. The exchange expanded its business steadily from the latter part of the nineteenth century until the war period of the early 1940s, at which time it became part of a national consolidated exchange. The TSE was separated again in 1949, this time as a mutual, nonprofit exchange trading in stocks and government bonds; during the 1960s and 1970s it added corporate bonds and convertible bonds to its operations. In 1969, as the Japanese industrial base and economy expanded, the exchange started tracking the broad Japanese stock market through the new Tokyo Stock Price Index (TOPIX), which later became an important reference for its futures contracts. The TSE introduced its first futures contract, on 10-year Japanese government bonds (JGBs), in 1985. Following the natural progression of its core stock trading business, the exchange introduced TOPIX futures and options in 1988 and 1989 (after regulatory changes permitted the creation of index contracts), as well as contracts on US Treasury bonds (which were ultimately delisted), 5-year JGBs, various TOPIX sector indexes and single stock options on TSE-listed companies. In order to support its strong JGB derivatives business, the exchange also developed innovative products related to calendar spread trading in 5- and 10-year bond futures and basis trading (simultaneous execution of cash and futures) in 10-year bonds. In recent years the TSE has also sought to strengthen its operations by developing alliances with other global derivative exchanges, including the CME and LIFFE; these alliances cover a broad range of areas, including joint product development/marketing, cross-platform access, technology-sharing and mutual trading offsets (the exchange has also sought to arrange similar alliances in securities trading, particularly with Asian exchanges). In 2000, TSE's overall securities operation expanded as it absorbed sister stock exchanges in Niigata, Hiroshima, and Fukuoka. Structurally, the exchange converted back to a "for profit" corporate entity in 2001.

Trading in both securities and derivatives occurred on the floor of the exchange from its reorganization in 1949 until April 1999 – at which point the TSE closed down its physical facility and moved to a pure electronic environment. In practice, the exchange had implemented securities trading technology in the early 1980s, so the move to a fully electronic environment was widely expected. It is worth stressing that TSE, like the OSE, is a stock exchange that has added derivatives capabilities, rather than an exchange created through the merger of established stock and derivative exchanges. Accordingly, most of TSE's efforts are still devoted to its main business of securities listing and trading.

The TSE is an exchange that is coping with structural changes in the marketplace by placing greater emphasis on corporate efficiencies, alliances, technology, and new products. Considering the themes of Chapter 2, we note that TSE:

- Is organized as a "for-profit" commercial company (and will follow with a public flotation in the future)

- Has started to forge global exchange alliances (e.g. CME, LIFFE)
- Has migrated completely to an electronic environment
- Offers additional clearing and nontrading services to supplement its revenues
- Has developed new products on a relatively regular basis (though ones that remain strongly linked to its core equity and JGB expertise)

24.2   CORPORATE STRUCTURE

Though TSE commenced its operations as a for-profit corporation in the late nineteenth century, it spent the second part of the twentieth century as a mutual, nonprofit company. In July 2000, however, a "demutualization committee" was formed to investigate the possibility of converting the exchange to a corporate entity in order to focus greater attention on profit/cost efficiencies and prepare the way for future capital markets access (to fund technology and potential alliances/joint ventures). In November 2001 the TSE adopted the committee's recommendation by demutualizing. The exchange is now organized as a for-profit holding company known as TSE Inc.; a public flotation is expected in the medium term. From an internal business perspective, the TSE features divisions focused on securities trading and listing, derivatives, clearing and settlement, and technology/information services.

24.3   TECHNOLOGY PLATFORM/INFRASTRUCTURE

The TSE began implementing a technology platform as early as 1982, when it introduced the Computer-Assisted Order Routing and Execution System (CORES) platform for stock and bond trading; the system was ultimately adapted to handle derivatives trading (i.e. the CORES FOP platform). CORES FOP, which features trade entry, routing, and matching, feeds directly into the exchange's Central Depository and Clearing System (CDCS) for clearing and settlement. In order to compute and manage margins, the TSE's clearing division uses CME's SPAN. In 2002 TSE introduced new securities trading systems for convertible bonds and exchangeable bonds and will likely replace CORES and its sister system, FORES, in the medium term.

24.4   CLEARING

The TSE's clearing division acts as a central counterparty on all derivative transactions. To reduce risk to the exchange, the TSE requires all clearing members to post margins and contribute to a clearing member deposit fund. From a technology perspective, the TSE uses SPAN to compute margins and CDCS (originally developed in October 1991, but since upgraded) to clear and settle all trades.

24.5   PRODUCT OFFERINGS

The TSE offers derivative contracts on key Japanese equity and fixed income benchmarks. Within the equity sector, the exchange offers (see Table 24.1):

- Options on individual Japanese stocks (listed on the TSE)
- Futures and options on Japanese indexes, including TOPIX and S&P/TOPIX 150, as well as narrower subindexes, including the TOPIX Bank, Electronic, and Transportation sectors

Table 24.1   TSE's equity derivatives

Reference	Futures	Options
Individual stocks	–	✓
TOPIX index	✓	✓
TOPIX Sector indexes	✓	–
S&P/TOPIX 150 index	✓	✓

Table 24.2   TSE's fixed income derivatives

Reference	Futures	Futures options
Japanese government bonds (5 year)	✓	–
Japanese government bonds (10 year)	✓	✓
5-year JGB calendar spreads	✓	–
10-year JGB calendar spreads	✓	–

In the fixed income sector, TSE trades (see Table 24.2):

• Futures and futures options on medium-term interest rates, including 5- and 10-year JGBs
• Futures on 5- and 10-year JGB calendar spreads

As noted earlier, the exchange also features a cash/futures basis facility for 10-year bonds.

24.6   REGULATION

Several different authorities regulate the TSE. Financial contracts, including those listed on the TSE, fall under the scope of the SEL. The SEL, which has been amended several times in recent years to allow for new products and trading mechanisms, dictates the operations that must be maintained in order to ensure client and market integrity; audits of these rules are conducted on a regular basis. The Ministry of Finance and the JSDA provide further regulatory oversight.

24.7   WEBSITE

The TSE website provides details on contract specifications and data/price data sources: www.tse.or.jp

Part III
The New Marketplaces

Emerging Exchanges

As noted in Chapter 1, a number of countries have created national exchanges to help promote growth in their local financial markets and move them closer to the "industrialized mainstream" of the global markets.

OVERVIEW OF STRUCTURE

An examination of a handful of emerging exchanges – typically those that have been in existence in current form for less than a decade and which are based in rapidly growing, though still emerging, economies – reveals that most offer derivative contracts that are critical to the management of local micro- and macro-risk exposures. These generally include contacts on:

- Short-term rates (interbank, bankers' acceptance, or Treasury bill rates)
- Medium/long-term rates (the local government bond rates)
- Exchange rates (typically expressed in terms of US$ or euro)
- Equity indexes (as a broad representation of the local equity market)
- Individual stocks (usually the largest capitalization local stocks)
- Commodity references (often related to local export or import goods)

In most cases emerging exchanges have been quick to embrace technology. Though not all of them are capable of funding comprehensive, customized front- to back-office processes, most have attempted to create or purchase relevant technologies' modules. In fact, some emerging exchanges (e.g. KOFEX, SAFEX) have only existed as electronic exchanges, suggesting that their technology platforms are actually quite robust. Like advanced exchanges, most emerging exchanges feature clearinghouses with multiple layers of protection to mitigate the effects of credit risk (e.g. margins, guarantee funds, member prequalification, and so on). Emerging exchanges generally lack the product/revenue diversification of advanced exchanges; most, for example, do not yet offer third-party clearing services or license technology to others. Many, however, have started to create alliances with other regional or international forums in order to expand product, client, and market depth. From a corporate structure perspective, emerging exchanges may be organized as mutual or corporate entities – no form of ownership appears to dominate.

Though the world of emerging exchanges is large and growing we select, for illustrative purposes, several regional exchanges that appear to be moving into the mainstream of futures and options. In particular, we consider:

- Bolsa de Mercado e Futuros (BM&F), located in Brazil
- Mercado Mexicano de Derivados (Mexder), located in Mexico
- Korea Futures Exchange (KOFEX), located in South Korea
- Malaysian Derivatives Exchange (MDEX), located in Malaysia
- South African Futures Exchange (SAFEX), located in South Africa

25

Bolsa de Mercado e Futuros
(BM&F) – Brazil

25.1 BACKGROUND

Brazil's Bolsa de Mercado e Futuros (BM&F) was established in early 1986 to trade financial futures and options. BM&F remained focused on local equity and fixed income contracts, which were traded primarily among domestic institutions, until it decided to expand its operations by acquiring another of the country's main exchanges, the São Paulo Commodity Exchange (BMSP); BMSP was originally established in 1917 to trade commodity futures on coffee, live cattle, and cotton. A third exchange, the Brazil Futures Exchange of Rio de Janeiro (BBF, established in 1983), was absorbed by the BM&F in June 1997 in order to integrate all of Brazil's futures trading under a single umbrella. The resulting entity, which preserves the BM&F branding, management, and physical trading floor, offers clients access to a broad range of commodity and financial contracts.

In order to broaden its international scope, scale, and presence, BM&F joined the Globex alliance in January 2000; its clients now have access to contracts traded on the CME, Euronext, SGX, MEFF, and MX, while international clients using Globex can access BM&F's local contracts. To expand its product and service base, the exchange has also taken the lead in offering third-party clearing services: the BM&F Derivatives Clearinghouse clears OTC derivative contracts, while a newly formed BM&F Foreign Exchange Clearinghouse is preparing to clear currency-related contracts. BM&F has also expanded its trading base by purchasing the Sisbex secondary bond market trading exchange; though activity is still relatively quiet, the exchange hopes to boost volume over time. In addition to product growth through acquisition and alliances, BM&F has actively introduced a series of new derivatives. For instance, in 2001 it created a forward rate contract based purely on interest rates (with no currency effects that might distort the value). It is also creating new contracts on a Brazilian-based American Depository Receipt (ADR) stock index and, through its commodity exchange unit, contracts on freight and cattle.

BM&F is an emerging exchange that is actively enhancing its operations in order to remain competitive. Considering the themes of Chapter 2, we note that BM&F:

- Is organized as a "for-profit" commercial company
- Has fully embraced the concept of mergers and alliances (e.g. its own acquisitions of BMSP and BBF, its participation in the Globex alliance, its purchase of Sisbex)
- Has started enhancing its technology platform (though it continues to trade primarily on a physical basis)
- Offers additional clearing services to supplement its revenues (e.g. OTC derivatives and foreign exchange clearing)
- Has been active in creating new types of derivative contracts and is represented across a broad product spectrum

25.2   CORPORATE STRUCTURE

BM&F is organized as a profit-making corporate entity. The exchange group is organized into distinct business units, including the exchange operation itself, BM&F Derivatives Clearing-house, BM&F FX Clearinghouse and Information Services.

25.3   TECHNOLOGY PLATFORM/INFRASTRUCTURE

Though BM&F trades primarily on a physical, open-outcry basis, it has adopted elements of advanced technologies in its exchange operations and is preparing to introduce additional functionality over the medium term. For instance, futures and options trades are input and processed through the exchange's Global Trading System (GTS), which gives members remote and after-hours capabilities. The initial version of GTS was introduced in September 2000, while an enhanced version, capable of handling cross-trading and new products/maturities, was implemented in late 2001. A new Margin Calculation System (MCS), capable of computing margin requirements of trade portfolios, was also introduced in 2001. To access contracts traded on other Globex alliance exchanges, BM&F members use the Euronext-developed NSC trading system.

25.4   CLEARING

The BM&F clears all listed (as well as select OTC) contracts through a centralized, in-house department; the division makes use of the MCS and GTS systems referenced above. The exchange relies on several layers of protection in order to ensure the integrity of its operations and the creditworthiness of all transactions; safeguards include initial and variation margins, direct clearing member liability, and three mandatory member-financed guarantee funds (e.g. the special fund, clearing fund, and guarantee fund). Clearing members are jointly and severally liable for the contract default of any other member;[1] accordingly, all clearing members are required to meet minimum financial requirements related to net capital, profitability, and so forth.

25.5   PRODUCT OFFERINGS

BM&F offers financial and commodity contracts; within the financial category, it lists and trades contracts on equities, interest rates, and exchange rates. In equities, the exchange lists (see Table 25.1):

Table 25.1   BM&F's equity derivatives

Reference	Futures	Options
Bovespa index*	✓	✓
Bovespa index volatility	✓	–

*Also available as a flex option.

---

[1] Clearing members, in turn, can turn to commodities broker houses or "locals" to seek restitution on a defaulted contract; once again, these entities must meet established minimum requirements.

Table 25.2   BM&F's fixed income/currency derivatives

Reference	Futures	Options
Interbank deposit (1 day, real)	✓	✓
Interbank deposit (1 day, US dollar)	✓	✓
FRA on US dollar spread	✓	✓
Interbank deposit (long-term)	✓	✓
Interbank deposit (resettable)	✓	✓
Interbank spread forward	✓	✓
Front-loaded bond	✓	–
US dollar/Brazilian real*	✓	✓
Euro/Brazilian real	✓	✓

*Also available as a flex option.

Table 25.3   BM&F's commodity derivatives

Reference	Futures	Options
Gold*	✓	✓
Fuel alcohol	✓	–
Arabica coffee	✓	✓
Corn (real-denominated)	✓	✓
Cotton	✓	✓
Live cattle (real-denominated)	✓	✓
Soybean	✓	✓
Sugar	✓	✓

*Also available as a standardized forward contract.

- Futures and options on Brazilian equity indexes, including the Bovespa index and the Bovespa volatility index

In the fixed income and currency sector, BM&F lists (see Table 25.2):

- Futures and options on short-term interest rates, including interbank deposits and forward rate agreements (FRAs)
- Futures and options on medium-term interest rates, including "front-loaded" bonds
- Futures and options on exchange rates, including the US$ and euro

BM&F's trades various commodity contracts, some of which date back to BMSP's earliest days. Specifically, the exchange lists (see Table 25.3):

- Futures and options on gold
- Futures and options on fuel alcohol
- Futures and options on arabica coffee, corn, cotton, soybeans, sugar, and cattle

25.6   REGULATION

BM&F's operations are regulated by various authorities, including the Brazilian Securities Commission (CVM), which oversees all activities in the derivative markets (including those related to listed and OTC contracts) and the Brazilian Central Bank, which is responsible for the overall strength of the financial marketplace and institutions/forums executing financial transactions. The CVM, which carries out resolutions of the National Monetary Council (the highest ranking authority in the Brazilian financial system), also devolves certain regulations and responsibilities to exchanges (such as the BM&F) so that they may operate in a self-regulatory capacity.

25.7   WEBSITE

The BM&F website provides details on contract specifications and data/price data sources: www.bmf.com

26
Mercado Mexicano de Derivados
(Mexder) – Mexico

26.1 BACKGROUND

The creation of the Mercado Mexicano de Derivados (Mexder) was the result of efforts by the Mexican Stock Exchange (Bolsa Mexicana de Valores (BMV)) and several other securities industry groups[1] to create a local derivatives marketplace. After nearly 4 years of preparation, Mexder received its operating license in early 1998 from the Bank of Mexico and the National Banking and Securities Commission and began operating on a trial basis in August of that year. Formal trading started in December 1998, once Mexder's clearinghouse was established. For the first 2 years of its existence Mexder operated on a physical, open-outcry basis; in May 2000, however, it abandoned physical trading in favor of electronic trading centered on an in-house platform. Though the exchange's charter permits trading in both futures and options, the exchange's efforts have been focused solely on futures; options will be introduced in the medium term, once sufficient expertise and liquidity have been gained in futures.

As Mexder is a relatively young exchange it has not had an opportunity to form global alliances, create a broad range of products, or develop third-party clearing or information services; significant work remains to be done in these areas. Revisiting the themes of Chapter 2, we note that Mexder:

- Is organized as a "for-profit" commercial company
- Has migrated completely to an electronic environment

26.2 CORPORATE STRUCTURE

Mexder is organized is a commercial, for-profit company. The Mexder holding company owns and operates the main exchange, as well as the exchange's clearing operation (Asigna). From an internal business perspective, the exchange group is divided into the units focused on exchange operations, clearing, and technology/information.

26.3 TECHNOLOGY PLATFORM/INFRASTRUCTURE

Though Mexder commenced operations as a physical exchange, it immediately started developing an electronic platform and, by 2000, was able to move all operations off the exchange floor. The core of Mexder's technology is the SENTRA system (Sistema Electronico de Negociacion, Transaccion, Registro y Asignacion). SENTRA acts as a trade entry, crossing and execution router that also passes executed trades to the SIVA module for clearing and settlement, and to the SIVA 25 module for dissemination of price information. Risk analysis

---

[1] Including the Asociacion Mexicana de Intermediarios Bursatiles (AMIB) and Indeval.

and margining occur through the SDC Compass module, which communicates directly with the Asigna clearinghouse.

26.4   CLEARING

All trades executed on Mexder are cleared and settled through the Asigna clearinghouse, a wholly owned subsidiary of the exchange group; Asigna thus acts as a counterparty on all transactions. In order to properly protect exchange operations, the clearinghouse reviews the financial status of all clearing members, sets clearing member limits, and requires posting of margins and contribution to a guarantee fund. As noted, Asigna uses the SIVA and SDC Compass modules of Mexder's technology infrastructure.

26.5   PRODUCT OFFERINGS

As indicated above, Mexder's product offerings are limited to futures contracts on fixed income and equity references (though commodity contracts may be added in the medium term). In the fixed income sector, Mexder lists (see Table 26.1):

- Futures on short-term interest rates, including 28-day interbank rates and 91-day Treasury bill rates (CETES)
- Futures on medium-term interest rates, including 3-year Mexican government bonds
- Futures on US dollar/Mexican peso FX rates

In the equity sector, the exchange lists and trades (see Table 26.2):

- Futures on individual Mexican stocks
- Futures on the Mexican IPC equity index

26.6   REGULATION

The Bank of Mexico has granted Mexder its official operating status and the Securities Commission sets exchange rules and ensures ongoing compliance; the Commission has also granted

Table 26.1   Mexder's fixed income/currency derivatives

Reference	Futures	Options
Peso interbank (28 day)	✓	–
Peso Treasury bills (91 day)	✓	–
Mexican Gov't Bonds (3 year)	✓	–
US dollar/Mexican peso	✓	–

Table 26.2   Mexder's equity derivatives

Reference	Futures	Options
Individual stocks	✓	–
Mexican IPC index	✓	–

Mexder self-regulatory status and requires that it oversee its own operations through regular monitoring and reporting.

26.7   WEBSITE

The Mexder website provides details on contract specifications and data/price data sources: www.mexder.com.mx

27
Korea Futures Exchange
(KOFEX) – South Korea

27.1 BACKGROUND

The Korea Futures Exchange (KOFEX) – designed as an all-electronic forum for equity, fixed income, and commodity derivative trading – was given approval to operate by the Korean government under the Futures Trading Act of 1995 and became operational in early 1999. KOFEX was not, however, Korea's first futures exchange; the Korea Stock Exchange (KSE, the country's main equity marketplace), listed and traded futures on the Korea Stock Price Index 200 (KOSPI 200) prior to the formation of KOFEX (in December 2000 KOFEX received approval to trade the KOSPI contract, and the business was transferred from the KSE to KOFEX; KSE is no longer involved in Korea's listed derivatives market). Though Korea has had a fairly restrictive policy toward offshore investment and activity in its financial markets, it liberalized foreign access in July 1998 (in advance of KOFEX's launch date) to help ensure free and easy participation by a broad range of international institutions. This strategy appears to have been effective, as strong interest in KOFEX's contracts (particularly its stock index futures) has made it a very active trading locale.

KOFEX is a relatively new emerging exchange that already features some characteristics of advanced forums. Though the exchange remains mutually owned and has not yet had time to achieve significant revenue diversification or negotiate cross-border alliances, we note, per the themes in Chapter 2, that it:

- Features an all-electronic trading environment
- Has created benchmark contracts that have achieved strong liquidity in a relatively short time period

27.2 CORPORATE STRUCTURE

KOFEX is organized as a mutually owned, limited liability organization. Though the liability of clearing members is technically limited, the exchange reserves the right to call on members to cover any shortfalls in the event of a catastrophic loss. No plans regarding potential demutualization have been put forth.

27.3 TECHNOLOGY PLATFORM/INFRASTRUCTURE

As indicated, trading on KOFEX is purely electronic in nature and is thus heavily dependent on a robust platform. The exchange has adapted OM's CLICK and SECUR platforms to allow for local trade entry, routing, matching/execution, and processing; as part of the customization process it has designed a fully integrated process in a real-time environment. The KOFEX version of the CLICK platform supports member systems and third-party APIs for ease of connectivity.

27.4   CLEARING

All transactions executed through KOFEX are cleared by the exchange itself; KOFEX features no independent clearinghouse subsidiary so members executing trades face KOFEX as counterparty. All clearing members are required to post appropriate margins and contribute to the exchange's "good faith deposit" fund and guarantee fund. KOFEX also monitors the financial standing of its clearing members on a monthly basis to ensure they have sufficient resources to meet potential obligations. In the event of default, the exchange is structured to cover losses in the following sequence: margins and deposits, KOFEX loss reserves, fund deposits provided by members, credit insurance, and bank letters of credit (with further calls on clearing members if needed).

27.5   PRODUCT OFFERINGS

Given its relatively recent development, KOFEX still features a small number of futures and options contracts (though it intends to expand into additional areas as local financial markets permit). However, all essential equity, fixed income, and commodity references can be traded via KOFEX. In the fixed income sector, the exchange lists (see Table 27.1):

- Futures on short-term interest rates, including 3-month Korean won certificates of deposit (CDs)
- Futures and futures options on medium-term interest rates, including 3-year Korean Treasury bonds
- Futures on the US dollar/Korean won FX rate

In the equity sector, KOFEX features (see Table 27.2):

- Futures and options on Korean equity indexes, including the KOSPI 200 and KOSDAQ 50

In the commodity sector, KOFEX lists (see Table 27.3):

- Futures on gold

Table 27.1   KOFEX's fixed income/currency derivatives

Reference	Futures	Options	Futures options
CD interest rates (3 month)	✓	–	–
Korean Treasury bonds (3 year)	✓	–	✓
US dollar/Korean won	✓	✓	–

Table 27.2   KOFEX's equity derivatives

Reference	Futures	Options
KOSPI 200 index	✓	✓
KOSDAQ 50 index	✓	✓

Table 27.3 KOFEX's commodity derivatives

Reference	Futures	Options
Gold	✓	–

27.6 REGULATION

The Futures Trading Act of 1995 (and its amended versions of 1998 and 1999) establishes the operating framework for KOFEX's activities; the Ministry of Finance and Economy, under the terms of the Futures Trading Act, has approved the exchange and licensed its activities. The Financial Supervisory Committee (FSC) reviews the operations of the country's futures industry organization, the Korea Futures Association (KFA), while the Financial Supervisory Service (FSS), an executive arm of the FSC, regularly audits KOFEX's activities.

27.7 WEBSITE

The KOFEX website provides details on contract specifications and data/price data sources: www.kofex.com

Malaysian Derivatives Exchange
(MDEX) – Malaysia

28.1 BACKGROUND

The Malaysian Derivatives Exchange (MDEX) was formally established in late 2000, though one of the founding exchanges traces its history back to 1980. Specifically, the Kuala Lumpur Commodity Exchange (KLCE), Southeast Asia's first derivative exchange, introduced futures trading on crude palm oil and rubber, two major Malaysian exports, in 1980. Though early trading was successful a new clearinghouse, the Malaysian Futures Clearing Corp (MFCC), had to be formed in 1985 after client defaults in the palm oil market left the KLCE with large losses. From 1986 to 1990 KLCE continued to expand its operations, introducing new contracts on tin, cocoa, and palm olein. At approximately the same time the Malaysian government started preliminary work on the establishment of a new exchange, the Kuala Lumpur Options and Financial Futures Exchange (KLOFFE), to trade equity contracts. In late 1995, after the creation of a dedicated clearinghouse (the Malaysian Derivatives Clearinghouse (MDCH)), KLOFFE began trading futures on the Kuala Lumpur Stock Exchange Composite Index (KLSE CI). Several months later KLCE incorporated a separate financial exchange of its own, the Malaysian Monetary Exchange (MME), to list and trade short-term interest rate futures (on the 3-month Kuala Lumpur Interbank Offer Rate (KLIBOR)).

Recognizing the opportunities for savings and efficiencies, MDCH and MFCC merged their clearing operations in late 1997 – the "new" MDCH thus became responsible for clearing contracts on all of the country's derivative exchanges (i.e. KLCE, MME, and KLOFFE). Nearly one year later KLCE absorbed the MME subsidiary back into its operations and renamed itself COMMEX Malaysia. The KLSE, in turn, acquired KLOFFE in order to rationalize exchange operations and bring the cash and derivative markets closer together; it also began discussions with COMMEX about merging the derivative operations of the two exchanges. In December 2000 the parties agreed to merge COMMEX and KLOFFE into MDEX, and trading on the new exchange started in June 2001. Later that year the exchange moved to an all-electronic platform and closed down its open-outcry trading floor (both COMMEX and KLOFFE had operated as physical exchanges). As part of the merger rationalization process, MDEX abandoned many of KLCE's original commodity contracts (which had become largely dormant, particularly after the Malaysian government imposed capital controls in 1998).

MDEX is an emerging exchange that has rationalized and focused its activities in order to remain efficient and viable. Considering the themes of Chapter 2, we note that MDEX:

- Is organized as a "for-profit" commercial company
- Has fully embraced the concept of mergers (e.g. its own consolidations of KLSE/KLOFFE and COMMEX/KLOFFE, as well as its combinations of clearing functions)
- Features a robust technology platform that has allowed it to abandon open-outcry trading

28.2   CORPORATE STRUCTURE

MDEX is structured as a for-profit corporation that is publicly held by investors. MDCH, the exchange's clearing entity, is wholly owned by the exchange. From an internal business perspective the exchange operates through divisions focused on derivatives, clearing, technology, and information.

28.3   TECHNOLOGY PLATFORM/INFRASTRUCTURE

MDEX moved to an all-electronic environment in late 2001, based on the KATS trading system it had developed in the late 1990s. In fact, KLOFFE, MME, and KLCE had all pursued technology solutions during the 1990s, so the new combined exchange incorporated technology with relative ease. KATS provides for electronic execution and trade matching, and connects to back-office modules. In early 1999 the exchange acquired Insoft and, through the purchase, access to the R&N Back Office System, which it uses to process trades.

28.4   CLEARING

MDCH, the ultimate survivor in the cycle of Malaysian clearinghouse consolidations, acts as counterparty on all clearing member trades flowing through MDEX; all transactions executed by clearing members are registered with MDCH, which then becomes the central counterparty. To preserve the integrity of the exchange, all clearing members post initial/variation margins, lodge a security deposit, and contribute to a clearing fund.

28.5   PRODUCT OFFERINGS

Though the "pre-MDEX" KLCE featured a number of commodity contracts, most were delisted as part of the merger process. As a result, MDEX has acquired more of a financial character, listing and trading futures and options on the country's main financial benchmarks. In the fixed income sector MDEX trades (see Table 28.1):

- Futures on short-term interest rates, including 3-month KLIBOR
- Futures on medium-term interest rates, including 5-year Malaysian government securities

In the equity sector, the exchange lists (see Table 28.2):

- Futures and options on the main Malaysian equity index, the KLSE CI

In the commodity sector, MDEX lists (see Table 28.3):

- Futures on crude palm oil

Table 28.1   MDEX's fixed income derivatives

Reference	Futures	Options
KLIBOR (3 month)	✓	–
Malaysian government securities (5 year)	✓	–

Table 28.2   MDEX's equity derivatives

Reference	Futures	Options
KLSE CI index	✓	✓

Table 28.3   MDEX's commodity derivatives

Reference	Futures	Options
Crude palm oil	✓	–

28.6   REGULATION

MDEX's activities, as well as those of MDCH and all MDCH clearing members, are regulated by the Securities Commission (SC), which operates under the authority of the Malaysian Ministry of Finance and the Futures Industry Act of 1993 (as amended in 1995). The SC specifies all exchange rules and audits for compliance on a regular basis.

28.7   WEBSITE

The MDEX website provides details on contract specifications and data/price data sources: www.mdex.com.my

South African Futures Exchange (SAFEX) – South Africa

29.1 BACKGROUND

The South African Futures Exchange (SAFEX) traces its origins to the 1980s when Rand Merchant Bank (RMB), one of South Africa's leading financial institutions, sponsored informal trading in "standardized" bond and equity contracts – acting as a de facto exchange, clearinghouse, and market-maker. Realizing the value of the products that were being traded, but desiring a more robust environment, 21 local financial institutions joined together in September 1988 to create the all-electronic SAFEX and the Safex Clearing Company (SAFCOM). Preparatory work followed, and in early 1990 SAFEX and SAFCOM were ready to take over financial futures trading from RMB. In August 1990 the new exchange and clearinghouse received authorization from the South African government under the Financial Market Control Act of 1990, and formal trading commenced. The earliest contracts traded on SAFEX were based on 3-month banker's acceptances, the long bond, the dollar price of gold, and three Johannesburg Stock Exchange (JSE) indexes; in 1995 SAFEX added an agricultural division to offer commodity futures on maize and wheat. Over the next few years the exchange continued its product development efforts, adding new financial and agricultural products at regular intervals (e.g. options on futures, individual equity options, and various agricultural options; in 1999 SAFEX abandoned equity options in favor of stock futures and options on stock futures).

In May 2001 SAFEX received a purchase offer from the JSE, which was interested in bringing the local cash and derivative markets closer together and increasing operating efficiencies. In late 2001 JSE became sole owner of SAFEX, but agreed to retain the exchange's branding, clearinghouse, and financial/agricultural divisions.

SAFEX successfully built a "ground up" derivative operation in less than a decade, and then merged with another major local forum to achieve a greater competitive advantage. Considering the themes of Chapter 2, we note that SAFEX:

- Is organized as a "for-profit" commercial company
- Has embraced the concept of mergers (e.g. its own sale to JSE, under the proviso that it retains its name and branding)
- Operates strictly on an electronic basis
- Has actively developed new types of derivative contracts and is represented across a broad product spectrum

29.2 CORPORATE STRUCTURE

SAFEX operates as a wholly owned, commercial subsidiary of the JSE, while SAFCOM is wholly owned by SAFEX. The JSE itself, originally founded in 1887, is organized as a "for-profit" corporation.

29.3   TECHNOLOGY PLATFORM/INFRASTRUCTURE

Trading on SAFEX has always been conducted electronically, suggesting that technology has been an important part of the exchange's strategy. The exchange introduced a new technology platform – the SAFEX Advanced Trading System (ATS) – in May 1996 and has enhanced it on a regular basis since that time. The ATS functions as a deal booking and price publication system. Through deal booking, members can execute electronically deals agreed by phone, or they can use "point and click" technology and accept bids or offers shown on-screen. Through price publication, members can publish prices where they will bid or offer, or request pricing information from other members. Trades executed through ATS flow electronically to SAFCOM for clearing and settlement.

29.4   CLEARING

All futures and futures options trades executed through SAFEX are cleared through SAFCOM, which becomes a counterparty on every transaction submitted by a member. To ensure the safety of the exchange, SAFCOM reviews the financial standing of all clearing members (and sets limits for each one), requires margins on all transactions and member contributions to a guarantee fund.

29.5   PRODUCT OFFERINGS

SAFEX lists and trades derivatives that relate to South Africa's primary equity, fixed income, and commodity references. Within the equity sector, the exchange lists (see Table 29.1):

- Futures and futures options on individual South African stocks
- Futures and futures options on the JSE index and select JSE subindexes

In the fixed income/currency sector, SAFEX's products are centered on the country's key benchmarks, including (see Table 29.2):

- Futures and futures options on short-term interest rates, including 3-month JIBAR (Johannesburg Interbank Acceptance Rate)
- Futures and futures options on long-term interest rates, including 5- to 25-year government bonds and a government bond index
- Futures and futures options on US dollar/South African rand FX

SAFEX's commodity contacts are based on the country's key agricultural products, including (see Table 29.3):

Table 29.1   SAFEX's equity derivatives

Reference	Futures	Futures options
Individual stocks	✓	✓
JSE All share index	✓	✓
JSE Industrial index	✓	✓
JSE Mining index	✓	✓
JSE Financials index	✓	✓

Table 29.2   SAFEX's fixed income/currency derivatives

Reference	Futures	Futures options
JIBAR (3 month)	✓	✓
Government bonds (5 year, RS150)	✓	✓
Government bonds (10 year, RS153)	✓	✓
Government bonds (15 year, RS157)	✓	✓
Government bonds (25 year, RS186)	✓	✓
Government bond index	✓	✓
US dollar/South African rand	✓	✓

Table 29.3   SAFEX's commodity derivatives

Reference	Futures	Futures options
White maize	✓	✓
Yellow maize	✓	✓
Wheat	✓	✓
Sunflower seeds	✓	✓
Soybeans	✓	–

• Futures and futures options on white maize, yellow maize, wheat, sunflower seeds, and soybeans

29.6   REGULATION

The Reserve Bank of South Africa (RBSA) regulates the activities of SAFEX and SAFCOM (as well as JSE, as parent of the exchange and its clearer). The RBSA authorizes SAFEX's activities and requires adherence to established rules; it audits the exchange for compliance on a regular basis.

29.7   WEBSITE

The SAFEX website provides details on contract specifications and data/price data sources: www.safex.co.za

Electronic Communication Networks and Electronic Exchanges

OVERVIEW OF STRUCTURE

In the first two chapters of this book we discussed the emergence of technology in the world of exchange-traded derivatives and how it has fostered a new level of competition. In this section we review some of the electronic exchanges that have emerged in this new environment. In examining the structure and scope of a small number of electronic exchanges we notice that they are true hybrids: centralized, technology-enabled forums capable of offering standardized execution and trading and, in some cases, clearing and information services. While they still lack the trading liquidity that characterizes the leading exchanges, they represent an important alternative for those seeking risk management products and are forcing established exchanges to focus on improving their own efficiencies and flexibility – hopefully to the benefit and advantage of all users.

Not surprisingly, many electronic trading platforms have been created over the past few years in order to capture a portion of the financial markets in general, and the derivatives market in particular. Some of these platforms appear viable, some are questionable, and still others have already "crashed and burned." While it is difficult to predict ex-ante which will survive in an extremely competitive environment, we propose that the ultimate winners may be those offering superior services based on:

- Efficient execution
- Broad product choice
- Tight pricing
- Secure clearing and
- Friendly, powerful technologies

Our intent in this section is not to review all of the electronic trading platforms that are dealing in exchange-traded activities. Rather, we select several different forums that appear to be challenging established notions of what an exchange-traded market should actually be; each of the forums we consider approaches the market in a slightly different fashion, highlighting distinct business models that can be employed. In this section we review:

- Intercontinental Exchange (ICE), a true hybrid exchange that is combining OTC and exchange-traded products and clearing services in an advanced electronic environment

- BrokerTec Futures Exchange (BTEX), a regulated platform developed by established financial institutions to focus on a narrow segment of the market
- OneChicago (OC), an exchange created through the cooperation of three well-known competitors, that offers new products through an all-electronic delivery mechanism
- International Securities Exchange (ISE), a exchange that has transformed its long-established operations quite dramatically, converting from a "traditional" exchange to one featuring leading-edge technologies and a flexible product platform
- European Electricity Exchange (EEX), an exchange that has combined and restructured existing marketplaces in order to create a niche in a deregulating industry

Though the business approaches may be different, the end goals are largely the same: to compete actively and effectively in the listed derivative market through the use of advanced technology and alternate business models.

30

Intercontinental Exchange (ICE)

30.1 BACKGROUND

US-based Intercontinental Exchange (ICE) is one of the "new breed" of purely electronic exchanges that draws on leading technology, conventional trading, and cooperative partnerships. ICE, headquartered in Atlanta, was established in 2000 by seven leading energy companies and financial institutions. The original partners provided ICE with the liquidity it needed to start trading and were ultimately joined by another seven companies who supplied additional equity and liquidity. Though not strictly a "traditional" exchange (i.e. one dealing in standard futures and options), ICE offers standardized dealing terms on certain spot and OTC contracts (e.g. swaps, options, forwards, and spreads based on liquid references such as WTI crude and Henry Hub gas); as such, its standardized OTC contracts begin to look like exchange futures and options. Unlike conventional exchanges, ICE features no membership structure; authorized users can trade on the platform and simply pay a fee per contract.

In order to build on its initial trading success ICE has entered into various alliances. For instance, ICE and LCH have created a venture to clear European OTC energy derivative contracts (e.g. UK gas, French and German power and coal, through the EnClear platform); not only does the LCH endeavor provide additional revenues, it draws in more users by giving them the ability to mitigate the effects of credit risk in the OTC market. ICE has also negotiated a similar alliance with BOTCC to clear US OTC power contracts. ICE is also sole owner of the IPE, the London-based energy futures and options exchange discussed in Chapter 6. Following its acquisition of IPE, ICE put forth a plan to migrate IPE's contracts to a new electronic platform and has since invested considerable capital in an effort to realize the plan; its ultimate goal is to offer customers a broad range of OTC and listed products through a flexible platform.

ICE serves, in many ways, as a model for future exchange endeavors. Considering the themes of Chapter 2, we note that the exchange:

- Is organized as a "for-profit" commercial company (though one that is still privately held by the partner companies)
- Has fully embraced the concept of mergers and alliances (e.g. its acquisition of IPE, its alliances with LCH and BOTCC)
- Operates solely in an electronic environment
- Offers additional clearing and nontrading services to supplement its revenues
- Has been active in creating new types of "standardized" OTC and listed products

30.2 CORPORATE STRUCTURE

ICE is a private corporation owned by 14 corporate partners, including AEP, Aquila, Duke, El Paso Energy, Reliant Energy, Mirant, Royal Dutch Shell, TotalFina Elf, Continental Power Exchange, BP Amoco, Deutsche Bank, Goldman Sachs, Morgan Stanley and Société Générale. IPE Holdings, the owner of the IPE, is itself wholly owned by ICE.

30.3   TECHNOLOGY PLATFORM/INFRASTRUCTURE

ICE features a comprehensive technology platform that allows users to access a broad range of products through a flexible, open access interface (which permits a considerable amount of user-defined customization). The core of the platform, the Commodity Trading System (CTS), supports trade execution, order book management, trade matching, credit counterparty filtering and reporting; the exchange is supplementing CTS's functionality with a "paperless back office" platform that allows for electronic straight-through-processing. In 2002 ICE contracted with financial technology provider eSpeed to employ its "Wagner patent" technology process, which ensures US clients have digital access to IPE's contracts through the ICE platform.

30.4   CLEARING

Since ICE's primary business is OTC-based, and the exchange acts as agent rather than principal between counterparties, buyers/sellers must bear one another's credit risk. Only if ICE-provided clearing services are used does the ICE-sponsored clearing venture become a counterparty to a transaction. As noted above, in August 2001 ICE and LCH created a clearing alliance for OTC transactions, allowing market participants to face the new clearing service rather than each other – this mitigates credit risks and permits customers to manage their exchange-traded and OTC positions on a portfolio basis. Under the clearing arrangement, margins on ICE's OTC products are set by the LCH and all clearing processes follow LCH's well-established model.[1] The BOTCC arrangement, based on US power contracts, operates in a similar fashion. IPE trades, as indicated in Chapter 6, are cleared through the LCH, with every buyer and seller facing the LCH as a counterparty once trades are matched. It should be noted that as a result of its 100% ownership of IPE, ICE is also an indirect minority owner of LCH.

30.5   PRODUCT OFFERINGS

ICE features a broad range of commodity-based derivatives, including:

- Contracts on energy (oil, natural gas, electric power)
- Contracts on precious metals
- Contracts on weather

The products listed by ICE are not strictly exchange traded futures and options; they are "standardized" OTC forwards, swaps and options, based on US and international references, with enough common features that some liquidity can develop as customers trade in and out of their positions (see Table 30.1). Contracts are available in both physical and financial form.

30.6   REGULATION

ICE is an SRO that oversees its own operations based on guidelines and regulations set forth by the CFTC and the NFA. The CFTC is an independent government agency established in 1974 to administer the federal commodity laws. CFTC has authority over futures, options, and leveraged contracts involving commodities and indexes of securities. It is responsible for

---

[1] As part of the process the LCH applied with the CFTC to become a Derivatives Clearing Organization.

Table 30.1 ICE's commodity derivatives

Reference	Forwards, swaps	Options
Oil	✓	✓
Natural gas	✓	✓
Electricity	✓	✓
Weather*	✓	✓
Gold	✓	✓
Silver	✓	✓

*Based on temperature indexes in select reference cities.

reviewing terms/conditions of national markets/contracts, ensuring that contracts meet normal market flows and conducting daily surveillance. CFTC works closely with, and audits, the NFA.

30.7 WEBSITE

The ICE website provides details on contract specifications and data/price data sources: www.intcx.com

31
BrokerTec Futures Exchange (BTEX)

31.1 BACKGROUND

BrokerTec Futures Exchange (BTEX) was created in 2001 by several large financial institutions as a purely electronic marketplace for trading US Treasury futures; the primary sponsor of the project is BrokerTec, a large interdealer broker in government securities. The exchange received regulatory approval (e.g. Designated Contract Market status and approval as a Derivatives Clearing Organization) in June 2001 and launched operations several months later with futures trading on several US Treasury benchmarks (product expansion plans call for Treasury options trading in the medium term). In order to increase efficiencies and attract more trading volume, BTEX's clearing arm and Government Securities Clearing Corp (GSCC) entered into a cross-margining arrangement in April 2002 which permits cross-margining of buy/sell and repo positions held in GSCC against futures positions carried on BTEX.

BTEX is a relatively new exchange that has been created from the "ground up" by emphasizing regulatory authorization, robust technologies, and specialized product focus. Considering the themes of Chapter 2, we note that the exchange:

- Is organized as a "for-profit" commercial company (though one that is still privately held)
- Operates solely in an electronic environment, through a robust and flexible platform
- Is beginning to form strategic alliances (e.g. GSCC cross-margining) in order to build a larger base of business

31.2 CORPORATE STRUCTURE

BTEX was established as an independent company operating within the BrokerTec group; the BrokerTec Clearing Corp (BCC) unit, in turn, is wholly owned by BTEX. In mid-2002 BrokerTec received a purchase offer from ICAP plc, a large UK-based financial broker, and agreed to merge its operations with ICAP's. BTEX was not included as part of the agreement and remains independently owned and managed (though it has entered into long-term service agreements with BrokerTec to use the firm's technology and infrastructure).

31.3 TECHNOLOGY PLATFORM/INFRASTRUCTURE

Since BTEX was designed as an electronic trading platform, it features robust technology that is both flexible and scalable. The main execution and trade matching system is built on OM's platform, which has been customized to meet BTEX's needs. The system emphasizes open architecture that lets members access the OM-powered trading engine through proprietary front-end modules, third-party-supplied APIs, or BTEX's own customized OM CLICK front-end. The open structure also permits straight-through-processing and real-time feeds for position and margin management. The exchange has purposely designed the platform with

Table 31.1   BTEX's fixed income derivatives

Reference	Futures	Options
US Treasury notes (5 year)	✓	–
US Treasury notes (10 year)	✓	–
US Treasury bonds	✓	–

enough flexibility to allow it to speed order matching times as volumes increase and add new products as they are introduced.

31.4   CLEARING

Clearing of futures trades executed on BTEX passes through two stages. In the first stage, BTEX's clearing subsidiary, BCC, backed by member margins and a $70mn guaranty fund, acts as central counterparty on all transactions. In the second stage BOTCC, which clears for NYBOT (see Chapter 15), provides BCC with clearing and processing services.

31.5   PRODUCT OFFERINGS

Given BTEX's relatively short history, it is no surprise that its product scope is still rather limited. Though the exchange intends to add more contracts over the medium term, it has also indicated that it intends to remain focused on its key specialization, e.g. US fixed income futures and options. The exchange currently lists (see Table 31.1):

• Futures on medium- and long-term interest rates, including 5-, 10-, and 30-year US Treasury securities

31.6   REGULATION

Since BTEX is authorized as a Designated Contract Market it is regulated by the CFTC (as outlined above). The exchange also adheres to the oversight and surveillance criteria set forth by the NFA.

31.7   WEBSITE

The BTEX website provides details on contract specifications and data/price data sources: www.btecfutures.com

32

OneChicago (OC)

32.1 BACKGROUND

Following the repeal of the Shad Johnson Agreement in 2000, which prohibited US trading of futures on single stocks, the Chicago complex – CME, CBOT, and CBOE – joined forces to create a new, electronic joint venture exchange offering futures on single stocks and narrow, industry-based, indexes. The intent was to leverage the market expertise of the exchanges, as well as their increasingly sophisticated technologies and clearing functions, to create a "cooperative" marketplace. Since all three exchanges had expressed interest in trading stock futures following deregulation, there was concern that the market would become fragmented; far better, in the view of exchange officials, to work cooperatively, thereby ensuring a deep and liquid market. After several delays, OC started futures trading in late 2002 with contracts on over 70 large capitalization stocks and 8 narrow indexes; further stocks and indexes will be added over time. In contrast to the physical trading that characterizes all three Chicago exchanges, OC is entirely electronic – it features no trading floor or open-outcry trading.

OC serves as a good example of a cooperative exchange venture that might become more prevalent in the future. Considering the themes of Chapter 2, we note that the exchange:

- Is organized as a "for-profit" commercial company (privately held by its partner companies)
- Has fully embraced the concept of alliances (e.g. by definition, as it is the product of an alliance between three otherwise fierce competitors)
- Operates solely in an electronic environment

32.2 CORPORATE STRUCTURE

OC is a private, for-profit company that is jointly owned by the CME, CBOE, and CBOT. Despite ties to the three exchanges, OC has its own independent management team and corporate accountabilities.

32.3 TECHNOLOGY PLATFORM/INFRASTRUCTURE

OC makes use of technologies that the various Chicago exchanges have developed for their own business needs (see Chapters 11–13 for additional information). Members and participants can use a broad range of interfaces – indeed, the entire OC architecture is based on front- and back-office flexibility. For instance, in the front-end users can execute trades through CBOEdirect, CME's GLOBEX 2, independently developed APIs, or proprietary software. Trade processing can be accomplished through CBOE Trade Matching or GLOBEX 2 (though all order matching eventually passes through CBOEdirect), while clearing occurs through the OCC's platform or CME's Clearing 21.

Table 32.1 OC's equity derivatives

Reference	Futures	Options
Single stocks	✓	–
Airline index	✓	–
Biotech index	✓	–
Computer index	✓	–
Defense index	✓	–
Investment bank index	✓	–
Oil services index	✓	–
Retail index	✓	–
Semiconductor index	✓	–

32.4 CLEARING

The OCC acts as principal clearinghouse for OC futures trades, meaning members face the OCC as counterparty (see Chapter 12 for additional detail). However, users can also elect to clear through the CME, and members that belong to both the OCC and CME can cross-margin their positions for more efficient management of funds.

32.5 PRODUCT OFFERINGS

OC's sole mission is to provide clients with trading and risk management opportunities in the "narrow" equity markets, through futures. As such, the exchange does not offer option contracts (which is the preserve of the CBOE) or contracts on broad indexes (which remains the domain of the three parent exchanges). OC lists (see Table 32.1):

- Futures on individual US stocks
- Futures on narrow indexes, including airlines, biotechnology, computers, defense, investment banks, oil services, retailers, and semiconductors

32.6 REGULATION

OC is an SRO that oversees its own operations based on guidelines and regulations set forth by the CFTC and the NFA.

32.7 WEBSITE

The OC website provides details on contract specifications and data/price data sources: www.onechicago.com

International Securities Exchange (ISE)

33.1 BACKGROUND

The International Securities Exchange (ISE) was originally established in the US in the 1970s as a national securities exchange specializing in US equity options trading (eight options exchanges were initially created, though that number has since declined to five). ISE is not, therefore, a "new" exchange from a chronological perspective; however, since it has dramatically changed its corporate structure and operating methods in recent years we consider it a model of what other exchanges might look like in the near or medium term.

ISE became the first exchange in the US to trade options electronically through an auction market method – instituting its electronic access membership as early as 1992 – and converted all of its operations to a new, leading-edge electronic platform in May 2000 (which it has since upgraded). Since its founding ISE has grown to become the third largest US options forum (after CBOE and ASE); unlike other US exchanges, however, it is focused solely on individual equity options and features no index options. Since ISE operates on an electronic basis, it has no floor brokers; all orders are input by registered broker/dealers directly into the electronic order book. The broker/dealers act as market-makers, providing liquidity in specific options.

ISE is a relatively unique example of an established forum that has dramatically altered aspects of its operations in order to compete more effectively against open-outcry markets and ECNs. Returning to the themes of Chapter 2, we note that the exchange:

- Is organized as a "for-profit" commercial company (privately held by its partner companies, though expecting to float publicly in the future)
- Operates solely in an electronic environment

33.2 CORPORATE STRUCTURE

ISE was organized as a mutually owned organization from its creation in 1973 until May 2002, at which time it demutualized. The exchange is now structured as a privately held company but expects to float its shares publicly in the future in order to raise more capital for expansion.

33.3 TECHNOLOGY PLATFORM/INFRASTRUCTURE

ISE's technology is based primarily on OM's architecture, adapted to suit the specific needs of the exchange. The exchange uses a version of OM's TORQUE platform for front-end quotes and market information, and CLICK as an order input and routing mechanism. The entire platform was upgraded in late 2001 to accommodate greater processing speed and transaction complexity (including options spreads, straddles, and so on).

Table 33.1   ISE's equity derivatives

Reference	Futures	Options
Individual stocks	–	✓

33.4   CLEARING

All transactions executed on the ISE are cleared directly through the exchange, which acts as a central counterparty on all trades. To ensure exchange integrity, members are required to post appropriate margins and contribute to a guarantee fund.

33.5   PRODUCT OFFERINGS

ISE's product offerings are limited to options on single stocks; it commenced with a handful of listings and has gradually added more as interest and volume have expanded. The exchange intends to add new equity options over time, but is not planning expansion into other asset classes (see Table 33.1).

33.6   REGULATION

The ISE's operations are regulated by both the SEC and the CFTC. In addition, the exchange has implemented its own market surveillance process.

33.7   WEBSITE

The ISE website provides details on contract specifications and data/price data sources: www.iseoptions.com

34

European Electricity Exchange (EEX)

34.1 BACKGROUND

The European Electricity Exchange (EEX) was formally created in 2002, when two of Germany's competing power exchanges, the Leipzig Power Exchange (LPX) and the original Frankfurt-based EEX, merged into a new, all-electronic, entity. LPX and the original EEX were both founded in 2000 to offer risk management services for participants in the deregulating German power market (the single largest marketplace for electricity in Europe, after Russia). LPX and EEX started their operations by trading in spot power for both base and peak load periods; in spring 2001 EEX added standard power futures to its activities. The combined platform now trades spot and futures contracts based on the German Physical Electricity index (Phelix); additional power-related contracts are expected to be added in the future.

EEX is an exchange that has created for itself a niche through a key merger and special focus on a new and important market. Considering the themes of Chapter 2, we note that the exchange:

- Is organized as a "for-profit" commercial company (privately held by its partner companies)
- Has fully embraced the concept of mergers (e.g. its own combination of LPX and the original EEX)
- Has expanded its clearing services to the OTC market
- Operates solely in an electronic environment

34.2 CORPORATE STRUCTURE

EEX is organized as a private corporation under the laws of Germany; the primary exchange and clearing division are known as collectively as EEX AG. Eurex, the European derivatives exchange discussed in Chapter 4, is a minority owner of EEX.

34.3 TECHNOLOGY PLATFORM/INFRASTRUCTURE

When creating a delivery and execution platform for its products and services, EEX opted not to build its own infrastructure, but to make use of Eurex's proven technologies. As such, all EEX front-, middle-, and back-office functions flow through a version of the Eurex platform that has been adapted to handle the specific requirements of spot and futures power trading. The EEX version accepts orders and checks for immediate execution opportunities; those not executed are passed to the order book where the matching engine searches by price and time priorities. Buyers and sellers automatically receive execution information and trade confirmations. EEX's platform supports open interfaces to connect the exchange engine to third-party APIs or proprietary interfaces.

Table 34.1   EEX's commodity derivatives

Reference	Futures	Options
Phelix base load	✓	–
Phelix peak load	✓	–

34.4   CLEARING

EEX AG, the main exchange holding company, clears all transactions and thus acts as central counterparty for every buyer and seller. The exchange is backed by the resources of approved clearing members, primarily large banks that have clearing licenses, who are required to post margins on all transactions and act as a "first line of defense" in the event of default (taking over the positions of any counterparty that fails). Participants that do not have clearing licenses must route their orders through a clearing member.

In addition to clearing EEX futures contracts, the exchange also clears OTC contracts that are identical in characteristic to its standardized contracts (e.g. same reference and maturity); these trades are collected through the EEX EFP facility and cleared through normal channels.

34.5   PRODUCT OFFERINGS

Though EEX intends to expand into other energy-related derivatives in the future, its operations are still limited to power. Specifically, the exchange offers (see Table 34.1):

* Futures on base load and peak load power referenced through the Phelix index

34.6   REGULATION

Regulation of recognized exchanges in Germany is the responsibility of individual state governments; in the case of EEX the Saxony Ministry for Economics and Labor is responsible for overseeing EEX's activities and making sure that it complies with Exchange Supervisory Authority decrees, including those detailed under the German Stock Exchange Act. In addition, since derivative contracts fall under the purview of the Federal Banking Supervisory Office, the EEX must adhere to regulations promulgated by the Banking Office; the Federal Authority for Financial Services Supervision also ensures that EEX (and other exchanges) are not involved in manipulation of market prices.

34.7   WEBSITE

The EEX website provides details on contract specifications and data/price data sources: www.eex.de

Summary

The exchange-traded derivatives sector of the twenty-first century is shaping up to be radically different than the one that existed through the latter part of the twentieth century. As we have noted throughout this book, many forces are at work in reshaping the competitive landscape; the most important of these forces include:

- Deregulation
- Globalization
- Product/market competition
- New technologies
- Disintermediation and
- Commercialization

As a result of these forces, the exchange community has attempted to redefine itself – to tactically and strategically redirect investment, initiatives, and direction – in order to remain vital and relevant in the financial sphere of the twenty-first century. Pressure to adapt has been, and will continue to be, considerable.

As we have noted, success in redefining exchange operations leads to new business opportunities, revenue growth, and shareholder (or member) profitability – all of which permit an exchange to prosper. Failure to adapt is damaging, and can lead to a decline in business, loss of independence through acquisition, abandonment of products, and – in the extreme – outright closure.

Though different exchanges have accepted the challenge in different ways, most have come to recognize the need to focus on one, or more, of the following tactical and strategic changes in order to remain relevant in the new environment:

- Adapting corporate structure
  - Demutualizing
  - Floating publicly
  - Merging or acquiring
  - Forming alliances/ventures
- Abandoning open-outcry trading (partially, if not completely)
- Implementing new technologies
- Enhancing market access and product choice
- Expanding clearing and settlement services

An examination of exchange activities since the mid-1990s reveals that many of the world's leading exchanges have accepted the realities of the new environment and realigned their operations in order to compete more effectively with the OTC and ECN sectors.

Table 1 summarizes the most significant changes made in recent years by the largest established and emerging exchanges.

Table 1 Summary of structural changes of major global exchanges

Exchange	Structural changes
BM&F	Created as a private "for-profit" company, acquired other exchanges, migrated partially to an electronic environment, introduced new products and services
BI	Consolidated cash/derivative markets, demutualized and floated publicly, migrated fully to an electronic environment
CBOE	Formed key alliances and joint ventures, migrated partially to an electronic environment, introduced new products and clearing services
CBOT	Formed key alliances and joint ventures, migrated partially to an electronic environment, introduced new products and clearing services
CME	Demutualized, formed key alliances and joint ventures, migrated partially to an electronic environment, introduced new products and clearing services
Eurex	Created as a private "for-profit" company, consolidated operations of two existing exchanges, migrated fully to an electronic environment
Euronext	Created as a public "for-profit" company, consolidated operations of three existing cash/derivative exchanges, acquired two other established exchanges, formed cross-exchange alliances, migrated fully to an electronic environment, introduced new products
HKEx	Consolidated cash/derivative markets, demutualized and floated publicly, migrated fully to an electronic environment
IPE	Sold operations to leading-edge ECN, migrated partially to an electronic environment
KOFEX	Migrated fully to an electronic environment, introduced new products
LIFFE	Demutualized and floated privately, sold exchange operations to larger exchange group, migrated fully to an electronic environment, introduced new products and services
LME	Demutualized, migrated partially to an electronic environment
MDEX	Consolidated cash/derivative markets, demutualized, migrated fully to an electronic environment
MEFF	Created as a private "for-profit" company, consolidated aspects of cash/derivative markets, migrated fully to an electronic environment, created cross-exchange alliances
Mexder	Created as a private "for-profit" company, migrated fully to an electronic environment
MX	Created as a private "for-profit" company, acquired other exchanges, migrated fully to an electronic environment
NYBOT	Created through mergers/consolidations, migrated partially to an electronic environment
NYMEX	Acquired other exchanges, formed cross-exchange alliances, migrated partially to an electronic environment, introduced new products and services
OM	Demutualized and floated publicly, acquired other exchanges, formed cross-exchange alliances, migrated fully to an electronic environment, introduced new products and services
OSE	Demutualized and floated publicly, migrated fully to an electronic environment, introduced new products
SAFEX	Sold operations to larger exchange group (consolidating cash/derivative markets), migrated fully to an electronic environment, introduced new products
SFE	Consolidated aspects of the cash/derivative markets, demutualized and floated publicly, acquired another exchange, formed cross-exchange alliances, migrated fully to an electronic environment, introduced new products and services
SGX	Consolidated cash/derivative markets, demutualized and floated publicly, migrated partially to an electronic environment, formed cross-exchange alliances, introduced new products
TGE	Acquired other exchanges, migrated fully to an electronic environment, introduced new products
TIFFE	Formed cross-exchange alliances, migrated fully to an electronic environment, introduced new products
TOCOM	Acquired other exchanges, migrated partially to an electronic environment, introduced new products
TSE	Demutualized, formed cross-exchange alliances, migrated fully to an electronic platform, introduced new products and services

At the risk of generalizing, it appears that major European exchanges have embraced the concepts of corporate/"for profit" status, electronic trading and cross-border alliances, mergers and acquisitions aggressively; many of them have also opted to consolidate national cash and derivative trading under single umbrellas. Major North American exchanges have actively developed new products and cooperative alliances, and implemented aspects of electronic trading, but continue to cling to open-outcry and, in some cases, mutual ownership. Japanese exchanges appear to be engaged in a game of "catch up": after several years of preserving the status quo, they have started investing in technologies and arranging cross-border alliances, but lag other forums in terms of new products, commitment to robust electronic platforms, and conversion to corporate status. Interestingly, Southeast Asia/Pacific Rim exchanges are at the leading edge of change, having, in many cases, combined cash and derivative markets, consolidated exchange operations, introduced new products, converted to corporate status, and abandoned physical trading.

As the marketplace for exchange-traded derivatives continues to change over the coming years – through national and cross-border exchange mergers, cash/derivative market consolidation, new technologies, regulatory clarification and liberalization, and so forth – the sector will undoubtedly evolve even further. Though exchange leaders have made considerable strides in refining their operations over the past decade, they will need to focus on further strategic changes in order to offer clients the best possible products and services and shareholders and members the best possible returns. By doing so, exchanges, and the products they offer, should continue to represent an important element of the global financial marketplace.

Glossary

Alternative Trading System (ATS): See Electronic communications network.

American option: An option that can be exercised at any time prior to, and including, the maturity date.

Application program interface (API): A software layer that connects network processes and platforms with proprietary or third-party "front-end" graphical user interfaces.

Arbitrage: A strategy, involving simultaneous purchase and sale of an underlying asset, which produces a riskless profit.

Backwardation: See normal backwardation.

Basis: The price differential between an underlying asset reference and a derivative contract used as a hedge; the basis arises from differences in supply/demand, reference indexes or friction costs (including financing, storage, insurance, transportation).

Basis point: One-hundredth of 1%, commonly used as a measure of interest rates.

Basis risk: The risk arising from differences in the basis between an asset and its derivative hedge.

Block trading facility (BTF): A facility offered by certain exchanges where two parties agree to cross (buy/sell) a large transaction away from the exchange in order not to skew prices; once a transaction is concluded through the facility it is registered with the exchange.

Business-to-business (B2B) exchange: An electronic commerce exchange where networks are used to connect institutional buyers and sellers of assets, goods, or services.

Butterfly: An option position, formed through long high and low strike options and short middle strike options (or vice versa for a short butterfly), that is taken when the market is expected to trade within a range. The payout of a long butterfly is similar to a short straddle without the extreme downside; the payout of a short butterfly is similar to a long straddle without the extreme upside.

Calendar spread: A position, taken in order to capitalize on perceived discrepancies in the forward market, where the purchaser buys a shorter-term contract and sells a longer-term contract, or vice versa. Also known as a time spread.

Call option: A contract that gives the buyer the right, but not the obligation, to purchase an underlying asset at a set strike price at some future date. In exchange for the right the buyer pays the seller an option premium payment.

Call spread: An option position created by buying and selling call options with the same expiry date but different strike prices (e.g. the purchaser of a call spread buys a closer-to-the-money call option and sells a farther out-of-the-money call option, the seller of a call spread does the reverse). The spread limits the gain/liability to an area defined by the two strikes.

Cheapest-to-deliver: An asset deliverable under a listed derivative contract that carries the lowest cost; by identifying the cheapest-to-deliver asset, profits can be maximized.

Clearing: A process where all exchange contracts traded during a trading session are registered and reassigned to the clearinghouse. Once reassigned the clearinghouse becomes the official trade counterparty.

Clearinghouse: A subsidiary or division of an exchange that is responsible for clearing listed trades, computing and collecting daily margins, and arranging for settlement of financial or physical assets underlying futures and options contracts. The credit risk normally associated with derivatives is neutralized as participants face the clearinghouse, rather than each other, as counterparty.

Clearing margin: Margin posted by a clearing member with the exchange.

Clearing member: An exchange member that is permitted to clear trades directly with the clearinghouse, and which can accept trades for clearing from nonclearing members.

Close-out: A process of establishing an equal and opposite derivative position in order to neutralize or offset the effect of an existing position.

Collar: A combination of a long call option/short put option or short call option/long put option with the same expiry date. The long position (which requires payment of premium) is intended to provide risk protection or speculative opportunity, while the short position (which results in receipt of option premium) helps defray, or eliminate, the cost of the long option. See also zero cost collar.

Collusion: An illegal practice where exchange members agree to execute a transaction at a prearranged price.

Commercial paper: Short-term, unsecured borrowing instruments for highly rated financial and industrial companies.

Commodity pool: A pool of investment funds, similar to a mutual fund or unit trust, that is invested in commodity futures and options.

Commodity trading advisor (CTA): An investment advisor that develops and executes investment strategies for commodity pools.

Condor: An option position, formed through long high and low strike options and short middle-high and middle-low strike options (or vice versa for a short condor), which is taken when the market is expected to trade within a range. The payout of a long condor is similar to a short strangle without the extreme downside; the payout of a short condor is similar to a long strangle without the extreme upside.

Contango: A market state where futures prices are above expected spot prices and fall as maturity approaches.

Contract month: The month on which futures and options contracts are offered for trading; some contracts are offered on a quarterly cycle (e.g. March, June, September, December), while very liquid contracts may be offered more frequently (e.g. monthly). (Some contracts are deliberately designed with short maturity periods, such as overnight or intraday; these, however, are exceptions rather than the norm.)

Convergence: The gradual drawing together of spot and futures prices as contract maturity approaches.

Convexity: A measure, along with duration, of the interest rate sensitivity of a fixed income instrument, such as a bond or a loan. Convexity measures the change in the duration of a bond for a given move in interest rates.

Correlation: The price relationship that exists between two underlying references, generally based on historical data. Perfect positive correlation ($+1$) means a unit change in the price of one reference leads to the same unit change in the price of the second; perfect negative correlation (-1) means they move in equal and opposite directions; correlation of 0 is another way of indicating the references are uncorrelated. Correlation is frequently used to determine hedge ratios.

Cost of carry: The future value of costs and benefits associated with maintaining a position (which typically includes the cost of financing, insurance, transportation, and/or storage, less any benefits derived from lending the asset). Cost of carry is used to determine theoretical futures prices.

Crack spread: A contract spread in the energy market that reflects the differential between the price of crude oil and the price of a refined product, such as gasoline or heating oil. (A similar concept, known as a spark spread, is found in the electricity markets, and reflects the differential between the price of natural gas and the price of electricity.)

Credit derivative: A derivative contract that is based on the credit risk of a reference counterparty. Credit derivatives are available in the form of default swaps/options (with payouts based on the default of a counterparty) or spread options (with payouts based on the credit spread movement of a counterparty).

Credit risk: The risk that a counterparty to a contractual obligation will fail to perform as expected under the terms of the contract, leading to a loss.

Cross-asset hedge: A proxy or substitute hedge used when a perfect match is not available. While a cross-asset hedge can remove directional risk it may leave residual basis risk.

Cross-margin agreement: An agreement between two or more exchanges that permits margin requirements to be computed on a net, rather than gross, basis. Such an agreement avoids "double counting" of margins for long and short positions, allowing more efficient use of assets.

Curve risk: The risk of loss arising from changes in the price of the reference asset at different maturity intervals.

Customer margin: Margin posted by the FCM or client with the clearing member to cover the requirements of trades that have been executed and covered by the member's clearing margins.

Dealer market ECN: An electronic communications network where clients face a sponsor as price-maker and counterparty.

Deliverable grade: The specific type and quality of asset (financial or physical) that must be delivered under the terms of the exchange futures or options contract.

Delivery date: The specific date(s) of an exchange contract period during which delivery of a physical asset can be made.

Delivery point: The specific location where a physical asset referenced through an exchange contract can be accepted for delivery or storage.

Delivery risk: The risk of loss arising from failure by one party to a contract to deliver cash or assets after it has already received assets or cash from the other party.

"Defaulter pays" model: A clearinghouse security model where exchange assets (e.g. margin) of the defaulting party are initially used to cover the loss; ultimately, however, the clearinghouse is likely to need enough capital to cover any residual loss.

Demutualization: The process of converting a mutual, member-owned, organization into a private or public company controlled by investors. Demutualization separates exchange membership from ownership.

Derivative: A contract that derives its value from some underlying reference asset. A derivative may be traded on an exchange or over-the-counter.

Directional risk: The risk of loss due to upward or downward moves in asset prices. Also known as market risk.

Electronic commerce: A sector of the economy based on conducting business in an electronic environment, through business models that rely on computers, networks, and telecommunications.

Electronic communications network (ECN): An electronic platform that is designed to accommodate electronic trading of financial or physical assets in either cash or derivative form.

Electronic portal: An integrated electronic interface where the sponsoring institution or exchange provides clients with a broad range of market information, research, pricing, analytics, and/or trade execution.

Electronic ticket: An electronically generated and communicated information "slate" used by certain exchanges to convey details of a trade; a typical electronic ticket is updated by relevant parties as new information is added during the trading and clearing process. The ticket ultimately represents a binding transaction.

Equity warrant: A long-term financial option contract written on single stocks, baskets, or indexes. Equity warrants are very similar to equity call and put options, except that they tend to have much longer maturities (e.g. 3–5 years). Certain stock and derivative exchanges list equity warrants as a supplement to their underlying securities or futures business.

European option: An option that can only be exercised on the maturity date.

Exchange: A central marketplace, approved by relevant regulatory authorities, which exists either in physical or electronic form. An exchange provides the facilities needed to bring together buyers and sellers and allow appropriate price discovery. An exchange does not set prices or trade for its own account.

Exchange for physical (EFP): A facility offered by certain exchanges where two parties can agree to exchange a futures contract for a physical asset at the agreed futures price quoted on the exchange. Before an EFP transaction can be concluded through the facility it must be registered with the exchange.

Exchange-traded derivative: a derivative contract (future, option, futures option) that is traded on a formal exchange. Also known as a listed derivative.

Exercise price: See strike price.

Expectations: A framework that relates theoretical futures prices to the expected spot price at contract maturity rather than the prevailing spot price. Under the expectations model, the current futures price is equal to the expected spot price at maturity.

Financial settlement: A derivative contract that requires settlement in financial/cash, rather than physical, terms.

Flexible exchange (flex) option: A standardized option contract that gives buyers and sellers a certain amount of flexibility in selecting key features, including strike price, exercise style, and maturity date.

Forward contract: A customized, over-the-counter contract requiring the future purchase or sale of a reference asset at a predetermined forward price. A forward contract features no intervening cash flows, simply a final cash exchange at the conclusion of the contract.

Front-running: An illegal practice where a floor trader executes a transaction in advance of a customer trade in order to capture favorable price movements.

Futures call: An exchange option contract giving the purchaser the right, but not the obligation, to buy a futures contract at a prespecified strike level.

Futures commission merchant (FCM): An intermediary standing between a client and clearing member that develops and executes client strategies, conveys information, and so forth. FCMs are the only entities, apart from clearinghouses, that can hold customer funds and may be structured as independent organizations or divisions of larger financial institutions. In the US, FCMs must meet certain minimum financial requirements (e.g. net capital) and must be a member of the National Futures Association.

Futures contract: A standardized contract traded on an exchange involving the future purchase or sale of a reference asset at a predetermined price. A futures contract features daily revaluation and settlement of margins.

Futures option: An exchange option contract giving the purchaser the right, but not the obligation, to buy or sell a futures contract at a prespecified strike level.

Futures put: An exchange option contract giving the purchaser the right, but not the obligation, to sell a futures contract at a prespecified strike level.

Hedge ratio: The result of a statistical process (e.g. linear regression) that indicates the price relationship between a reference asset and a proxy hedge contract; the ratio reflects how much of a derivative contract is needed to hedge the reference exposure.

Hedger: A party that seeks to minimize, or neutralize, risk through the use of derivative contracts.

Horizontal services: Clearinghouse services that are extended from one exchange to other exchanges.

Hybrid ECN: An electronic communications network that incorporates the features of both dealer market and regulated ECNs.

Illiquidity: Lack of contract activity (i.e. volume or turnover) resulting from insufficient interest by buyers and/or sellers. An illiquid market is characterized by large differences between buying prices (bids) and selling prices (offers), and often requires use of alternative hedging or speculating strategies that are more economical to execute.

In-the-money: An option that has current (or intrinsic) value, e.g. the spot price is greater than the strike price for a call option, or less than the strike price for a put option. It can be exercised for immediate financial gain.

Initial margin: Security (e.g. cash, letter of credit, certain high-quality securities) posted by the buyer and seller of exchange contracts at the inception of each transaction. Initial margin is typically computed based on the price volatility of the asset underlying the contract and is used to protect the clearinghouse against counterparty default. Also known as original margin.

Intermarket spread: A speculative derivative position that seeks to take advantage of price differences between two distinct, but related, markets/assets; the spread attempts only to capitalize on movements in the spread, or basis, rather than the absolute direction, of the references.

Intermediate: The process of standing between two parties to a financial transaction in order to supply a necessary service, such as transaction execution or credit risk mitigation.

Introducing broker: An intermediary standing between a client and an FCM that develops and executes client strategies. Since the broker cannot hold customer funds, it must deal through an FCM.

Last trading day: The final day on which trading in a given contract can occur.

Liquidity: A measure of contract activity. A liquid contract features strong buying and selling interest and small differences between buying prices (bids) and selling prices (offers). An illiquid contract features little turnover and large differences between bids and offers.

Long hedge: A long position in a derivative contract that seeks to protect a natural short position.

Long position: A purchased or owned position that benefits from price appreciation.

Low exercise price option (LEPO): An option with a strike price set very close to zero. By establishing a low strike price the option's value fluctuates very closely with that of the underlying reference asset.

Maintenance margin: The minimum margin each party to an exchange transaction must preserve. Once the maintenance margin level has been breached, variation margin must be posted.

Margin: Security (e.g. cash, letter of credit, certain high-quality securities) posted by the buyer and seller of an exchange transaction at the start of the trade (initial margin) and periodically thereafter (variation margin).

Mark-to-market: The daily process of revaluing exchange transactions based on closing prices. The revaluation process can lead to calling or returning of margin.

Mini contract: A contract designed primarily for use by retail customers. Minis are structurally identical to other exchange contracts but are offered in much smaller denominations that make them suitable for retail clients. Given their small size, minis are usually only traded through electronic mechanisms (even on physical exchanges).

Mutual Offset System (MOS): A formal arrangement between two exchanges where contracts initiated on one exchange can be transferred to, or closed out on, another exchange.

Mutual organization: A corporate structure where members, rather than external investors, own the organization.

Naked position: An outright long or short position that is not protected by an offsetting hedge.

Nearby contract: The current, or closest, contract on a reference asset, often the most actively traded.

Next nearby contract: The second closest contract on a reference asset.

Nonclearing member: An exchange member that is not permitted to clear trades directly with the clearinghouse; nonclearing members must clear trades through a clearing member.

Noncompetitive trading: An illegal practice where a floor trader executes a transaction without exposing it to the market at large.

Normal backwardation: A market state where futures prices are below expected spot prices and rise as maturity approaches.

Notional value: The dollar value of a derivative contract, typically determined by multiplying contract size and closing price.

Open interest: A measure of contract liquidity, generally computed as the number of outstanding futures or options contracts.

Open-outcry: A trading process/mechanism based on physical interaction between floor traders. Through verbal discussion or hand-signals floor traders agree on purchase and sale terms.

Option: A derivative contract giving the purchaser the right, but not the obligation, to purchase (call option) or sell (put option) an underlying asset at a predetermined strike price and date.

Out-of-the-money: An option that has no current (or intrinsic) value, e.g. the spot price is less than the strike price for a call option, or more than the strike price for a put option. It cannot be exercised for immediate financial gain.

Out-trade: A trade that cannot be reconciled during the clearing process as a result of discrepancies between buyer and seller.

Over-the-counter (OTC) derivative: A customized derivative contract.

Physical settlement: A derivative contract that requires settlement in physical, rather than cash/financial, terms.

Premium payment: A cash payment made by an option buyer to an option seller. By accepting the premium, the seller is obligated to perform under the terms of the option contract when the buyer exercises its rights.

Present value: A financial computation where a future cash flow or financial amount is discounted back to current terms through use of a relevant interest rate.

Price discovery: The process of bringing together buyers and sellers so that a fair price for a reference asset can be determined without manipulation or price controls.

Price limit: A cap placed on an exchange contract that limits the amount of price movement that can occur during a particular trading session.

Put option: A contract that gives the purchaser the right, but not the obligation, to sell an underlying asset at a set strike price at some future date. In exchange for the right, the buyer pays the seller an option premium payment.

Put spread: An option position created by buying and selling put options with the same expiry date but different strike prices (e.g. the purchaser of a put spread buys a closer-to-the-money put option and sells a farther out-of-the-money put option, the seller of a put spread does the reverse). The spread limits the gain/liability to an area defined by the two strikes.

Regulated ECN: An electronic communications network that is authorized by regulatory authorities to operate as an exchange.

Regulatory consolidation: Combining different national regulators under a single "umbrella" in order to ensure unified treatment of markets, products, and forums that provide similar/identical benefits.

Regulatory cooperation: Assistance between regulators on items of mutual interest – within, and across, national boundaries.

Regulatory harmonization: The process of making certain that rules for exchanges are generally similar from country to country; this can help minimize cross-border regulatory arbitrage.

Regulatory parity: The process of creating a "level playing field," or equivalent rules, for marketplaces that perform similar functions.

Repurchase agreement: A financial contract that effectively acts as a collateralized funding mechanism: the repurchase agreement (repo) party enters into a simultaneous agreement to sell, and then repurchase, securities with a reverse repurchase agreement (reverse repo) party. While the reverse repo party holds the securities, the repo party has use of the cash proceeds (i.e. it has been granted a loan).

Rolling hedge: A hedge strategy, generally applied to long-term positions, that requires the hedger to purchase or sell the most liquid contract, close it out prior to maturity, reestablish it with the next contract, and so forth, until the final exposure being protected enters the liquid (or active) part of the market. The hedger effectively "rolls" the hedge from one contract to the next. Also known as a "stack and roll" hedge.

Sector options: Option contracts that reference entire industry sectors (e.g. banks, automobiles, telecoms).

Short hedge: A short position in a derivative contract that seeks to protect a natural long position.

Short position: A sold or borrowed position that benefits from price depreciation.

Softs: A range of commodity derivatives that normally includes cocoa, coffee, sugar and orange juice and so forth.

Speculator: A participant that uses derivatives to take advantage of market movements (e.g. direction, basis, curve, volatility) in order to generate a profit.

Spot market: The current, or cash, market for an asset.

Spot price: The price of an asset in the cash, rather than forward/futures, market.

Squeeze: A lack of deliverable grade assets into a futures/options contract that can lead to price distortions.

"Stack and roll" hedge: See rolling hedge.

Straddle: A combination of a put option and a call option with the same strike price and expiry date. The purchaser of a straddle attempts to protect against changes in market volatility rather than market direction.

Strangle: A combination of a put option and a call option with the same expiry date but different strike prices. A strangle is similar to a straddle, except that the purchaser generally expects a greater amount of volatility.

Strike price: The agreed price at which an option can be exercised. Also known as exercise price.

Strip hedge: A hedge, comprised of sequential derivative contracts, that is designed to approximate the sequential cash flows of the underlying reference asset.

"Survivor pays" model: A clearinghouse security model where risk and losses arising from a counterparty default are pooled and shared among clearinghouse members.

Swap: A customized, over-the-counter contract requiring the exchange of periodic cash flows until final maturity. Swaps can be purchased or sold on a broad range of financial and commodity references.

Synthetic long position: A combination of a long call option and a short put option, struck at the same price, which replicates the economics of a long position.

Synthetic short position: A combination of a long put option and a short call option, struck at the same price, which replicates the economics of a short position.

Tailing a hedge: A process where a proxy hedge is discounted using a present value factor in order to take account of the fact that exchange-traded positions are marked-to-market and settled every day.

Theoretical futures price: The "no-arbitrage" price of a contract, equal to the spot price plus the cost of carry.

Tick value: The price increment of an exchange-traded derivative contract.

Time spread: See calendar spread.

Trading units: See notional value.

Variation margin: Incremental security (e.g. cash, letter of credit, certain high-quality securities) posted by the buyer or seller of an exchange contract as the position is revalued each day. Variation margin is called once the maintenance margin level has been breached.

Vertical services: Clearinghouse services that are extended from traditional futures/options clearing to cash and over-the-counter derivatives clearing.

Volatility: A measure of financial/physical asset price movement. Volatility is often measured in statistical terms, such as standard deviation (variation around the mean, or average, value).

Zero cost collar: A collar strategy where the premium paid on the long call or put is precisely offset by the premium received on the short put or call, resulting in zero cost. See also collar.

Selected References

Selected books and articles

Ahn, J., J. Cai, and Y.L. Cheung (2002), "What Moves German Bund Futures Contracts on Eurex," *Journal of Futures Markets*, Vol. 5.

Banks, E. (1996), *Asia Pacific Derivative Markets*, London: Macmillan.

Banks, E. (2001), *e-Finance*, New York: John Wiley.

Chance, D. and R. Trippi (eds) (1993), *Advances in Futures and Options Research*, Vol. 6, Greenwich, Connecticut: JAI Press.

Chance, D. and R. Trippi (eds) (1994), *Advances in Futures and Options Research*, Vol. 7, Greenwich, Connecticut: JAI Press.

Commodity Futures Trading Commission (1999), "The Global Competitiveness of US Futures Markets Revisited," Washington, DC: CFTC.

Commodity Futures Trading Commission (1999), "Opportunities for Strategic Change: CFTC Strategic Plan 2000–2005," Washington, DC: CFTC.

Cornell, B. and M. Reinganum (1981), "Forward and Futures Prices: Evidence from the Foreign Exchange Markets," *Journal of Finance*, Vol. 36, pp. 105–106.

Daigler, R. (1993), *Managing Risk with Financial Futures*, Chicago: Probus.

Das, S. (1994), *Swaps and Financial Derivatives*, 2nd edn, Sydney: Law Book Company.

Dubovsky, D. (1992), *Options and Financial Futures*, New York: McGraw-Hill.

Duffie, D. (1989), *Futures Markets*, Englewood Cliffs, New Jersey: Prentice-Hall.

Ederington, L. H. (1979), "The Hedging Performance of the New Futures Markets,"*Journal of Finance*, Vol. 34, pp. 157–169.

Errera, S. and S. Brown (1999), *Fundamentals of Trading Energy Futures and Options*, Tulsa, Oklahoma: Penwell.

Feduniak, R. and R. Fink (1988), *Futures Trading: Concepts and Strategies*, New York: NY Institute of Finance.

Figlewski, S. (1986), *Hedging with Financial Futures for Institutional Investors*, Cambridge, Massachusetts: Ballinger.

Francis, J., W. Toy, and J.G. Whittaker (eds) (1995), *Handbook of Equity Derivatives*, New York: McGraw-Hill.

Grabbe, O. (1986), *International Financial Markets*, New York: Elsevier.

Grindal, I. (1988), "Flexible Risk Control and Arbitrage," *Futures and Options World*, June.

Grossman, S. and M. Miller (1988), "Liquidity and Market Structure," *Journal of Finance*, Vol. 43, pp. 617–637.

Hieronymus, T. (1977), *Economics of Futures Trading*, New York: Commodity Research Bureau.

Horn, F. and V. Farah (1979), *Trading in Commodity Futures*, 2nd edn, New York: NY Institute of Finance.

Hull, J. (1993), *Options, Futures and Other Derivative Securities*, 2nd edn, Englewood Cliffs, New Jersey: Prentice-Hall.

Iati, R. (2001), "Adapting to the Inevitable," *Futures Industry*, pp. 1–4.

Institute for Financial Markets (2002), *Futures and Options Factbook*, Washington, DC: IFM.

International Organization of Securities Commissions (2001), "Issues Paper on Exchange Demutualization," Madrid: IOSCO.

Kane, E. (1984), "Regulatory Structure in Futures Markets," *Journal of Futures Markets*, Vol. 4, pp. 367–384.

Kleinman, G. and R. Stagg (eds) (2000), *Commodity Futures and Options*, London: Financial Times.

Kolb, R. (1999), *Futures, Options and Swaps*, London: Blackwell.

Kuberek, R. and N. Peffey (1983), "Hedging Corporate Debt with US Treasury Bond Futures," *Journal of Futures Markets*, Vol. 3, pp. 345–353.

Luskin, D. (1987), *Index Options and Futures*, New York: John Wiley.

McDonald, R. (2002), *Derivative Markets*, New York: Addison-Wesley.

Markhan, J. (1987), *The History of Commodity Futures Trading and its Regulation*, New York: Praeger.

Miettinen, P. (2002), "Advances in OTC Trade Processing," *Global Energy Business*.

Peck, A. (ed.) (1985), *Futures Markets: Their Economic Role*, Washington, DC: American Enterprise Institute.

Pennings, J. and R. Leuthold (1999), "Futures Exchange Innovations," Working Paper, Office for Futures and Options Research, University of Illinois.

Rawsley, A. (2001), "Clearing Skies for European CCP," *Futures and Options World*, September, pp. 41–45.

Risk Publications (1997), *Managing Metals Price Risk*, London: Risk Publications.

Smithson, C. (1998), *Managing Financial Risk*, 3rd edn, New York: McGraw-Hill.

Stein, J. (1986), *The Economics of Futures Markets*, Oxford: Basil Blackwell.

Stoll, H. and R. Whaley (1988), "Futures and Options on Stock Indexes," *Review of Futures Markets*, Vol. 7, pp. 224–248.

Stoll, H. and R. Whaley (1993): *Futures and Options*, Cincinnati, Ohio: Southwestern Publishing.

Taleb, N. (1997), *Dynamic Hedging*, New York: John Wiley.

Selected trade publication websites

Selected articles from:
Applied Derivatives: www.appliederivatives.com
Commodity Research Bureau: www.crbtrader.com
Derivatives Week: www.derivativesweek.com
Derivatives Strategy: www.derivativesstrategy.com
Euromoney: www.euromoney.com
Futures Industry Magazine: www.futuresindustry.org
Futures Magazine: www.futuresmag.com
Futures and Options Magazine: www.fow.com
Institutional Investor: www.institutionalinvestor.com
Risk Magazine: www.riskwaters.com

Selected regulatory/industry websites

Selected guidelines, research publications and working papers from:
Australian Securities and Investment Commission: www.asic.gov.au
Bank for International Settlements: www.bis.org
Commodity Futures Association of Japan: www.nisshokyo.or.jp
Commodity Futures Trading Commission: www.cftc.gov
Financial Services Agency (Japan): www.fsa.go.jp
Financial Services Authority (UK): www.fsa.gov.uk
Futures Industry Association: www.futuresindustry.org
International Organization of Securities Commissions: www.iosco.org
International Swap and Derivatives Association: www.isda.org

Monetary Authority of Singapore: www.mas.gov.sg
Ministry of Finance (Japan): www.mof.go.jp
National Futures Association: www.nfa.futures.org
Reserve Bank of Australia: www.rba.gov.au
Securities and Exchange Commission: www.sec.gov
Securities and Futures Commission (Hong Kong): www.sfc.org.hk
World Federation of Exchanges: www.world-exchanges.org

Exchange and clearinghouse websites

Investor, product, market and education articles and pamphlets from:
Board of Trade Clearing Corp: www.botcc.com
Bolsa de Mercados e Futuros: www.bmf.com
Borsa Italia: www.borsaitalia.com
BrokerTec Futures Exchange: www.btecfutures.com
Chicago Board of Trade: www.cbot.com
Chicago Board Options Exchange: www.cboe.com
Chicago Mercantile Exchange: www.cme.com
Clearnet: www.clearnetsa.com
Clearstream: www.clearstream.com
Eurex: www.eurexchange.com
Euronext: www.euronext.com
European Electricity Exchange: www.eex.de
Hong Kong Exchanges and Clearing: www.hkex.com
Intercontinental Exchange: www.intcx.com
International Petroleum Exchange: www.ipe.co.uk
International Stock Exchange: www.iseoptions.com
Korea Futures Exchange: www.kofex.com
London Clearinghouse: www.lch.com
London International Financial Futures Exchange: www.liffe.co.uk
London Metal Exchange: www.lme.co.uk
Malaysian Derivative Exchange: www.mdex.com.my
Mercado Español de Futuros Financieros: www.meff.es
Mercado Mexicano de Derivados: www.mexder.com.mx
Montreal Exchange: www.m-x.ca
New York Board of Trade: www.nybot.com
New York Mercantile Exchange: www.nymex.com
OM/Stockholmsborsen: www.omgroup.com
OneChicago: www.onechicago.com
Options Clearing Corp: www.optionsclearing.com
Osaka Securities Exchange: www.ose.or.jp
Singapore Exchange: www.sgx.com
South African Futures Exchange: www.safex.co.za
Sydney Futures Exchange: www.sfe.com.au
Tokyo Commodity Exchange: www.tocom.or.jp
Tokyo Grain Exchange: www.tge.or.jp
Tokyo International Financial Futures Exchange: www.tiffe.or.jp
Tokyo Stock Exchange: www.tse.or.jp

Index